# METAPHYSICAL ART

# METAPHYSICAL ART

## Massimo Carrà

with Patrick Waldberg and Ewald Rathke

Translation and Historical Foreword by Caroline Tisdall

PRAEGER PUBLISHERS
New York · Washington

BOOKS THAT MATTER

Published in the United States of America in 1971
by Praeger Publishers, Inc., 111 Fourth Avenue,
New York, N.Y. 10003

English translation and Historical Foreword
© 1971 in London, England, by Thames and Hudson Ltd
Original edition © 1968 in Milan, Italy, by Gabriele Mazzotta editore

Library of Congress Catalog Card Number: 79–116640

*Printed in Great Britain*

# Contents

# Historical Foreword

**Caroline Tisdall**

Metaphysical painting was never an extensive formal movement like cubism or futurism. It represented a state of mind common to a group of painters for whom the plastic reappraisal of reality, as practised by the cubists, was less important than a reallocation of reality's component parts, each more or less realistically depicted, and sometimes combined with incongruity or overt fantasy. The poet Alberto Savinio, De Chirico's younger brother, described it as a *way of seeing*, and this is perhaps the best means of grasping the link between the painters represented in this collection of documents, and of understanding the contribution to twentieth-century perception made by their painting.

The precise chronology of the intensive period of metaphysical activity from 1916 to 1921 has been confused by the deliberately misleading accounts of it written by its two main exponents, Giorgio de Chirico and Carlo Carrà, both of whom claimed the entire credit for its invention. Their memoirs illustrate their varying versions of their meeting and collaboration in Ferrara in 1917, which was crucial to the development of metaphysical painting. De Chirico, in his memoirs, written in 1945, describes Carrà's reaction in this way: 'When Carrà saw me painting he went to Ferrara, bought canvas and colours, and started painting, but very badly, the same subjects as me, with admirable unabashedness and *sans-gêne*. Obtaining a long leave of convalescence, he hurried off to Milan with these "metaphysical" paintings, and hastened to organize an exhibition of them, hoping to persuade his contemporaries that he was the sole and only inventor of metaphysical painting, and that I was only an obscure and modest imitator. This was very naïve, since my paintings done in Paris were already known.' Yet in Carrà's 1942 autobiography the only mention of De Chirico is tucked into a list of more obscure names: 'My casual encounters with Ravegnani, Govoni, De Chirico, Savinio and De Pisis were moments of great joy for me.'

Admittedly most metaphysical stories are contradictory, but the subsequent rivalry between the two painters should be borne in mind, since it helps to explain some of the contradictions in the documents that follow, most of which were written after their short period of collaboration. It should also be remembered that when they met in 1917 both painters had distinguished achievements behind them: Carrà as a leading member of the futurist movement in Italy, and De Chirico as the sole exponent of his personal vision of the enigmatic in Paris.

Giorgio de Chirico was born in 1888 in Volo, a seaport in Thessaly, Northern Greece. His father was an Italian railway engineer who spent most of his life working in Greece, an enigmatic figure described by De Chirico as pale, formal, and very much a nineteenth-century gentleman. The image of his father, whose memory has haunted De Chirico all his life, and fragments of this background of Greece and railways were to reappear in his painting. For De Chirico no detail of this childhood full of 'metaphysical and provincial events' was insignificant, for much of his visual vocabulary was culled from such scenes remembered.

De Chirico and his younger brother Andrea (who later changed his name to Alberto Savinio) were solicitously encouraged by their mother to develop their artistic leanings, De Chirico as a painter and Savinio as a musician. For a short time, after a series of private tutors, De Chirico attended the Polytechnic School in Athens. After the death of his father in 1905, the family moved to Munich. They travelled via Italy, where in Venice De Chirico saw the work of Tintoretto, Titian and Veronese, though at the time they interested him less than eating cream cakes in Florian's. In Milan he had his first contact with 'modern art': he encountered the Italian blend of symbolism as practised by Previati, whom De Chirico admired, and the work of the pointillist Segantini, who influenced the futurists considerably but made little impression on De Chirico.

The foundations of De Chirico's early style, and of the 'Nordic' strain of metaphysical painting, were laid in Munich, principally through contact with the magic realism of Arnold Böcklin, and the philosophy of Nietzsche.

Böcklin was one of the most literary nineteenth-century German romantic painters of Italianate mythical and melodramatic scenes, whose work has never been described more enthusiastically than by De Chirico in the article published in 1921 in *Il Convegno*, and reprinted in this collection. He admired above all Böcklin's ability to make the unlikely seem instantly credible, the unreal real, and the real unreal. It should, however, be remembered that by the time he wrote this article he had already come into contact with Apollinaire's theory, so crucial to metaphysical painting, that 'authentic modern art is distinguishable by the element of surprise'. De Chirico was struck by Böcklin's use of the tragic aspects of statuary, veiled figures and enigmatic, inexplicable situations, as can be clearly seen if *The Enigma of the Oracle*, painted in 1910, a year after he left Munich, is compared with Böcklin's *Odysseus and Calypso*, of 1881–3 [47, 46]. Böcklin's use of complicated tempera and varnish techniques also appealed to De Chirico.

Besides Böcklin he admired Franz Stuck and Alfred Kubin – whose hallucinatory city squares and frozen monuments (particularly *Vision of Italy* of 1904–5) have much in common with De Chirico's later Italian squares – as well as Max Klinger, whose work he describes in an article published, like that on Böcklin, in *Il Convegno*. De Chirico was particularly struck by Klinger's gift of mingling scenes from contemporary life with ancient visions, his theatricality and his feeling for the romanticism of modern life (in no way similar to Baudelaire's). In De Chirico's work, however, the overt theatricality that ultimately weakens the work of these German painters is replaced by a much subtler grasp of the power of 'jarred reality', strange juxtapositions that are potent because they seem credible.

In the writings of Nietzsche, De Chirico found confirmation of his own melancholy and mystical tendencies. In *The Birth of Tragedy*, Nietzsche describes the 'symbolic dream picture', which reveals to the artist his state of unity with the primal source of the universe; he also communicates his foreboding that beneath apparent reality another reality lies concealed. De Chirico's metaphysical painting was the first to question this 'apparent reality'. Nietzsche's call for a poetic reappraisal of everyday objects and scenes to reveal the more profound meaning beneath superficial appearances is clearly reflected in the series of Italian squares painted in Paris, and is particularly crucial for an understanding of the Ferrarese metaphysical still-lifes. Nietzsche described Turin, surely the most metaphysical of Italian towns, with its vast open squares and nineteenth-century frockcoated monuments, as the only suitable place for him, and his evocation of its atmosphere impressed De Chirico: 'The innovation is a strange and profound poetry, infinitely mysterious and solitary, based on the mood of an autumn afternoon when the weather is clear and the shadows are longer than in summer, for the sun is beginning to be lower. Turin is the city where this extraordinary phenomenon is most apparent.' Paintings like *Melancholy of a Beautiful Day*, and *Delights of the Poet* [56], both of 1913, are perfect illustrations of this.

In Munich De Chirico also came into contact with the philosophy of Arthur Schopenhauer and Otto Weininger. In *Parerga and Paralipomena*, Schopenhauer put forward the theory that 'to have original, extraordinary, and perhaps even immortal ideas one has but to isolate oneself from the world for a few minutes so completely that the most commonplace happenings appear to be new and unfamiliar, and in this way reveal their true essence'. Schopenhauer also maintained that the gift of considering men and objects as mere phantoms and dream pictures was the criterion of philosophical ability. Moreover, a link can be traced between his writing on apparitions, especially his advice to place monuments on low plinths so that they appear to walk among men, and De Chirico's manipulation of the ghostlike appearance of statues. De Chirico found Weininger's writings helpful for an understanding of the work of Böcklin; and his theory of the emotive power of basic geometric shapes, like the square, circle and triangle, is worth remembering when considering De Chirico's later metaphysical still-lifes.

In the summer of 1909 the family left Munich, which De Chirico later described as the birthplace of two great evils, modern art and Nazism, and went to Milan, where Savinio hoped to produce his opera *Carmela*, and then on to Florence. There in 1910 De Chirico painted *The Enigma of the Oracle* [47]. In this the influence of Böcklin is still clearly visible in the shrouded, silhouetted figure, almost a direct transcription of Böcklin's *Odysseus and Calypso* [46]. This same year, however, marks the end of his Böcklinesque period, and the beginning of his use of adjusted reality, long foreground shadows, and emotive perspective. 'Who can deny the troubling connection that exists between perspective and metaphysics?' De Chirico wrote, and in the *Enigma of an Autumn Afternoon*, inspired by Piazza Santa Croce, there appears the fusion of nostalgia and Nietzschian poetry that characterizes De Chirico's painting right up to the Ferrarese period.

From Florence the family set off for Paris, stopping off in Turin where De Chirico, still steeped in Nietzsche, was impressed by the city's nineteenth-century neoclassicism

9

and its monuments, frockcoated and equestrian. He was ill here, troubled as so often in his youth by intestinal disorders (to which the extreme melancholy of his painting has at times been ascribed!).

In the course of his years in Paris from 1912–15, De Chirico evolved most of the images of his metaphysical painting: the towers [51; 55; 67]; the mysterious architectural settings, as in *Enigma of the Hour* of 1912 [56] and *Melancholy of Departure* of 1914 [77]; the deep and dislocated perspective, as in *The Joys and Enigmas of a Strange Hour* of 1913 [73] and *Mystery and Melancholy of a Street* of 1914 [91]; and the incorporation of inexplicable still-life objects. Some of these are instantly recognizable, like the artichokes in *The Square*, of 1913 [61], and the fruit in *The Dream Transformed* [68] of the same year; but most significant are the recurring juxtapositions of known and unknown elements, like the delineated ball with the rubber glove and plaster-cast head in the *Song of Love* of 1913 [60], or the solid scroll and two-dimensional cross with the plaster feet and egg in the *Self-portrait* of 1913 [63]. Paintings of 1914, like the *Sailors' Barracks* [86], already embody 'the absolute realization of the space that separates the various objects and establishes a new astronomy of things which are bound to the planet by the law of gravity' (De Chirico, 'On Metaphysical Painting', 1919). Most remarkable of all is *The Endless Journey* of 1914 [84], for in this there appear both the blackboard with diagrams and the manikin figure of the Ferrarese period.

The manikin theme was probably inspired by a character created by Savinio, a man without voice, eyes or face, who appears in his 'Chants de la mi-mort', published by Apollinaire in *Les Soirées de Paris* in 1914. In De Chirico's work Apollinaire had recognized one of the qualities he admired most: 'To describe the fatal character of contemporary things the painter uses that most modern recourse – surprise.' Apollinaire had been impressed by the two Santa Croce-inspired 'metaphysical landscapes', as he himself called them, shown with the *Self-portrait* [52] at the Salon d'Automne of 1913, and had introduced De Chirico to the celebrities of cubist Paris, though De Chirico later professed to have found his famous Saturday soirées boring. In 1914 he painted the famous portrait of Apollinaire [81], which the sitter considered prophetic of his 1918 trepanation operation.

Cubism itself had little effect on De Chirico's painting. He referred to the cubists as 'slaving away in the midst of their sterile and arid systems', whilst he himself was discerning 'the first ghost of a more complete, profound and complicated art'; however, it is impossible to ignore the personalized cubism of some of the later metaphysical interiors. The cubists proposed a visual reassessment of reality, whereas De Chirico was interested in the dislocated reality of the dream. They both drew on basic geometric shapes, but De Chirico referred to Weininger's emotive forms, not to Cézanne. He was not exploring the structure of known objects, but inventing new ones. At this time he wrote: 'To be really immortal a work of art must go beyond the limits of the human: good sense and logic will be missing from it. In this way it will come close to the dream state, and also to the mentality of children.'

During the winter of 1914–15 the manikins became the main theme of De Chirico's painting, and the evocations of Italian architecture that had preoccupied him for five years became a backdrop for them. In the summer of 1915 he and Savinio were called up and left Paris (with their ever-present mother) for Ferrara. Here they both became clerks in military headquarters, eating and sleeping at home, an arrangement that enabled them to continue their activities, and to absorb the atmosphere of Ferrara.

An important catalyst in this period of metaphysical art was Filippo de Pisis. De Pisis was then 21, witty and extrovert, more interested in writing than in painting, which he did not take up seriously until 1922. He had been exempted from military service, and lived in an exotic room crammed full of incongruous objects in his parents' house in Ferrara. It was he who introduced De Chirico and Savinio to the extraordinarily sensuous atmosphere of the town, and explored with them its squares, the Castello Estense (which appears in several works of this time, such as *A Girl's Pastimes* [107]), and above all the old Jewish quarter, with its specialist shops selling military decorations, draughtsman's instruments, maps and fancy biscuits, all of which were incorporated into De Chirico's paintings.

In his memoirs (1945) he wrote: 'The appearance of Ferrara, one of the loveliest cities in Italy, had made a deep impression on me, but what struck me above all, and inspired me from the metaphysical point of view in which I was then working, was the appearance of certain interiors, certain window displays, certain shops, certain houses, certain quarters, for instance the old ghetto, where one could find sweets and biscuits in exceedingly strange and metaphysical shapes.'

Until this time De Chirico had placed still-life objects in *exterior* settings, but in the winter of 1915–16 he started the great series of metaphysical *interiors*. These evolved from paintings like *The Philosopher and the Poet* [104] and *The Astronomer* [109] of 1915, semi-interior scenes with windows overlooking piazzas, and manikins contemplating diagrams. In these evocative rooms the objects – biscuits, set-squares and rulers, medals, etc. – are woven into an increasingly complex web of spatial and geometric juxtapositions [119; 120; 122–34]. The colour becomes richer, and the texture more crusty and varied, so that the edible objects appear almost sculpturally tangible. Distortion of perspective is used as a powerful dislocating device: 'Who can deny the disturbing relationship that exists between perspective and metaphysics?' wrote De Chirico. Remarkable among the interiors are the *Metaphysical Interior with Small Factory* of 1916 [113], and the *Great Metaphysical Interior* of 1917 [137], in which De Chirico places a framed exterior view in a claustrophobic room, thereby adding another dimension of ambiguity, a picture within a picture, as René Magritte realized.

In January 1917 Carlo Carrà arrived in Ferrara, and the short period of close contact between the two painters began. Before considering the part played by Carrà in metaphysical art, a summary of his life is necessary. Unlike De Chirico, Carrà did not draw on details of his life and experience to any great extent, not at this time at least. His painting until a few years before his arrival in Ferrara had been diametrically opposed to De Chirico's enigmatic vision; De Chirico had in fact reacted against the futurist turmoil of which Carrà had been a prominent exponent.

Carlo Carrà was born in 1881, seven years before De Chirico, in Quargnento in Piedmont. At the age of twelve he left home and became apprentice to a mural painter, moving to Milan in 1895. Eleven years of this training gave him sound technical experience and the love of Italian tradition that was to assert itself so strongly after the futurist period. In 1899–1900 he worked in Paris as a decorator at the Exposition Centennielle, and visited London, where he was impressed by Turner and Constable. In 1905–8 he studied at the Brera academy in Milan, where he was taught by the academic painter Cesare Tallone. Like the other members of the futurist group his style at this time was heavily influenced by the divisionism of Segantini and the symbolism of Previati, whose work De Chirico had seen in 1905. Carrà later destroyed most of his pre-futurist paintings, and his dating of works is often as unreliable as De Chirico's.

By 1908, when he met Umberto Boccioni, he was already well known in the Milanese art world, and was organizing exhibitions for the Famiglia Artistica. During the next six years of intense futurist activity there developed between the two painters the rivalry that also characterizes his relationship with De Chirico. In 1910 he signed the first Futurist Manifesto with Boccioni, Aroldo Bonzagni, Romolo Romani and Luigi Russolo, and until 1915 was one of the most active members of the movement. Paintings of 1910–11 like *Leaving the Theatre* and *Funeral of the Anarchist Galli* attempt an emotional embodiment of the futurist dictum 'All things move, all things run, all things change rapidly', so far removed from metaphysical concerns.

The years 1911–12 mark two significant developments in Carrà's work and thought. In 1911 the futurist painters came into contact with cubism, and made their first visit to Paris, where they met Apollinaire. The influence of cubism is clearly reflected in Carrà's *Woman and Absinthe* of 1911. In 1912 they held an exhibition in the Bernheim-Jeune gallery in Paris, and the wording of the catalogue reflects the more subjective turn that Carrà's work had taken: 'We must show the invisible which stirs and lives beyond densities, that which we have to our right, left and behind us, and not just the little square of life artificially enclosed as though framed by the wings of a stage.'

In Carrà's painting there appeared a new concern with the life of inanimate matter, with construction, and with the painting of states of mind. He was depending less on physical observation, and more on conceptualization of line, shape and space. By 1913, when he painted *Simultaneity*, he was attempting to reconcile futurism and cubism, to achieve a unity of the static and movemented qualities he later quoted as being the two essential ingredients of painting. In this same year he evolved his vision of a 'total art', incorporating sounds, noises and smells, and of 'anti-grace', the rejection of 'nice' standards of beauty, a theme still evident in 1916 (see ill. 1). In 1914 both he and Boccioni wrote free-association texts influenced by Marinetti's *parole in libertà* ('words in freedom'). Carrà was a copious writer, both then and during his metaphysical period, contributing to many of the avant-garde publications, among them *Lacerba* (the futurist magazine), *La Voce*, *Valori Plastici*, *Il Convegno*, *La Raccolta*, *La Brigata*, and *L'Esprit nouveau*.

By the spring of 1914 the unity of the futurist group was already threatened. Boccioni's book of that year *La Pittura e la scultura futurista* seemed to Carrà to give him insufficient credit for his concept of the total art of sounds, noises and odours. He wrote to Severini of the 'profoundly *passéiste* nature of Marinetti's and Boccioni's tireless and not very reflective activity', and of Marinetti's social and pedagogical concerns as being of little value to 'pure artists', a sentiment that Boccioni too came to share. Another visit to Paris in 1914 helped Carrà over a crisis in his painting, which he felt had concluded nothing. On his return from Paris he started work on a series of collages, the most successful of which was *Circular Synthesis of Objects*. These were the result of his impatience with 'stubborn pictorial materials', and formed both a continuation of his free-association writing, and a foreshadowing of the explosive word games of Dada.

In 1915 he produced *Guerrapittura*, a book of drawings, free-association compositions and collages, with reprints of some of his earlier articles. The book was in an aggressive vein, and signed 'Carrràààà' to give it a more staccato effect. Yet at the same time his new concern for *concrete forms* placed in space had led him to a study of Giotto.

In his autobiography Carrà dates his break with futurism at the end of 1915, though his painting still showed traces of it as late as 1917, when he was still signing his works as a futurist. He describes his disaffiliation as the result of a labour of conscience, a need for a more measured art. Most decisive was his desire to identify his painting with history, and particularly with that of Italy, to achieve a reconciliation of tradition and revolution, of nature and art, that he felt had been lost. For him futurism's doctrine of the mystique of machines was superseded. Paintings of 1915–16 show him seeking out a new style, introducing elements of cubism, Douanier Rousseau, Giotto, and his own brand of primitivism and 'anti-grace' in painting. It should be remembered, particularly in the case of the *Drunken Gentleman* [8], that he backdated works of this period, or reworked them later. The croquet stick, shadows and background of the *Drunken Gentleman* were painted in after seeing De Chirico's paintings.

The writings of 1915 and 1916 included in this volume, 'The Compass-Rose of Will' and 'Orientalism', were originally published in *La Voce*, and still contain emotionally evocative futurist juxtapositions, but also references to Giotto and Uccello, the 'Christian city', and the 'music of summer mornings', all of which indicate his search for a more mystical mode of expression. In 1916 he published articles on Giotto and Uccello, also in *La Voce*. He claimed that these two painters had helped him towards an understanding of spatiality, Euclidian geometry and the constructive value of angles. In them he found the 'primitive and universal principle, true for all times, climes and latitudes', the concern for 'ordinary things' that is characteristic of his later painting. He wrote: 'He who abandons everyday things falls inevitably into the absurd, i.e. into the spiritual and plastic void.'

He was now looking for a way of expressing the spiritual atmosphere of Giotto and Uccello, which he felt had been obliterated by naturalism. Paintings of 1916 already reflect his concern with the 'magic realism' that was to become a central feature of his work after the metaphysical period. He became increasingly concerned with the relationships between objects and the emotive space that separates them, as is clear in paintings like the *Antigrazioso* [4].

Carrà arrived in Ferrara in January 1917, and, like De Chirico, was allocated to office work in military headquarters in Pieve di Cento. In Ferrara he also met Savinio and De Pisis, and was able to keep up his activity as a writer, contributing poems (as did Savinio) to Bino Binazzi's Bolognese publication *La Brigata*. A few months later both he and De Chirico entered Villa Seminario, the army infirmary, suffering from nervous disorders (a fact the surrealists were later to pounce on in their interpretation of De Chirico's work). Here they were able to paint, and their brief period of close contact began. It was very brief; Carrà produced at the most twenty canvases, then, obtaining convalescent leave, he hurried off to Milan, where in December 1917 he held a large exhibition of his futurist and metaphysical paintings in the Chini gallery. He thus secured for himself the first showing of metaphysical work in Italy, a fact that caused considerable resentment on De Chirico's part.

De Chirico's metaphysical inventions, his evocative iconography and dislocated reality, were undoubtedly a solution for Carrà. In De Chirico's themes he found a crystallization of his own tendencies towards a return to the spirituality of Italian fourteenth- and fifteenth-century painting. It was in 1917 that De Chirico painted his greatest metaphysical works, such as the *Great Metaphysical Interior* [137], and Carrà followed through his earlier progress carefully: Carrà's *Solitude* [14], *Penelope* [19] and *Oval of Apparitions* [21], for example, are closely related to De Chirico's *The Philosopher and the Poet* [104], *Hector and Andromache* [118; 147], and *The Disquieting Muses* [138].

But within this adopted framework Carrà achieved a very different effect. In his so-called metaphysical paintings there is little of De Chirico's sense of mystery and foreboding. The attention centres instead on the relationships between the objects depicted and the distance that divides them, what Carrà described as the 'secret magnificence' of the world of ordinary things. This was already present in his work to a certain extent before his arrival in Ferrara. In *The Drunken Gentleman* of 1916 [8], for example, there exists a relationship, a tragicomic dialogue between the man, who needs the bottle, and the bottle, which needs the man to fulfil its function. Even his manikins, like *Penelope* [19], are not so much strange and inexplicable presences as oddly constructed human figures. *The Metaphysical Muse* [15], though composed of elements borrowed from De Chirico's metaphysical vocabulary, completely lacks his baroque theatricality. Any looming presence that the figure and the surrounding objects acquire is due principally to the compositional device of contrasting their large scale with the constricting space around them.

Carrà's most successful works of this period, like the *Still-life with Set-square* [10], and *The Horseman of the West* [III], both of 1917, illustrate his more purely painterly qualities, his search for a new embodiment of the primitive, and his attempt on one hand to synthesize the sensations of movement and stillness, and on the other to resolve form and colour relationships in a concrete way. The *Still-life* is particularly monumental in its simplicity, and is frequently cited by Italian critics as proof of the 'Italianness' of Carrà's metaphysical work, De Chirico representing the 'Nordic' strain.

Carrà continued to paint in a metaphysical vein until 1921, his last work in this style being *The Engineer's Mistress* [34]. He then turned to his own primitivistic 'magic realism', influenced by André Derain, of which *Pine Tree by the Sea*, of 1921 [37], and *The House of Love*, of 1922 [39], are typical, embodying the architectonic austerity that became his criterion.

Looking back in 1942 he summed up the experience of these years in this way: 'In effect, metaphysical painting was for me a search for a better relationship between reality and intellectual values; as such the ideas of modernity and tradition no longer form a dualism, but connect and merge. I understood tradition and modernity as two halves of the same sphere. The sphere turns and the half below comes to the top; in this way the revolutionary can become traditionalist and vice-versa.'

De Chirico was not demobilized until the end of the war, and his first opportunity of showing his metaphysical paintings was in an exhibition shared with Carrà at the Epoca gallery in Rome in July 1918. It should be remembered that most of the documents that follow were written after their period of close collaboration, and that a metaphysical aesthetic as such was formed after the most representative works had been painted. In 1919 Carrà published his book *Pittura Metafisica*, of which in fact only one chapter was directly concerned with metaphysics. This was attacked by De Chirico a year later in *Il Convegno*. In 1919, both painters contributed articles to the magazine *Valori Plastici*, the editor of which, Mario Broglio, did much to spread knowledge of their painting, both through his publication and later through the travelling exhibitions he organized, particularly in Germany.

After his return to Rome De Chirico became increasingly obsessed with technique, and this led him back to a study of the Old Masters. In 1919 he underwent a revelation in the Villa Borghese, as he recounted in his memoirs: 'It was in the museum of the Villa Borghese one morning, standing before a Titian, that I received the revelation of what great painting is: in the gallery I beheld tongues of flame, outside, through the vastness of the bright sky, a solemn clangour echoed over the city, and trumpets blared announcing a resurrection.'

And De Chirico set out on a lifelong crusade to resurrect *la bella pittura* and to become himself an Old Master, with a series of paintings and copies influenced by a wide variety of painters: Lotto, Michaelangelo, Dossi, Signorelli, Rubens, Raphael, Delacroix and Courbet, with neoclassicism and the baroque as his two extremes. At the same time he evolved a style of painting 'from nature' using very oily, rich paint, as in the *Still-life with Salami* [151], and the *Sacred Fish* [152], both of 1919. At times during the 1920s he reverted to metaphysical subject matter, reworking old themes and iconography in a mannered style and with brushwork reminiscent of Rubens and Delacroix, as in *Hector and Andromache* of 1924 [155] and *Seated Manikin* of 1926 [161].

Alberto Savinio (see Massimo Carrà's introduction, p. 25) had stopped composing in 1915. During the Ferrarese period he was undoubtedly an important catalyst in the formation of metaphysical ideas, until transferred by the Italian Army to Macedonia in 1917. In the mid-1920s he started painting, continuing the strangest aspects of De Chirico's iconography, mingled with the witty whimsicality that comes across clearly in his writings of 1918–21. In later years he took up ballet composition.

The metaphysical works of Giorgio Morandi (1890–1963) were painted in Bologna, independently of De Chirico and Carrà, whose paintings Morandi had seen in reproduction. He was never given to writing statements or articles, and is represented here only by reproductions [VII; VIII; 178–90]. Morandi lived, worked and died in his native Bologna, which he rarely left, and never travelled outside Italy. He studied at the academy there from 1907–13, when he was much influenced by Cézanne, again through reproductions. In 1914 he was represented, strangely enough, in two futurist exhibitions in Rome, and met Carrà briefly at a futurist evening at the Teatro del Corso in Bologna. That same year he was impressed by an exhibition of Cézanne watercolours, and studied Giotto in Assisi and Padua. In 1915–18 he concentrated on still-lifes and self-portraits, many of which he destroyed. Paintings of 1918–20 incorporate metaphysical iconography – four of them contain manikin heads – but are closer to the technique of the Parisian purists, though more emphatically modelled.

With these, and all his paintings, he was seeking eternal *order*, rather than psychological disturbance. For him the rounded manikin head, for example, was a pleasing object, the equivalent of a bottle, his concerns being formal. When he dropped metaphysical iconography there was no dramatic change in a style that remained remarkably consistent all his life. His work of this time was illustrated and exhibited with that of De Chirico and Carrà, and De Chirico admired it particularly, writing of it in 1922 as 'the metaphysics of the most humble objects, objects man looks at *without recognizing them*'.

# Introduction: Quest for a New Art

**Massimo Carrà**

In the years after 1910 the realization spread among European artists that cubism and futurism, which were in some ways the offspring of impressionism, could not satisfy completely, definitively – as had at first been imagined – the need to find an expressive form that matched the social, psychological and spiritual changes, in fact the life ushered in by the new century. There was now a need for 'a new definition of things', which had been attempted to a certain extent by the Douanier Rousseau in France in the opening years of the century, and this explains the many references to his work. It was Carrà who clearly revealed the inability of cubism and futurism to go beyond the ultimate results of impressionism when he wrote in 1914: 'They are still concerned with a materialistic form of description of the object, which in no way goes beyond the stage of naturalistic reproduction.' What was now needed was something quite different and was motivated by a fervid desire for a real knowledge of the disquiet that pervaded the spirit of modern man in his great crisis of transition, against which the war that was being fought rose up like a commanding and terrible 'superimposition' of reality. This is certainly not a return to classicism, as some over-hasty critics believe, but rather an inspiration to the intellectual and moral discipline of which the participating painters themselves speak with complete awareness.

Werner Haftmann puts it this way, in his *Painting in the Twentieth Century*: 'Pittura Metafisica did not contribute a new kind of painting, but a new vision of things. This group of painters experienced the world of things as alien and mysterious – reflecting the modern attitude towards reality. There was something disquieting about the way an inanimate object, seemingly withdrawn into its solemn steadfastness, could affect human emotions. Any old thing forgotten in a corner, if the eye dwelt on it, acquired an eloquence of its own, communicating its lyricism and magic to the kindred soul. If a neglected object of this kind were forcibly isolated, that is, divested of its warmth and of the protective coat of its environment, or even ironically combined with completely unrelated things, it would reassert its dignity in the new context and stand there, incomprehensible, weird, mysterious.'

### GIORGIO DE CHIRICO
It has already been said that the points of departure among the metaphysical painters were various, as were their interpretations of it. Let us first of all examine the case of De Chirico, a painter who had not passed through the heat of the futurist or cubist fires, but had observed them from a very different angle, remaining untouched by

them as he had been by the fauves and the expressionists. De Chirico the painter was formed in Germany, and his anti-naturalistic argument seeks support in the extremes of German romanticism, idealistically neoclassical and at the same time very inclined towards the literary values of mystery and symbols.

'To find the daemon in everything' is the task that De Chirico set himself in a writing of 1918. And this 'daemon', that is, the mysterious appearance concealed behind every object is revealed to the artist in certain magical or 'abnormal' moments of his creative contemplation: a nostalgia that is melancholy, and vice versa; in a whimsical game of references and allusions, paradox and impasse.

Literary examples were obvious, and it was De Chirico himself who chose Nietzsche as an example of an artist who knew how to gather these 'happy moments of the metaphysical', attributing to him the merit of having taught 'the non-sense of life, and how this non-sense can be transformed into art. . . . The fearful void discovered in this way is itself the inanimate and calm beauty of matter.' To this void and illogic De Chirico assigns the meaning of magic, the means of capturing the 'daemon'. Another name that De Chirico puts forward is that of Jules Verne, who had a very fundamental influence on him. The reference to the sad ghost Phileas Fogg who walks in a spectral London square may be a superficial one, but it is a literary analogy that pleased De Chirico, who from 1911 onwards more than once populated his Italian squares with ambiguous and melancholy characters not so very far removed from Phileas Fogg. Otto Weininger should be added to this list of influences outside the field of painting (significantly, he spoke of the 'determination of the profundity of things'), and so should Schopenhauer, with his writings on apparitions. Added to these was the weight of De Chirico's classical and neoclassical culture, rather like his nostalgia for his Aegean childhood mingled rather haphazardly during his time in Munich with the study of painters who infused classicism with the aspirations of the imagination. The names of these are easily traced: on one side are Poussin and Claude Lorrain (and even Mantegna in his archaeological period after 1460), on the other Arnold Böcklin and Max Klinger, and the more decidedly romantic Caspar David Friedrich, and besides these some examples of Bavarian rococo architecture, strangely balanced as it is between romantic impetus and classical repose. His Mediterranean origins in Greece left him with a feeling of aspiration and of nostalgia like that of artists north of the Alps, 'repeating the experience of Von Marées, Böcklin and Klinger' as Lamberto Vitali observed.

It seems that De Chirico resolutely pursued this tone of fantasy and fiction, that an element of narrative was dear to him more for its magic than for its discursive contents. His means to this end included many subtle mannerisms, even subterfuges: violent light flowing from the sides to penetrate the composition in a melodramatic way, raw shadows and impetuous colours, presences as ambiguous as absences, real or imagined, but suggested, images between mystery and suspense, Nordic nostalgia for the unknowable, and intellectual irony. All these elements used with, at times, over-skilful mastery create the impression of a great theatrical inspiration. As Roberto Longhi writes: 'He evoked ancient painting in a nostalgic theatrical way, and introduced the monsters of cubism, transforming them realistically and not without irony into manikins: the fifteenth century became the stage setting for the metaphysical puppet opera, with its stone guests.'

De Chirico specified his concern with metaphor, dream and minute narration: 'We are constructing in our painting a new metaphysical psychology of things. The absolute awareness of the space that an object must occupy in a painting, and of the space that divides each object from the others, establishes a new astronomy of things connected to our planet by the fatal law of gravity.'

De Chirico is primarily concerned with this narration rather than with the forms and images of the composition, and pours into it the various and contradictory elements of his adventurous and bizarre spirit. The second reality which is born of the meeting between the object and its representation is for him above all a psychic reality, consisting in the poetic emotion of the painter himself. It is his own presence and influence that imposes this meaning and value – logical and figurative – upon the things painted.

De Chirico gives this example of a chain of circumstance: a man is sitting in a room with a birdcage, some books, some pictures. 'Let us suppose that, for inexplicable reasons independent of my will, the thread of this necklace should break: who can say how I would see the seated man, the cage, the pictures, the bookshelf: who can imagine my amazement. . . . But the scene itself would not have changed, I would just be seeing it from a different angle. And here we arrive at the metaphysical appearance of things.'

The rupture of the habitual logic of situations and of spaces is for De Chirico the way of revealing the magical and mysterious aspect hidden behind normal relationships and the habitual thread of our memories. To this result the theatrical element makes a splendid contribution, a skilful use of architecture as a pictorial transformation of visionary marquetry work. De Chirico, writing of this, refers to Klinger; it is clear that in De Chirico's case as well as in Klinger's, the decisive factor is the artist's disturbing personality, his psychic and philosophical make-up, his dreams, his culture and his taste, good or bad, without forgetting that metaphysical element of ambiguity that contributes so greatly to the creation of the atmosphere.

These lines by Jean Cocteau, from *Le Mystère laïc* (1928), are in themselves sufficient to clarify the link between De Chirico's 'magical' elements and the ideas of surrealist and other artists north of the Alps. 'I turned round abruptly. A beautiful youth was crossing the empty square on a bicycle. He was naked, with a bowler hat. He was Mercury. . . . Prophetic dreams are infrequent. Nearly always the strangeness of the dream is art. Impurity of the acts of the dream. Mix two colours to obtain a third. The dream mixes memories and obtains an actuality that has no relationship with any of the dreams it mixes. . . . In a dream one does not see a staircase or a room, one sees *one* room and *one* staircase. In all their minutest details. Realism of the dream. Poetic reality. . . . In a fierce place, behold, like a nude, a floor, an armchair, wardrobe and mirror. Nothing evokes a cinema set. A phenomenon reveals to the tourist the opposite of a ruin: the model of a projected apartment. . . . The origin of the furnished landscapes [of De Chirico] must be in some comic American film. Perhaps that in which the bailiffs carry away a house, dismantling it round the owner as he eats his lunch.'

De Chirico represents, then, one of the well-defined aspects of metaphysical painting, the Nordic one, closer to surrealism (Ernst's and Magritte's indebtedness to him are clear), nourished as it is on the lyrical realism of Schopenhauer and on Weininger's view of the surreal. In its intrinsic elements it has very little in common with the other aspect, represented by Carrà and by Morandi.

## CARLO CARRÀ

In this second aspect of metaphysical painting, that which can legitimately be defined as 'Italian', there are no elements of nostalgia for Greece or of German romantic escapism, Weininger's symbolism or Schopenhauer's oneiric representation. Rather than by the magic of the enigma, one is confronted by the enchantment of things captured in the 'stunned certainty of existence'. Its sources lie in the spiritual reassessment unleashed by futurism and cubism, in dissatisfaction with their quickly-discovered limits, and in the lesson of French impressionism and the subsequent efforts to go beyond it, the bitter and glorious experience of Cézanne, Seurat and Gauguin. Besides these, there was an overriding need to return to 'elementaries', to repeat the vital experiences of a whole pictorial tradition, to go from Rousseau to the Tuscan primitives. As Arcangeli wrote on the occasion of the metaphysical exhibition at the Biennale: 'De Chirico's spatial nostalgia stimulated Carrà to invent an intensely rhythmical and rigid compositional framework, the module of which was no longer the generic measure of the temples, but Giotto's abrupt cubes. The *mystère laïc* is nourished on bitter solitude, and metaphysical painting grows into a religious sense of fulfilment; meditation on form and artistic quality coincides in concrete terms with the scenario of these beautiful modern legends.'

The year 1917, when De Chirico and Carrà were soldiers in Ferrara, serves as a reference point, and marks the maturity of a phase in their art, but its importance should not be exaggerated. For years Carrà had already been undergoing his futurist and cubist crises: as early as 1914 his search became more frenzied and branched out in several directions. His collages of 1914 and 1915 bear witness to this, for in them cubo-futurism is reduced to the function of a vocabulary, imposed on a figurative syntax which is already orientated towards static images, and towards a composition designed to qualify the objects, to affirm their enchanted beauty. These are characteristics of Italian metaphysical painting, at least in so far as it is an art of austere simplicity. A declaration by Carrà clearly demonstrates the conscious intellectual and artistic process which did not break with that which had gone before, though neither did it absorb anything for convenience's sake. 'Metaphysical painting, being post-cubist and post-futurist, cannot nor does it wish to, deny these previous experiences, but rather seeks to resolve their function and achievement within itself.'

An eloquent example of this progression can be found in the work of Carrà himself, in an image that recurs from the earliest moments of futurism onwards and passes through four different versions over the years, and which reflects and confirms this determined linguistic research in all its successive stages, whether they be connected or at variance. It is the image of a man on horseback which first appears in a drawing of 1909–10, and is taken up again in 1913 in the tempera painting entitled *The Red Horseman*, and then again in a drawing of 1914 and in the collage *Pursuit* of the same year, and makes its final appearance in the emblematic oil painting of 1917 entitled *The Horseman of the West* [III].

The object here, as in nearly all the paintings of these years, is pursued and examined in its 'other' sense, but also in its true and elementary reality. This is what interested Carrà all his life.

Towards the end of the First World War, he himself defined his poetry of objects in his writings on 'ordinary things' which are direct clarifications of the second thread of metaphysical painting, and are valid, too, for the work of Giorgio Morandi. 'It is the ordinary things that act on our souls in such a way as to reach the extreme heights of grace, and he who abandons them inevitably falls into the absurd, both artistically and spiritually. . . . Ordinary things reveal those forms of simplicity that tell us of a higher state of being, which constitutes all the richness of the secret of art. But when these flashes of inspiration of ordinary things, so rarely repeated, illuminate art, they create those 'essentials' that are the most precious for us modern artists. . . . And since we can express ourselves only in signs, we turn our minds to this sense of peaceful poetry, and leave all false dreams of the fantastic to vulgar and rustic mentalities.'

The confusion of futurism's violent years now became the calm of a solitude in which meditation on form was translated with equally solitary artistic feeling. 'One can narrate a painting by De Chirico,' wrote Longhi, 'but in Carrà's work the fable is expressed, not so much by the ambiguous titles as by the intersections of bright and dull colours, by the magic of the impasto, and by the harsh meetings of segmented spaces amid the primitive little compartmented rooms.' The poetry of ordinary things also characterizes the *Antigrazioso* [4], the end product of a long series of collages which served to make him aware of the formal definition of the object. In the collages, he had already reached the threshold of his own brand of metaphysical painting; in the *Antigrazioso* he made the final step. Here the forms have the meaning of things, but in their painful terseness they suggest 'another' meaning. This tendency to go 'beyond the visible' is a constant thread that unites the collages of 1914–15 to the 'anti-grace' works of 1916, and to those of the fully fledged metaphysical period between 1916 and 1921. Carrà's apparitions are words in a figurative argument, in which even in 1921 there can already be glimpsed, in the light that rises from the horizon, and in the use of bluish and greenish tones, the presence of the sea, like a quiet rebirth of nature, as much in image as in form. An image which for Carrà contains flashes of light fierce enough to arrest reality itself. 'The painter must concentrate continually on the essentials, which is the way to achieve true architectonic austerity. This is the second reality; this is metaphysical painting: this is the premise on which our work is based.' Thus Carrà interprets the lesson of the old masters: pure form alone can attain a 'second reality', cutting through the doubt and disquietude of the modern consciousness.

## GIORGIO MORANDI

Morandi became a metaphysical painter much later than De Chirico and Carrà and probably did so because of the confirmation of the example of Cézanne (who had preoccupied him between 1911 and 1916), which he found in the works of Carrà. He was particularly impressed by the still-lifes of 1916 and 1917, including the *Drunken Gentleman* [8] and certain 'anti-graceful' heads, which struck him because of their cubist interpretation of Giotto. And then, almost as a counterpoint to cubist theories, there was the work of Renoir and the Douanier Rousseau. Morandi, reserved and patient as he was, chose the safest road to find himself. Between the first landscape of 1911), which heralds his whole purist evolution, and the compositions of objects of 1918 in which the 'things' begin to scan in a disciplined reality of pure geometry, he made a series of studies which were solitary, intense and lofty exercises in Cézannian terms, and which deal, by hints more than outright statements, with linguistic problems and propositions. His interest in Cézanne did not exclude Seurat; but above all he found justification in his study of the Renaissance painters and the primitives, Giotto, Piero della Francesca, Masaccio. His 'exile in the past' was the exile of a man who proudly knew that he was capable of interpreting his own time, but who, in avoiding both the adventitious and the merely polemical, sought ease and comfort in the lucid geometry of Arezzo, Florence and Padua, in the 'sweet perspective' that induced the solitude of poetic meditation. For him, too, 'ordinary things' were the most important, in a less dramatic but no less severe way than for Carrà. He sought a purity that was a means of creating style, indeed the very style itself.

His development followed logically from that first landscape in 1911: forms controlled by rigid mental discipline, lines, modelling, use of chiaroscuro, dialectical division of space and planes. But in 1918 something happened within him that caused a more decided move towards the shores of metaphysical magic. Although De Chirico's obsession with the enigma remained alien to him, Morandi still found much in De Chirico to interest him – as he did, intellectually, in Savinio. But what concerned him most were certain works by Carrà, as he himself stated; in them he saw, translated into essential pictorial terms, certain formal values, certain echoes of artistic awareness, that he, instinctively mistrustful though he was of all literary leanings, recognized as persuasive answers to his own formal and emotional questions. In all this Morandi found an aware and vital relationship with concepts of form belonging to the past. The result of this was a change in his evaluation and distribution of pictorial space, which now became evocative rather than concrete, and a harder use of light and of line. In his works of 1918, 1919 and 1920, the composition is based on the rigid presence of structural harmonies in which the gentle perspective introduces a silent depth to restore the balance of the three dimensions. His vocabulary widened to include decidedly metaphysical themes such as manikin heads, lines and spheres. Above all, he now took to the rarefied, mathematical atmosphere of metaphysical painting, and to the metaphysical view of the human being as a cipher suspended 'in the pneumatic void of these empty spaces, rulers, balls, and circled globes that seemed to play a tacit game of references, obliquities and momentary immobility.

Everything in it is the Cartesian daemon' (Arcangeli). And even the severity of his palette, white, earthy-yellow, brown and black, adds to the geometric rhythm of these vigorously structural values.

These works embody his natural bent towards contemplation and silent colloquy, his peaceful feeling for history, neither academic nor rhetorical but alive with solitude. His humble attachment to the mystery of reality and of life leads him to seek a faith far removed from irony or literature.

## ALBERTO SAVINIO

Between 1915 and 1919, when Alberto Savinio was a soldier in Ferrara, he was almost exclusively concerned with literature. He was a man of piercing, ironic intelligence and all-embracing curiosity, and in May 1914 had published, in Apollinaire's review *Soirées de Paris*, the 'Chants de la mi-mort' which are the most original and valid literary equivalent of metaphysical painting, especially that of his brother De Chirico. Savinio, too, was a great creator of ideas, and he too held that art is the man; when he started painting in about 1926–7 he was to say, as De Chirico had said, that one should not ask what the painting is, but rather what the artist is.

'I must say straight away: I am a painter beyond painting. For painters the painting is the end, for some painters it is a means. . . . My painting is not to be looked at, or judged as it is looked at, as one judges painting born directly of the eye, the brushstroke, the colour, the tonal relationships. My paintings do not finish where painting finishes . . . they were already born before they were painted. It is right that they also live beyond the painted surface.' These thoughts, written many years later, were those he had already voiced in the cafés of Ferrara in conversation with Carrà, De Pisis and De Chirico, who was perhaps the only one who completely agreed with him.

The link binding Savinio and De Chirico is extremely strong: Savinio invented his own surprising images; during the early years, he translated them into words as his brother translated them into a visual language. The give-and-take relationship between them is not clear, and perhaps will never be so. They certainly shared a common foundation of inventiveness, as well as their memories of and nostalgia for their childhood in the Aegean, a common cultural background and common anxieties and trepidations about life. It is in the 'Chants de la mi-mort' that the enigmatic and desolate image of the manikin first appears, that sexless, voiceless, cyclops figure that was to provide a measure of the existential anguish of the 'future city'.

Unlike De Chirico, Savinio distrusted the dream. In 1919 he wrote: 'Art, and I say this particularly for the benefit of certain idealists and mystics, has no point of resemblance with dreams.' He concentrated on irony in order to capture the spectral nature of reality, 'the very subtle but elementary reaction that might be called modesty'. And yet, like his brother, he was a metaphysical in what I have called the Nordic interpretation of the term; he was almost a surrealist before the term was coined, and more explicitly so than De Chirico. His was a very particular and intelligent surrealism which owed much to Alfred Jarry's *Ubu Roi,* and which was part of a generous and tumultuous fervour for life both real and imaginary, accentuating both symbolic transposition and the 'dark side'. His metaphysical inclination was directed instinctively towards the interpretation of images representing the links between 'yesterday', 'today' and 'tomorrow', in which the phantasms of the subconscious, evoked by the intelligence, are the sole actors in an interior world. The relationship between the unconscious and the intellect, between hallucination and lucidity, is therefore indissoluble. Painting, music, literature, the expressive means, do not matter. What does matter is the idea that is to be transcribed.

## AFTER 1921: DE PISIS, CASORATI AND SIRONI

In the early 1920's other painters appeared on the scene: Filippo De Pisis, Felice Casorati and Mario Sironi. For these men, however, metaphysical art was only a curiosity, a temporary adhesion, not a spontaneous and necessary revelation. They all soon rejected it. The artistic and intellectual climate had changed progressively, changed too much, and so had the concerns that preoccupied men of culture. After 1921 the time of ideograms had clearly passed.

De Pisis, then scarcely more than twenty years old, had been an attentive but uneasy witness of the Ferrarese metaphysical phase, and he himself had attempted to paint and write in this vein from 1916 onwards. But only in 1919 did he succeed in achieving that two-dimensional union of objects, disconcerted and full of imagination, that is like a pure rhythm of forms in space [191–92]. There is a reference to the metaphysical in this, but it is transformed without trace into a whimsical, elegantly cursive game.

In 1919 he wrote these lines, full of lively 'Ferrarese' spirit, and with a sense of mystery in the presence of De Chirico's 'astronomy of objects': 'The parallelepipeds of the rooms were alive with phantoms and returning spirits, the luminous openings assumed a deep sense of mystery and the twisted legs of the ninety-year-old tables and the red fenestrated tower reflected in the still green lake. A white curtain falling over the black panes of a high window above the rumbling street, one lost evening, can hold more enchantment than a cloudy sunset over the sea. Does our spirit long for the magic that has disappeared from the incorporeal vision? The suit hanging in folds (its shadows precise) from a coat-hanger decorated with shiny black scrolls, in a hermetic room in a second-class hotel, can tell us of the simple reality of things and dramatize itself in symbols.'

Perhaps this represents the 'geometrical apparition' as seen from a decadent viewpoint; in any case, it is De Pisis' personal contribution. In his painting he was never metaphysical to this extent; for this passage amounts to a literary transcription of a canvas by De Chirico.

After 1921, especially after his experiences in Rome in 1924, and his study of the baroque still-life painters and his contacts with *Valori Plastici*, De Pisis revised in a more concrete and serious way, his Ferrarese manner, his formal discipline, and the experience which he had shared with Carrà and De Chirico. The results of this are some singular works which are in a way a personal reply to his memories of 1916–17. One of these is the *Still-life with Eyes* of 1924, which already contains some surrealist elements, though the tone is cleaner and more flowing. In these works there can still be found the evocative atmosphere of the Ferrarese period, but the heightened expressiveness indicates an eighteenth-century culture which has nothing in common with the earlier metaphysical painting. This is clear in the *Sacred Fish* of 1925, which is neither enchanted nor ironic, but instead touchingly sensuous, expressive of De Pisis' tender yet bitter interpretation of the metaphysical.

Casorati was already over forty when he came under the metaphysical influence in 1921, after years of drifting in the seas of secessionism and Art Nouveau. His is a Nordic sort of figurative idealism, filtered through the aesthetic of pure visibility, and this background, together with his lucid, almost excessive mental control, carried him towards static forms and simple values of perspective and geometry, in which the stiffened magic of the metaphysical is strangely transformed into a completely cerebral relationship between the severity of the form and its abstracted typicality and neoclassicism.

Sironi, too, had an encounter with some of the metaphysical ideas. He was born into painting in the lively atmosphere of Giacomo Balla's Roman studio, in close contact with Severini and Boccioni. He then continued to paint in Milan in 1914–15, and so it was natural that he should pass through phases of divisionism and futurism, a futurism that had developed beyond the myths of dynamism in 1914 and come closer to cubism. Sironi's vocabulary is an urban one: houses, chimneys, the blind walls of the industrial suburbs, the domes that unexpectedly break the pattern of the roofs. Carrieri defined him as a 'metropolitan metaphysical', and his solitude, his desolate silence and his sinister magic, are neither those of Carrà's rooms nor of De Chirico's spectral squares: his is an architectonic solitude in which there remain visible traces of cubist construction. Where one finds lucid balance, energetic geometric values, a rarefied atmosphere and a precise scanning of space in the work of Carrà, Morandi and even De Chirico, in that of Sironi there are violent emotions, dramatic forms, order and disorder mingled in a whirlwind of volumes and tones.

## AFTER 1921: DE CHIRICO, CARRÀ AND MORANDI

And now let us examine briefly the development of metaphysical concepts after 1920–1, in the work of the three principal figures. In two of their cases the tendency is that indicated by Haftmann *à propos* of Carrà: to fuse the constructive concepts of modern French thought, the great traditional values of Italian art, and the solid definition of things.

In all three painters the magic experience of reality always continued, in other expressive forms. But in De Chirico's case it took a very particular turn, for he found he was able to find flashes of brilliance even within the terms of academic rules. He felt very much at ease in the classicizing atmosphere after the war (as he said: 'I honour myself with three words: *pictor classicus sum*'), and seems to have found an answer in translating plastic forms more explicitly in the imaginative terms of northern romanticism, whilst his inventiveness, still rich in figures and symbols, now turned towards the most showy examples of Renaissance eclecticism; this very fact gives some idea of the severe crisis he was undergoing. In this way his German formation is merged with the classical example, and also with the work of some of the Emilian painters, from Tura to Dossi, and Ercole de Roberti, even the lunar atmosphere of Schifanoia. The heroic myth is fused with the sensuality of certain Ariostian enchantments. The Roman villas, the wandering horsemen, the vast quantity of self-portraits painted between 1922 and 1924, demonstrate his desire for a style almost like that of Von Marées, seeking to be spectacular at all costs. The result is so sentimentally pompous that his abrupt and abusive criticisms of the greater part of modern painting, of Cézanne above all, seem perfectly consistent. With the third phase of his painting his congenital sense of irony, bizarrely mingled with a sincere readiness to accept the suggestions of history, permit him to transfer realistic images endowed with objective values into atmospheres that are still vaguely spectral.

In this sense De Chirico was following an ideal that had been present in his work since his pre-war days in Paris: to achieve an effect on the spectator using not merely pictorial means, but all the expedients offered by imagination, dreams and artifice. And even in this neoclassical style, with its cavalier disregard for the academic rules (as in the *Lucretia* of 1921 [153]), he is still disposed to use symbolist nostalgia. Thanks to pastiche, his interpretation of the modernity-tradition issue is full of life. As he said, his foremost intention in painting was to 'arouse in the spectator that tremor of surprise and curiosity that is one of the truest signs of genius in a work of art'.

The paintings done during the decade after 1924 [157–76], which include the *Archaeologists*, the *Gladiators*, the furnished landscapes and the horses by the sea, play on these three elements: compositional monumentality, plastic weight and a mysterious surprise which is of metaphysical origin. The structure is neoclassical; but there are also signs of surrealism, as in the suggestive outdoor interiors, and of the baroque, as in those masses of male nudes straining their muscles to the limit, and the games of perspective in the series of horsemen and of gladiators. In this decade his love of myth already apparent even before his Ferrarese period, is revealed even more strongly; Verne and Schopenhauer seem to reappear, resting in the shade in the garden of Armida.

Eclecticism? It is indeed, but on a very particular level, because in De Chirico's interpretation these contradictory forms often attain the status of authentic transfigurations of a reality imagined according to an inner rhythm. And one must admit that there is present that element of mystification which Cocteau claims is to be found at the beginning of every discovery. But all this is also proof of a disquiet – an obvious sign of our times – which for De Chirico means liberty to change and revive, to seek what he needs wherever he is likely to find it, to interchange tones and impressions according to opportunity and convenience, and indeed, to find in every object his own myth and his own imagination. On close examination, the fundamental characteristics of De Chirico the painter have not changed.

For Carrà the post-war period meant above all a profound moral crisis, expressed in the form of doubts about his own expressive language. In his autobiography he wrote of the 'gloomy desperation of the period immediately after the war', and in these years he painted very few canvases: only one in 1918, three in 1919 and none in 1920. He was again troubled by a fundamental problem: the relationship between the artist and objects, including nature.

'Painting', wrote Carrà, 'must embrace both the need for identification with objects and the need for abstraction. Under this double stimulus the painter realizes his capacity to release objects from contingency, purifying them and conferring on them an absolute value. In this way painting creates a new thing, a new entity. Painting as I understand it is neither the reproduction of physical phenomena, nor archaeology, nor aestheticism.' And again: 'For the spirit there are no contradictions, only transformations and developments: for me, to change direction in art does not mean to deny the past, but rather to widen it and to introduce into it an aesthetic concept, and in this way to discover new relationships, and to open one's eyes wider to understand a greater part of reality.'

The past for him meant his figurative experiences, from the Lombard realism and divisionism of his early years, to futurism, the 'anti-graceful' and the metaphysical. When Carrà again confronted reality in 1921, he justified it by saying that he considered nature to be the provoker of pictorial relationships, 'which by their very coherence are determined in rhythms of form, colour and light, in a harmonic construction with chosen spatial and architectonic values'.

An element of the metaphysical does remain in his work after 1921. The 'cosmic seriousness', the 'cosmic sadness', the 'unredeemed foundation of primordial gravity' of which Wilhelm Worringer speaks when referring to the 'new' Carrà after 1921, are the direct consequence of his metaphysical meditations verified by contact with this reality of the things in Nature. Without 'anti-grace', and without the language developed in Ferrara, his dimension of intelligence would not be capable of restoring to the image a more peaceful emotional simplicity which contains both the real and the imaginary. Lasting amazement in face of things and their existence, precise spatial relationships, a space agglomerant and cohesive, implicit in the solidity of the form, balance of linear and tonal values, magic of internal rhythm, rigid formal theorems, all these can be found in the hermetic canvases painted by Carrà when he came out of hospital in Ferrara. In works like the *Shooting Range* of 1928, or *Morning by the Sea* of the same year, 'the image is presented in quite a calculated pictorial order exemplified by the trestle that had also appeared in *Pine Tree by the Sea*, of 1921 [37], which relates to the triangle in the background which is repeated geometrically in the rigging of the sails' (James Thrall Soby). Indeed in very many of his later works there is a true structural constant that incorporates elements from every phase, and metaphysical concepts form an essential element in the calculated cadence of space and volume and in the relationship between volume and void. This constant and explicit affirmation is present in the *Mad Poet* of 1941, as in *The Balcony* of 1942 and *Manikin with a Doll* of 1955.

Of the three, Morandi was the artist who seems to have most extensively set aside the syntactical and lexical apparatus of metaphysical painting. Some critics see his metaphysical phase as an incidental encounter; others as a useful but rapidly superseded experience. His single-minded quest for a vital rapport with the object resolved itself not so much in an act of composition as in an essentially emotional act, an unostentatious commitment to analyse the object, with one eye on Cézanne's concept of space. The magical silence of his forms, and their poetic vibration, spring directly from the demands the artist makes on Nature. These demands are modest, even humble; but they are also capable of transformation into pure form. This, to Morandi, is the only way, in this century, to face up to the challenge of history.

And in this sense, Morandi is not really very far from the 'purist' position taken up by Ozenfant and Le Corbusier, who rejected, in the name of rationality and sensibility, all the 'secondary purposes' of art. (Morandi's affinity with them is, however, rather on the poetic and moral plane than on that of the substance of painting.) Purification, for all these artists, was the reflection of a constant endeavour to open the way to a stylistic perfection which was attainable only through sacrifice and self-denial. The reality that the artist must set out to represent is not that of the senses but – by the very nature of his being – its conceptual elaboration, achieved through a subtle process of reasoning.

For Morandi after 1921, nothing counted but what freed itself spontaneously from the work, without deliberate provocation, without affectation, without intellectual witchcraft. And without ever renouncing the use of a well-defined pictorial mood, Morandi was able to recall Chardin and Corot, and discreetly set out to correct certain of his pictorial methods, attenuating the crudity of his outlines, replacing his brutal light by a more delicate, enveloping light, muting his tonal relationships in more compact compositional blocks. But the primary elements in his painting, as in that of Carrà, are still simple geometrical forms, the sphere, the parallelepiped, the cone, the cylinder – universal sense data of which the artist avails himself in the course of the creative process. This process is basically one of transformation, adaptation, exploration and structuring. It is thus possible to pass, without strain and without compromise, from the elementary object to the complex plastic form which defines the objects and their relationships, preserving the link with their origins but avoiding the pursuit of the 'slice of life', the fragmentary reality. Creation and transfiguration: this Hegelian conception of art, which was in the thoughts of all the best artists in Europe in those tense post-war years, was the source of Morandi's preoccupation with humble, everyday objects in which a subjective analysis can legitimately attempt to reconcile nature and reason, beauty and truth, imagination and logical rigour. This is the much sought-for equilibrium which Morandi made his ideal; and in his quest for self-knowledge in painting he could not but be haunted by the lesson of metaphysical painting, which is that the almost paradoxical union of objectivity and emotional intensity is an attainable goal.

30

# DOCUMENTS

# Carlo Carrà

## Our Antiquity

Whatever else will our contemporaries find to reproach us with! And yet, if we too had forgotten our origins we would certainly be praised, but we would no longer be fit to carry out works of uncontaminated will.

Our ancient character is firmly rooted in severe law, almost as if to vegetate more comfortably in modern reality without destroying it.

Admittedly, it would at times be pleasant to leave this state of inebriation in which we live, were it not for the magic link which holds us bound to our poor 'savage gods'.

The hot winds of history arouse this spiritual disposition for new and profound things. They hint of calm music. The game becomes serious, my friends, and to sing this music too freely could also be dangerous.

We never knew 'indifference', but now our spasmodic passions have ceased to preach. We prefer to conceal ourselves from the eyes of the profane. We are alone in the profundity of our epoch, alone with our sin, and with our study.

By a strange anarchical paradox we have returned, almost without wishing to do so, to pure classicism.

What was it that breathed in our ears the sound of so many things we believed to be dead?

The truth is that we know of no greater happiness than that of listening to ourselves.

What is this feeling that provokes in us the jealousy that a thought of ours may tomorrow belong to many men, a jealousy greater than that provoked by the thought that our woman may cease to be ours?

If we too had reduced the spirit of art to a convenient calculation of algebra and daily bread, we would perhaps feel more secure, but also more mortified than we do. The enjoyments of easily-conquered paradises always leave us indifferent.

We too have sung the praise of the western orgies; then we felt it permissible to receive our brothers' indecision with the tenderness befitting our democratic habits. But now we have become more cautious, and no longer tolerate the riots which ambitious and disturbed people denominate 'artistic movements'. These villains always ensnare incautious youth, which, eager to make itself felt, fails to realize that its youthful adventurousness is prone to malevolence and ungrateful obduracy.

From this it can be discerned that we no longer wish to see ourselves confronted with uncertain premises. If it is not a sin of pride to do so, let us claim to have thrown overboard a good part of our corruptibility, or at least of our own belief in lying prophecies.

We have become aware of the truths that are said to be serious, and we do not accept that the veils have been lifted for the delight of the unworthy. It is an illusion that one can force this on those who do not wish it, and he who tries to do so, demonstrates such candour that he is pardonable because the need to give vent to the passions that torment him is manifest. He is unlike us, for with experience we have lost this candour and believe most firmly that that which is particular to the individual can never belong to a generation.

This general idea that bears such truth is understood by few, partly because it is of very little advantage to those who use it.

It is obvious that civilization corrupts men at their birth and consumes them, letting them believe that for them, sweetness is reserved for the future, for their old age. For this reason we see even artists settling down to earn money and considering art as a material convenience right from their tenderest years. Thus everyone looks after his own affairs, his predetermined aim being that his family should eat and drink and sleep heartily or, as the poet puts it in a sweeter way, in life they love above all 'venery, sleep, song and dance'.

Thoughtless natures like this imagine art and life to be divergent and contradictory; or they even consider art to be a sort of ill omen. If this is not admitted openly it is because no one dares to do so, it is through pure courtesy towards the few men of real value who have preferred study to the theatre, to sport, to eating and drinking.

Apart from this, what on earth can this our prolonged effort, our subtle intellectual work, so in contrast with worldly ornaments and enjoyments, mean to ordinary men, if they are unaware of its relationships? And then, of course, to smile at this grave labour is easy, costs nothing and endows the smiler with a knowing air.

The chameleon-like reproduction of visible reality is another ugly thing that has been imported from outside. In places where painters were not used to condensation of the elements of the body, they could now surrender, with deceitful ardour, as if it were a liberation, to theories that were born and resolved without being completed. And it was thus that the painting of so-called effects of light (which really concern only highly-strung stage electricians) came to be accepted.

What was needed was a return to the Italian idea of the original solidity of things, so that men would recognize the well-disguised deceit of the astute philosophies which are put into circulation with all the publicity necessary for the triumph of an industrial product.

But now that the inevitable intoxication has been slept off, matters are returning to a more determined state. In this way, linear delights will no longer be disrupted by ecstatic rotations of colour and we will no longer be pushed towards trivial and trembling mobility and tumultuous surfaces.

The appearance of even the smallest bodies is no longer changed by ephemeral distractions, our ends are no longer resolved in light which cannot celebrate weight.

The aims will change and by means of a second, richer, more diffuse and conscious transposition, reality will again be conceived with an inextinguishable spiritual ardour

which will comply more persuasively with form. After this, colour, and the picture.

Combinations of the module will return in valiant opposition, and with them, the golden section, giving a more ample spatial breath.

Tonal matter will be assembled homogeneously in all its immanent weight.

Internal discipline brings us to a more fulfilled significance, to a cubature pregnant with poetry.

And this is how we initiated the second period of our artistic development after having confronted the public in the Italian theatres, and brawled in the squares, for the advent of a new art.

Let us recover a little energy and courage, and all of us place ourselves in the hands of destiny, and let us not be beaten by our evil genius. We do not question the belief in an Italian art that we imbibed along with our mothers' milk.

We still have a belief and a hope, and we shall yet have our hour of consolation.

Solemn and deadly is the error of him who passes his years in vain, inconclusive dreams; and his condition is particularly hard nowadays.

The study which has as its object the nature of the beautiful is a desperate madness, carrying us above ourselves, and creating in our souls a sense of anguish which we are unable to overcome. And yet art, with its terrible and almost barbaric gaiety, consists above all of a reflexive love which magnifies the object on which it rests. It exists by virtue of the ability we have to dominate phenomena and the brute forces of matter.

The analytical life of bodies causes our desires to oscillate between twin poles: firm outline, and the ever-budding sensuality of explicit detail.

Another reason for the sudden extinction of the painting of the movement we invented can be found in the exaggerated predilection we had for the curved line.

Let it not be believed that these words are written to spit upon the dear memories of our extreme youth.

The problem is much more complex because of the various grades and qualities of the concurrent elements, and is now being radically displaced into certified formulae.

All intellectual preoccupations with subject matter and content can create tiresome misunderstandings, because in works which show signs of theology we see false content overwhelming the sensibility that generates all vital form. And yet we cannot admire the ingenuousness of the savages, nor endure that of the 'popular artists'.

Much water has flowed under the bridges of art, but the proprieties that preside over painting are yet to be clarified. They can be summarized in the following impulses of the spirit:

a) line (straight and curved in contrast) in proportional arrangements of individual forces,

b) the local tone of aspects of reality (simultaneous relationship of chiaroscuro and chromatic colour),

c) the first stage of the form having been attained, to find the balance of the volumes; that is, the synthesis which constitutes the definitive order within the painting. Let us not forget that art cannot be only the immediate reflection of a sensation; neither must forms remain as merely raw external expressions of the reality that surrounds us, or be limited to arresting the shadows of vibratory movement.

It was modern naturalism that led to the anecdotal, enclosing art and cutting off all its possibilities, limiting it to mere physical phenomena, for no beautiful brushwork can mask its spiritual sterility. Artful devices, pseudo-cleverness of angle and well-adjusted line are not sufficient substitute for the creative function that is lacking.

Nearly all artists still believe, with Monet, that painting must limit itself to the function of tickling the sensuality of our eyeballs. Such painters, of course, are inclined to believe that naturalist production in all its aspects is excellent.

He who does not feel the supreme harmony of volumes and the profound refinement of a totality of well-constructed forms could tolerate even the sterility and dilettantism which has already made its mark generally felt on art.

Is it to be wondered at that the coarse and misled public think of the artistic function as limited to a vague chromatic pseudo-sensuality which has nothing to do with the lyrical elation of the true realities of art? [. . .] Pictorial naturalism is being judiciously opposed by the young Italian school, but we shall see later the elements of frailty this opposition contains, and distinguish their irremediable errors in its rebirth.

A certain instinct is undoubtedly the foremost necessity for a painter, but it must be dominated, and gradually transformed from an impure force into clear consciousness, since real art denies anything produced solely by uncontrolled instinct. And this confirms the maxim that sensibility alone is not sufficient for the creative act.

The charm and the chromatic sinuosities of Signac once interested me; now that I am more mature, they seem to me even more trifling than those of Monet.

Let us have creation, then, and not the imitation of phenomena. Certain slight nervous stimuli make us smile; we can no longer mistake them for real spiritual joy.

The mislaid necessities of style are returning, or rather are reborn; and the artist, with greater purity than before, proclaims them irrefutably present.

Never has this problem been felt to be so important as it is today by those who are exponents of the collective spirit. It is the law of realization that presides over artistic representation. And so, say what you will, to reduce painting to a realistic recognition of human and natural appearances is almost equivalent to a disregard of the superior aims of art.

Artistic creation involves a watchful, diligent and attentive will, and demands a continued effort to prevent the 'apparitions' from being overlooked. Artistic creation, which is satisfaction of the imagination and intellect, is destined to stimulate in the beholder a particular meaning and a repetition of that satisfaction felt by the artist.

This said, it is not to be wondered at that simple temperaments of scant individual quality go astray among the flourishes of chimerical worlds, and that their sensations dissolve into such vague hypotheses that they are unable in any way to find adequate conclusions among the specific values of art.

In times like ours of the most unrestrained pseudo-artistic libertinage, everything is determined by abstract intelligence, and every work is at the most the more or less jaded result of an *a priori* mental attitude which holds up only as long as the theory that produced it exists. Whilst the universality of the real work of art cannot spring from specious assertions or content itself with uncertain stages of confused consciousness.

We find this same confusion in the ambitious and oracular simplifications indulged in by practical minds that have come to art through vanity, void of the disinterested love without which no form of art can exist.

Universality is given to the work by the perennial interest it arouses in us.

Now, most modern painting (the names announce themselves even if they remain unspoken) does not renew itself from within through original lyricism, but is determined by arbitrary concepts, oscillating between the counterpoint of drawing and the fantasy and glamour of the subject. With all this it is evident that anyone who cannot resist speculating on the intrinsic lyrical quality of the forms is drawn into a hypothetical position; his sensations melt into an imaginary world which despises the proportions of the real one. This world, in striving to reproduce itself larger than the real world, reduces itself to an even more minuscule size than the natural one. And so, strictly speaking, one could say that these young painters – in spite of their vaunted talent for assimilation and their vigorous spirit – are unable to make things concrete, so that reality comes across featureless and raw, as if shattered at birth.

I know painters who are said to be tormented by a thousand categorical interrogatives, and this may be true. But if this fact constitutes their nobility and their drama, for us it is not enough to know that their spirits are troubled and in continual crisis, or in continual process of purification.

Projects and programmes cannot be transcended unless one can manage to realise in depth the specific object of the 'apparitions', unless one answers these lofty interrogatives adequately. Others seek to veil their vacuity with cunning gaiety, nearly always forced and out of place. These are they who, at every hour of night and day, declare themselves to be the most modern, the most advanced and the most avant-garde. They nevertheless find redemption in the wretched existence of the poor Italian, full of desire to live.

The aesthetic conscience of our time is certainly not that to be found among the sentimentalists of art; in the manner of people without measure, they use curious circumlocutions to justify a vague idealism which tends towards emblematic forms without always managing to conceal their uncertainty. Far removed as these artists are from the very material that moulds even mistaken ideals, they fall back on theories, the substitutes for art. But if one were to examine their case more closely, one would find that they are encrusted with the remains of our erstwhile researches, and that they repeat them in an inferior form. But this is always true of those who need to make a sensation: through lack of thought they are content to navigate in a troubled current, convinced that no one will want to seek the meaning beneath the disturbance.

There will also be the stubborn ones concerned with a return that has already given fruit, not with one of those forms of imitation of the style of earlier painters, nor like those of Derain and Picasso, but rather with those 'complex visions' achieved with obstinate toil by Poussin, Ingres and Cézanne. And all this to re-enter the law of the ancient, but always new, *Mysterium mirabile*, able to manifest itself in real acts of spiritual consolation, without nausea and without remorse. . . .

Besides, it is not necessary to have participated in recent artistic events to understand that we were commanded to initiate the new orientation and to rise up against the blessed avant-garde of today who periodically shoot their gloomy chromatic machine-gun fire into the ranks of the ingenuous. And so Italian art lives and progresses. We must therefore go back to the germ of vitality that was in us, but in a new way, so that our emotion plunges deep into antique form, to reappear as an attractive pictorial creature – even though all this rancorous lyricism has taken us beyond every idea of finesse and grace.

We have understood, first and foremost, that one cannot progress with uncertain ideas and that our courage and our eagerness for historic gestures will not necessarily be diminished even if our youthful disquiet is stilled.

So it will be seen that the squalls will be somewhat calmed, and we will no longer be obsessed with finding at all costs an original way of interpreting reality, which will come of its own accord.

This means that our desire for polemic has been extinguished, at least the desire for certain infantile arguments which might almost have been designed to sabotage the work of re-education begun by us in 1910.

Right from the days of 'decomposition' there began in us that state of uncertainty that precedes great resolutions, because from that time we realized that the linear path led into an error opposite to that of the impressionists.

Nevertheless we felt that it was not necessary to make an abrupt break in continuity and so cut short our experimentation with energetic painting before we had exhausted its possibilities.

The principle that presides over an act of spiritual will is obscure, but we know that we must take note of all researches, even the ephemeral ones.

Whatever the passions that touch and agitate the souls of today may be, these crises of aspiration in our spirit must be greeted like the torment of our consciences, even though we ourselves may not realize their full significance. They say that rain follows sun, that wind follows rain, that snow follows wind, and that snow disappears in the sun. Such is the law that governs ideas. From any given emotion others arise, to make way in their turn for yet others. Such is the life of the seasons: this is the destiny of the human mind. . . .

Perhaps we are acting presumptuously in affirming that we are concerned with the interests of art in general, but if one ignores ironic subtleties, one must admit that there are cases and situations that have not yet been sufficiently considered.

There are silent efforts, unrecognized activity that seeks to make facts docilely follow desire; while the usual distributors of smoke seek and distribute diplomas of virtue. On the basis of these facts, it is necessary to attempt to bring a little clarity and proportion to things.

We shall not mention the particular conditions prevailing in art as a whole, unless directly relevant to our argument.

Let it not be thought, however, that we wish to isolate the problem of national art from the finality of European – universal – order, on which every artistic problem is directly dependent. We will dwell in detail on the task that the young are called to perform, a grave responsibility for anyone conscious of the situation in which Italian art, for various reasons, finds itself. To try to analyse these reasons could be to fall into the error of a man dissecting the human body in the hope of discovering not only the law of life but also that of human emotion.

On the other hand, to run joyously towards certain intoxications, shouting 'long live' or 'down with' according to one's sympathies or antipathies, is to lose contact with the concreteness of things. It therefore follows, if one cannot reasonably isolate the examination of a single part without considering the idea imparted by the parts, that one cannot form a general idea without considering its particular effects. Whether one proceeds from the general to the particular, or vice versa, whether one proceeds by synthesis or analysis, every artistic problem must be seen as connected in all its parts and with its necessary unity.

But we know that in the sum of experiences there arise so many new and unforeseen elements that unity either cannot be attained, or makes itself manifest in unexpected ways.

In aesthetic activity more than in any other human activity, one never attains the end one sets out to reach. But in days of great aesthetic disorganization, any support is good. Today, for men of imagination, tendencies of equal falsity contend for supremacy at the crossroads of obscure directions.

Light as a fountain, spiritualization slowly comes; but those who wish to understand are not intimidated by adverse forces.

We are no longer constrained by physical illuminations to play at blind man's buff with our thoughts. This is the theory of the card players who when they want spades and see clubs turn up, change their tactics.

It is easy to throw hurried accents into a mess of hypotheses of doubtful taste, or to outline improvised figures without clarity, precision or control. But even if there are infinite ways of erring, there is only one way to work correctly.

Overweening revolts are in vain, as is the search for the reasons for birth; but it is of great advantage to a man to know where he wants to go.

Planes and distinctions in judgment appear again. Consciousness is manifest in its totality. The outlines of ideas become as clear as those in geometry.

From elementary things one reaches the sphere of the sublime.

We know that the verdict on these problems cannot be given quickly, but our heart is consumed in a complicated operation, which desires that all be fused into a single song composed of multiple voices.

In this way spiritual form becomes evident, indivisible, necessary, like concave and convex coupled in a circle.

The conflict with the image of universal silence is tragic. Currents press in upon the spirit from every side and contrast the vision; but the liberty that moves it finally brings into existence that metaphysical reality that makes things eternal.

41

We will never fear that what we have said may turn out to be mere bravado. Our intention is to produce horoscopes. We are not like the people with absolute certainties, who for every love argue mechanics.

What does it matter that he who contemplates the plenitude of his spirit is taken nowadays for a foolish idolater who, hungry for nothingness, dissolves into Isis or Osiris?

These words were written on a day when we gave a name and a person and bodily limits, measured mathematically, to our inner voices. It was one of the many days of our enchantment, and we write these words in the joyful notebook of our intelligence. . . .

We are not concerned with an intimate and objective examination of a definitive form, because nothing is definitive, but with a form of art as yet scarcely sketched in, simple and elementary. And rather than a norm we set out to provide a suggestion in generic terms.

Nevertheless, the choice of new criteria and postulates is already a guarantee of seriousness and probity, if not yet a demonstration of new constructions of forms hitherto sought and imagined and invoked in vain.

But one could already demonstrate with readily accessible facts that metaphysical painting is nothing but an intuitive development of that which preceded it, and in actual fact it perhaps represents the first, imprecise, ideal projection; the first steps on intractable soil; an uncontrollable desire to go beyond purely sensory and materialistic forms, however superfluous it may seem to us to claim the roots of this form of art in the Italian tradition. We do not wish to base any claim on the future, because art, like history, passes through successive stages, though this does not alter its profound essence, and it carries the future within it.

As can be seen, we do not rest our case on originality, but rather on the discovery of origins which will lead to the achievement of rigorous and immutable forms. . . .

In this way we have realized that the gentle warmth of our present spring (our works are but the first buds of a vitalizing thaw) has incited many young people to shout about a new solar age. Quite apart from a certain obvious ingenuousness – which is always boastful by definition – it must be clearly understood what is meant when one says 'Italian Principle', because there are amongst us too many people who have grown lazy through antiquated mental habits, and who will use our orientation towards tradition as a way of attempting to impede the course of Italian spiritual life; and with stupid and preconceived references taken from the storerooms of the academy, they will attempt to cloud the waters.

Like the fortune-tellers in Dante's Inferno, these people meet the future with their heads turned to face backwards: not through wisdom or in order to experience that which has been created, but only because they are urged on by a desire to deny every new enterprise.

But since this is by now a diluted and vulgar axiom where intelligent people are concerned, let us pass on to examine what is meant by the word originality, which today has taken possession of the majority of young people. Perhaps this word constitutes the greatest and most disquieting misunderstanding to emerge from the workshops of the artistic peasantry in these recent years.

It is bitter for the sensitive man to see how arrogance, ostentation, frivolity, vacuity, wantonness and every excess nowadays are the most positive characteristics of today's artists.

From this arises the reciprocal concern shown by today's painters for surpassing each other in the incessant invention of new styles, supposing that they can capture the admiration of the public by such artifice, and neglecting the improvement of their real creative faculty; their output is consequently closer to bizarre eccentricity than to the real imagination which neither tires the mind nor diverts the attention from the substantial aims of art.

And it is precisely this pitiful mania for seeming original that prevents contemporary painters from realizing the varied graces of linear relationships, so essential in the production of that magic enchantment which used to be familiar to the painter.

So it happens that, while on the one hand we consider irksome the closed orders, the arthritic systems and the dead forms which the good old Academy's rules seek to put back into circulation, on the other we must rebuke the young painters who are neglecting the most elementary awareness and absolutely every necessity of study to follow their own fatuous whims; because in the last resort we should never forget that he who refrains from study of the great masters through fear of losing his native sensibility, will only succeed in creating a form of art without roots and without real excellence.

It would be as if some one claimed that it is possible to become a great poet without having any appreciation at all of language.

Even the earth would produce only wild plants, if the farmer's care and toil did not put it in condition to receive the seeds and participate in the nourishment of delicate produce.

This is what happens to the painter as long as he ignores the precious contribution made by the great masters over the centuries. He who fears to lose his native poetic sense should not devote himself to art or poetry, since these presuppose a knowledge of historical development and of the informative laws of expression.

Nevertheless, there are painters who, on seeing the works of the great masters, either acquire a false sensibility when they have none, or corrupt the natural sensibility they do have.

As can be seen, it is always a question of intelligence and moderation, because he who studies the masters with discernment, once he has overcome the technical difficulties which block his comprehension, will know how to accelerate the development of his native sensibility, and will be able to maintain, better than others, his own inspiration, the force within us that seeks out planes, lines and surfaces and co-ordinates them, creating unity from the discordant elements of sensation: a word which signifies what unexpected and irreducible emotions are aroused by objects.

But now if we return to the first point made in this discourse we will see the fundamental reasons on which the Principle of our art rests, which, since it has brought glory on the Italian name for centuries, can shine out again if we in our turn grasp the essential point. Albrecht Dürer – as Vasari said – had already understood the considerable profit to be had in burning his Northern frenzy with the help of such excellent fuel, as did later Poussin, Delacroix, Ingres, Cézanne and other eminent artists who nourished their dreaming spirits at this same ancient flame to carry out tangible and certified formulae, that is to say, the expression that characterizes the art that survives all eras.

Because, after all, the idea of Italian art is at the apex of every constructive aspiration and lends itself to perennial development.

Care should be taken, however, for this Principle can generate both beneficial developments and grave superstitions.

It is above all when the painter does not recognize his capacity and seeks to create works beyond his range, that it impairs his way of seeing greatness in simplicity and truth in the natural, and he slips, almost without realizing it, into the false and the mannered, and seeks to carry out his vision in the excesses of rhetoric.

Painters like this are men whose fixed purpose is to impose their own will; and, to create really excellent works, one must indeed study a great deal; but then one must leave to nature all her operative liberty.

Let it not be forgotten that the same right questions receive a thousand equally wrong answers.

It would be mistaken to believe that in our case a passion for works of style leads us to support those pictorial theories which obliterate that immediate spontaneity which works become frigid and any good result is nullified. We are deadly enemies of every sort of affectation, and although a clear statement of our position is necessary to give consistency to our inspiration we will always cover the side of art that should be kept hidden, so as not to fall into the usual sin of haughty charlatanism which constitutes the greatest danger to any artist.

A thing that sometimes astounds us is to see certain painters seek order and method beyond the laws of painting. These painters who let themselves be guided by chance believe, in all good faith, that they are representing our tradition and its fine content.

The present writer is free of preconceptions, but believes that he is not straying beyond the limits of truth in affirming that none of the dominating artistic tendencies of today fulfils the expectations of the epoch in which we live, nor the ardour of our new needs.

We too know that it is one thing to affirm that in all matters one must aim (like a mathematician) at the centre, and another to demonstrate how one reaches this point; and so, finding themselves unable to suggest precise precepts, writers about art should limit themselves to arousing in the souls of young painters the love and seriousness which are the only factors that enable action to take the place of hope.

To speak today of the art of invention as possessing a historical character is to recognize that art is quite different now from what it was fifty years ago, in the days of 'history painting': it arises from other impulses, lives in a different atmosphere, and is constrained by other needs. Then the problem was almost exclusively that of 'subject', today it is recognized that the excellence of a work does not consist entirely in being what is called 'beautifully worked out', although this is a necessity, but rather in the exclusion of every superfluity and in the equal intrinsic density of all its parts. This signifies a unification of extreme simplicity and maximum magnificence. Nor will the painter fail in his intentions if he considers the spirit of the times, rendering to every predecessor his due with purity and sincerity; this is real, not simulated gratitude. Everyone understands it in his own way, since only practice nurtures judgment, and even though today everything is reasoned in abstract theoretical concepts, for us painters everything consists of that sincerity which in the practice of art is nothing more or less than diffidence.

For us doctrine is a function that makes the genuine shine, but it is beyond changes of fortune or success.

Sincerity can be contradictory, but never empty of useful possibilities.

These words are perhaps insufficient to suggest to the reader the idea we have of sincerity which is after all, a natural attribute that could only be compared to the innocent smile of a sage.

Perhaps absolute sincerity, like purity, is not a thing to take lightly, but nowadays to smile at such things costs little and can also seem very intelligent.

From this it can be deduced that if we ourselves advocate respect for the 'Italian Principle' it is because we believe in a law of co-ordination of visible reality, without which the picture remains a fragment that aspires in vain to have a unified centre.

We do not care at all if criticisms rain down from all directions on our new and personal views.

What is certain is that if you take a close look at 'Impressionism', which was like a counter-altar to 'Italianism', you will not be amazed by Cézanne's reaction, nor by what you have read till now.

Apart from this, it is very natural that the antidote should have been found there, rather than anywhere else, in that country where the scourge had flourished most.

> *Changeons en notre miel les plus antiques fleurs;*
> *Pour peindre notre idée empruntons leurs couleurs;*
> *Allumons nos flambeaux à leurs feux poétiques;*
> *Sur des pensées nouveaux faisons des vers antiques.*

> Let us make our own honey from the most ancient flowers;
> To paint our ideas let us borrow their colours;
> Let us kindle our torches at their bardic fires;
> On thoughts that are new let us make antique verses.

1916–18; published in Carrà's *Pittura Metafisica,* Florence 1919

## Declaration

Looked at for a long time substance grows grey

The ephemeral force of words is lost in idle conjecture

Remote rules and measures and the extinct phantoms of the will are unaware that the sun has long since risen again

We are little suited to public administration and in commerce with men we use too much irony

These men swooped down to attack us but unperturbed we ventured into the language of secret sweetness

Then we became aware that a vague moisture was dulling our souls and that the mentalities which arose possessed abandoned inflections

But now our agitation assumes predominance with new direct needs

From the new planes which are not chimeric we see the first lines of our ideal parabola

Clear amazements rediscovered

The precise forms of harmonic proportion have pleasant union with things and destinies

A flash of beauty and we will forget whether our life will be secure

We make contact with new myths

The approaches to reality are always unexpected

We oppose the artifice that supports itself with implications of fantasy

We justify our perverse adventures and this love of vain dreams

Devilry of a bizarre race resolved in a fleeting singing pleasure

The great interrogatives

The obscure pretexts

Ah the scale of values

The wicked happiness of things that give themselves

Having entered a delirious geometry we now emerge not indifferent

They say that the will of prophets can dissolve the dark enigmas and hush the cosmic voices of the free and impure sea

Hence our invitations made us haughty

But in good time we realized that these things were done in mockery

The new needs have changed the terms in our hands

We feel a returning taste for calm and agreeable postures even if they present us with food for sadness

We are caught up in the web of fatality but prefer to absent ourselves from surprising things and light heartedly

To live in the indifferent breath of a piercing light could signify a self-surrender of the so loving defences

And I say that if there is something that cannot be hurt there is also something innocent that could be lost

Time which is right has imposed on us a limit which we do not intend to respect

To sustain the solitude we feel as men out of our epoch, a vague smile from the stars is sufficient

46

Let us not forget that we are passing through this very life fleeting and ignorant of its
    destined end
But neither let us forget that this depends upon the law of God who will give us the
    necessary light to bear the catastrophes that weigh upon us
At the beginning of our day time without limit cannot bar its door on us

> *Carrà è cheto:*
> *la meta smarrita*
> *vuol per sé la vita*
> *Carrà è lieto:*
> *cavalca senza freni*
> *ponti d'arcobaleni*

> Carrà is tranquil;
> The lost aim
> Wants life for itself
> Carrà is joyful:
> Unbridled he rides astride
> Bridges of rainbows

January 1918; published in Pittura Metafisica, Florence 1919

## Concerning Ordinary Things

I could write at great length here about the Principle of Metaphysical Painting, as I have come to know it, either through direct experience or through discussion, in order to throw light on its importance and the excellence of its aims, and its hopes of attaining them. But since I consider that style is not disconnected from matter, which plays as great a part in the excellence of art as our own efforts, I feel that one could say much about its qualities and its shortcomings. One cannot truly distinguish between material and style, and attribute to one of the two the excellence of a work, since the two are indivisible. Now, should it happen that a painter is not totally aware of these two constituent qualities, through lack of either intuition or practice, he will never teach himself the real and supreme truths of art. When for some reason a man is ill-disposed towards the effects of painting, he is neither moved by the toil involved nor delighted by the contemplation of natural things. And so, in this infantile state, he will scorn 'ordinary things' and take refuge in vain dreams of the marvellous, and seek in the realms of fantasy the reasons for his own incomprehension. But he who is ready and fit to receive and re-create any image whatsoever, and can express it becomingly, will prefer to concentrate his spiritual activity on natural things; he will renounce crude, childish fancies, because in them he can find no serious enjoyment, not out of insensitivity but because he has a better idea of the elements which go to make up art.
    (In fact, it is only the very unskilled aviator – or rather the false or imaginary one –

who despises the ground. We must be careful – advises a friend of ours – because our spirit, like the sin of pride, can don strange disguises.)

With the progress of the years, this habit of seeking harmony in the objects that surround us increases rather than diminishes, because we feel that, if we forget the real, all order and proportion perish, and with them the just evaluation of life and art – which ultimately signifies calling objects by their own names.

It is the 'ordinary things' that work on our souls in such a beneficial way that we attain the extreme summit of grace; and he who abandons them falls inevitably into the absurd, that is, the void, both plastically and spiritually. For this reason our opinion is that tranquil happiness is the most elevated rapture ever evolved by man, and that it was evolved by one man alone who observed a great deal, meditated profoundly, and suffered greatly too. For 'ordinary things' reveal the forms of simplicity that tell us of a superior state of being, which constitutes the splendid secret of art. But when the flashes of inspiration of 'ordinary things', so rarely repeated, illuminate art, they create those essentials that are the most precious for us modern artists. One could say that in this way we rise from the depths to the surface like flying fish.

And since we can communicate only by way of signs, we turn our minds to this sense of calm poetry and leave fantasy to vulgar and rustic natures.[. . .]

Women, children and primitive natures are subject to puerile criteria of value, and can ask nothing of 'ordinary things' apart from a certain immediate utility. In fact, when the eye of such a person rests upon concrete objects his diatonic indifference towards everything appertaining to pure taste would soon lead to an abundant dose of boredom and monotony. Hence we affirm that the spectral vision of reality is reserved for rare and completely rational individuals; phantasmagorical illusions are for artists of little power and discipline.[. . .]

In the fields of poetry and music, too, the only new path that has been opened up has brought confusion of means and aims. Indeed, though perhaps I should not say so, these arts, in borrowing many characteristics from painting, have lost some of their former majesty and distinction. It should have been sufficiently understood that all tendencies towards promiscuity in the arts generate harm for all concerned, since give-and-take does not preclude mutual deception.[. . .]

For if the truth be told, we have little time for those who tell tales of a new world every twenty-four hours and every morning fill the air with cries announcing the discovery of new wonders. It seems sufficient to us that the artist should have a clear idea of what he is doing hour by hour.

For our part, we who loved beautifully painted and well-defined things, will try to fulfil our vow with due devotion.

And since anything that is not completely clarified is no longer sufficient, we will attempt to exercise upon each of our promises an efficacious, imperative and dictatorial control, and so discriminate the beautiful from the excessive, the true from the imaginary, and the singular from the affected.

1918; published in *Pittura Metafisica,* Florence 1919

# Metaphysical Painting

*'The true element of poetry is a metaphysical truth, so that if physical truth does not conform to this it must be considered false.'*
GIOVANNI BATTISTA VICO

We believe only in 'Painting without adjectives', that is, in that 'pure form' of plastic activity that cannot admit such expedients and didactic embellishments as complicate more than they explain. All the same, we too adapt ourselves to these deformed times, and almost without repulsion we attach tendentious labels to all things just as modern custom demands. We know that it is unbecoming, as they say, to lead one's own defence, but every hour that passes reaps words spoken or printed which resound malignantly against us and our undertaking.

Perhaps, too, we are mistaken when, in all good faith, we say we believe that even a mediocre doctrine carried out with love moves us more than a greater doctrine manipulated without the lubricants of emotion. We say this, but at the same time we indulge in continual aesthetic reflections which, alas, revive the frozen landscapes of most abstruse cerebrality. Hence the very precepts and maxims that we expound overshadow the enthusiasm one would like to see illuminated.

And so here we are again, to declare that it would be a great good fortune if one could succeed in discovering the essential motives that move a true artist – who, incidentally, seems to us to be the most fragile man among our contemporaries and the one most easily beaten in the material competition of life. And this is partly due to the very nature of the discoverer and is even more the result of a false elaboration of values, accepted without examination, which have led to some misunderstandings that should be eliminated from the discussion.

And so it is that there has emerged the sort of product which now has currency in the picture market, and which is worse and more gaudy than traditional and academic painting, and which is at best comparable in effect with those slight electric shocks which used once to cost a penny at the fair, and which produced a tingling of the nerves, forcing the facial muscles into a vague idiotic smile that many confuse with a feeling of joy. One ought to know by now, after the passage of so many intellectual movements, that this is a limited art, able only to give life to a series of particular examples which by their external singularity can surprise and affect none but excessively ingenuous or easily misled souls.

The consequences of these artistic misunderstandings will go on making themselves felt for a long time in the present Babylon, unless we learn to distinguish and divide for ever things that are different by nature, just as the true is different from the false. The new tyranny seems already to have vanquished the old one.

This does not mean that we entirely reject that element of art that is really original, since the force of amazement furnished by this is indispensable for 'beauty', in the same way as a certain native inventiveness is necessary to prevent a people stagnating and hence becoming cut off from the competition of international life: never has this seemed truer than at the present moment in history.

But there are other reasons that clarify for us the fact that modern art seems to be a negation of our spirit, whilst in former times art was always a triumphal affirmation of it. The men of the past went wrong sometimes; but in these days of greater aesthetic disorganization, *any* pretext is sufficient to mask the void that rules supreme in the artist's soul.

This is because all our young painters, no sooner have they painted a canvas on which opaline planes, and distant shadowy villages, and distant tissue-paper margins no longer meet, than every one of them thinks he has achieved something lasting; whereas, if we consider carefully this sort of plastic lucubration, with its complete absence of every internal discipline, it reveals only an eccentric coquetry based on that sweet nothing that some tricksters pompously call 'universal art'.

Now if one were not aware that such lamentations have arisen at every time and from every place, and if one did not know that good and courageous painters have always been a minority, one would be inclined to believe that with the passage of time intellectual man has deteriorated considerably, and become increasingly querulous, diffident and vain.

We personally intend to ignore only the inferior forms and measures, in both the ancient and the modern. We do not adhere to the school that wants the corruption of one thing to lead to the growth of another; we cannot delude ourselves that we have lifted our equation to its ultimate power.

If we prove unable to place our judgment in accepted things, if we are unable to define once and for all what in art is corruptible and what merely transcendable, if the absolute flees because we run after words too much, if even the thing poorest in ideal content can create new and more intricate problems for modern man, it is because we bear in our hearts the image of a life which seeks to impose the weight of its greed.

Let us not forget that inventors who are free are impelled by genius, whilst the timid and the mediocre operate according to mechanical rules, which means that truth, in passing from hand to hand, is transformed into absurdity. They tell us that it is not for us to know the non-existent; they say that Nothingness cannot express itself, but what then is all this writing stuffed with puerile, ridiculous, formalist dignity?

The philosophers of art today love the expedient facility of vain formulae. They let us know that the incorruptible is at a higher level than the corruptible; they say that a work of art is nothing but an elated state of the intelligible; they tell us that in empirical evaluation the 'real' must be distinguished from the 'false'. They teach us that to understand the artistic act as a continual participation in creation is the equivalent of thinking of a spiritual movement that is above contingency and new and diverse every moment; thus appreciation of aesthetic phenomena, more vertiginous than those of the physical world, varies continually. But when they encounter a specific instance of 'artistic creation' they grope like men in a thick fog, and bleat like Dante's sheep pastured on wind.

From this it is clear that it is of no avail to bandy extravagant terms, and that all we know with certainty is that we must deny ourselves even a moment's compromise on essentials, so that in every one of our works a progression of beauty really shows itself. The creative spirit wanders in a dream in the fields of the absolute; but our skilled sensibility makes itself felt when we find ourselves confronted with an art that can be understood in more than one way. Because for us art has not yet been degraded from its original dignity. These are all things which can equally well be illusory, and which are of little interest to artists in general, but are inestimable for us because they make us feel that nature accepts us with that sincere tenderness that forms a noble part of our pride in our beautiful toil.

To work for 'beauty' is always an agreeable thing, but a great country, mature in civilization, as ours is, should not neglect too much the elements that constitute its artistic future. This thought will seem rather too practical to false idealists, but we think that if it were resolved in practice it would remove our only elements of inferiority compared with artists north of the Alps.

We would thereby be offered a better way of making ourselves known, with more numerous and perfect reproductions, and with more frequent exhibitions abroad, which would constitute a real advantage for our Italy, always so disregarded by other countries. The realization of this project needs the participation and help of those who claim to love our young art, but for this to be possible all problems and substantial differences must be clarified. I am not addressing the mass who have neither the time nor the possibility to do so; they are doomed to remain unmoved by spiritual movements.

We know that this is not the right time for 'sermons on Taste', but we affirm that one can already come across some works that declare of themselves that their authors have done everything possible to revive the artistic virtues of their race. For these young artists, originality and tradition are not two contradictory terms. But one must be completely just and say that only today, after a decade of passionate research, can they face judgment and sentence.

We who feel ourselves to be uncorrupted sons of a great race of constructors (Giotto, Uccello, Masaccio, etc.) have always concentrated on precise figures and expression, even when all the painters in Italy had gone astray and were cherishing the light blue and violet mists of impressionism. And at other times we have declared, as we do again today, that modern French naturalism (gnash not thy teeth in that ignoble tomb, proud Courbet of the barricades), which still holds the field, has never been able to extinguish our desire to give back to plastic art that ideal atmosphere without which the picture cannot transcend the ostentation of technique, since every fit of energy has been expended in the episodic analysis of external and fragmentary reality.

French naturalism, even that of the cubists in recent years, in disdaining problems that go beyond the material, has never managed to signify true and authentic reconstruction of modern values. The new needs of the modern spirit require firmly incised planes and a variety of integrating forces, but above all they demand that the characters of spiritual form be present, the elements that eliminate all arbitrariness in the composition, and offer us the means of controlling the pace and the route.[. . .]

Far from believing that we have completely exhausted the subject, let us conclude this part of the matter by saying that, just as there were impressionists, cubists, fauves and futurists with a set aim, there are already metaphysical painters with an equally set aim. And it is obvious that there is metaphysical art and metaphysical art, just as *Il y a Fagots et Fagots*.

Perhaps in ours one may find insufficiently prepared passages, but if one looks beyond their immediate effect it may be felt that in them the relationships are well-defined, as is the intimate correspondence of movement that generates them.

We will not boast of our incompatibility with current ideas. We will only say that in taking up painting it was not our intention to obscure those limits that lead back to true principles. Hence, if we have not always succeeded in respecting them, it is because it is not always easy to recognize that each art has its own nature.

Besides, the idea that the beauty of a form consists not so much in its points of relationship and proportion with reality as in its overall and generalized lyrical nature, leads one to slide easily into a harmful overrunning of frontiers and into the rhetoric that is always lurking ready to lay upon us the sweet burden of deceitful appearances.

Well away from all conventicles, we can discriminate the good and the bad better than others, but since we do not feel inclined to reprove the childish lunacy of those who inflict witchcraft and horoscopes on art, we do not ask ourselves whether, the present conditions in which the artist lives being unworthy as they are, art's flowering tomorrow will be abundant or meagre.

No one is less inclined than we are to believe that a new art can germinate from these new quarrels, and so we leave to the astrologers and other wizards the privilege of seeing and deciphering the cards of the future.

And although years and experience are accumulating, in us as in others, we must confess that never have we felt more destitute and devoid of prophetic faculties. And to think we even believed we represented an element of life and intactness of the 'Italian Principle' in this age, and of the ideal virtues which guide Italian art through time.

But, by heaven, these are things that nervous imbecility cannot concede, even if they hurl column after column of abuse upon us. Clearly, the fact that we represent something is evidently one of our many faults. All the simoniacs of Italy felt duty-bound to convince us of the insane use we were making of life. The ridiculous exaggerations, the explosive anathemas, the shrieks of all those pretentious and licentious dwarfs, were merely the external manifestation of the attitudes of the rest of that educated mob which attempts in the silence to destroy our aim to give back to the Italians that spiritual consciousness without which there can be no participation in the Europe of today. Among them are the usual angry little writers with their convulsive shudderings who, instead of keeping their impotence to themselves, devote themselves to covert and overt intrigue, and seek to mask their spiteful intentions from those ordinary men who, though their souls may be alien to distinguished achievements, nevertheless show an appreciation of those who toil for art. Among them, too, is the usual deadbeat, who is authorized, by those artists who are currently full of Moslem

1 Carlo Carrà as a soldier, 1917

3 CARLO CARRÀ *The Prodigal Son* 19

2 CARLO CARRÀ *Clown* 1915

4 CARLO CARRÀ *Antigrazioso* 1916

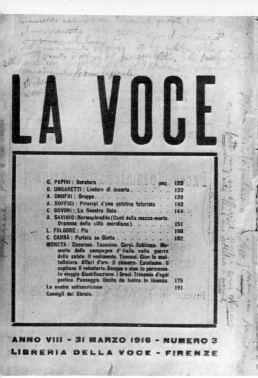

cover of the magazine *La Voce* No. 3 1916

6 CARLO CARRÀ *Composition TA* 1916

CARLO CARRÀ *My Son* 1916

8 CARLO CARRÀ *Drunken Gentleman* 1916

9 Carlo Carrà with his fiancée
Ines Minoja, 1917

10 CARLO CARRÀ
*Still-life with Set-Square* 1917

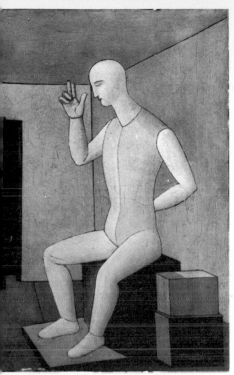

CARLO CARRÀ *The Idol Hermaphrodite* 1917

12 CARLO CARRÀ *Fortune Teller* 1917

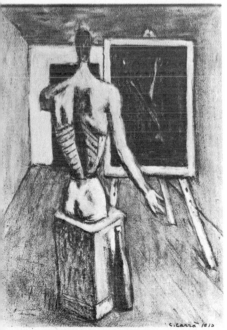

CARLO CARRÀ *Study for 'Solitude'* 1917

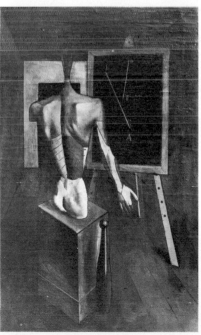

14 CARLO CARRÀ *Solitude* 1917

15 CARLO CARRÀ *The Metaphysical Muse* 1917

16 Carlo Carrà (right) as a soldier, 1917

17 Postcard from Ungaretti to Carrà, 1917
My dear Carrà, It's such a long time since I heard
from you! I have been in Paris and will return
there. I saw Apollinaire and Picasso: we talked
about you, of course. I have had several requests
for my contributions from the [review] *Raccolta*,
but have not sent anything yet, though not
through ill-will. I didn't have anything. Since
September my inspiration seemed to have dried
up. But now I have given birth. I am certain that
few men in Italy write poetry as pure as that
which has been born to me. In France there is
only Apollinaire. I will send them as soon as they
are ready. I am translating all my things into
French, they come out delightfully. You should
collaborate with me in a reprint of my book
because it would then be really precious. Fondest
regards, Ungaretti.

**18 Postcard from Apollinaire to Carrà, 1917**

My dear Carrà, Thank you for sending me Raimondi's little book and the catalogue of your exhibition which interested me a great deal. Perhaps it will soon be possible to organize something for the new painting here in Paris. If you have the opportunity ask someone who is coming here to bring me one of your paintings and some drawings, so that I can show them to those who might be interested. I will let you have them back, and anyway, I wish you great success. Your friend, Guil. Apollinaire.

20 CARLO CARRÀ *Metaphysical Square* 1918

19 CARLO CARRÀ *Penelope* 1917

21 CARLO CARRÀ *The Oval of the Apparitions* 1918

C. CARRÀ

# PITTURA
# METAFISICA

VALLECCHI EDITORE – FIRENZE

**22** Cover of the first edition of Carlo Carrà's book
*Pittura Metafisica*, 1919

**23** CARLO CARRÀ *The Daughter of the West* 1919

**24** CARLO CARRÀ *Metaphysical Drawing* 1921

**25** CARLO CARRÀ *The Builder's Son* 1918

6 CARLO CARRÀ *The Builder's Son* 1917-21

27 CARLO CARRÀ *Metaphysical Interior* 1921

28 CARLO CARRÀ *Drawing* 1919

29 CARLO CARRÀ *Lot's Daughters* 1919

30 CARLO CARRÀ *Lot's Daughters* 1919

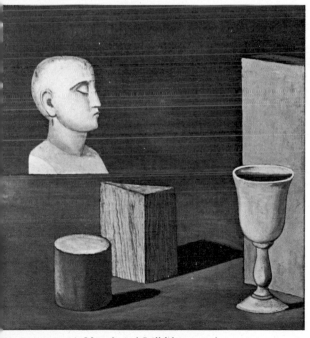

**31 Letter from Cardarelli to Carrà, 1920**
Dear Carrà, I am here in Bologna, and think I will stay here until the summer. Bacchelli has offered me a room in his old house. Such an offer would be difficult to refuse, and so for the time being I have postponed my idea of coming to Milan. However, we will see each other soon, and, if fortune is on my side, I hope to be able to finish 'The Fable of Genesis' soon. What are you doing? Write a couple of lines, care of the Post Office. Can I ask you to do me a favour? I probably have a lot of post waiting for me at the Post Office in Milan, would you just ask them to send it on to Bologna, to the address I have given you? Thank you so much, dear Carrà, and forgive me for bothering you. Could you send me something for the 'Ronda'? I ask this on Bacchelli's behalf, too, and he also sends you his fondest regards. Try to remember, and don't abandon us. My regards to your girl friend. Happy Easter. Your loving friend, V. Cardarelli.

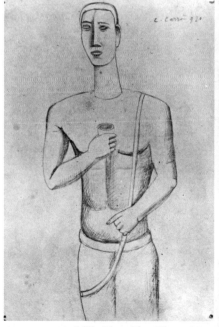

32 CARLO CARRÀ *Metaphysical Still-life* 1919

33 CARLO CARRÀ *The Man with a Glass* 1920

34 CARLO CARRÀ *The Engineer's Mistress* 1921

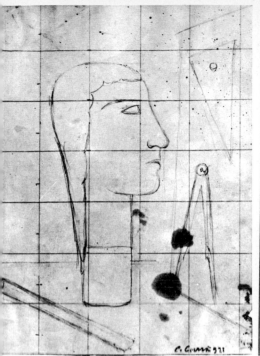

CARLO CARRÀ *Study for 'The Engineer's Mistress'* 1921

36 CARLO CARRÀ *St Anne's Mill* 1921

CARLO CARRÀ *The Pine Tree by the Sea* 1921

38 Carlo Carrà at work at Belgirate,
Lago Maggiore, summer 1922

39 CARLO CARRÀ *The House of Love* 1922

fury against the 'images of painting', to uphold with frantic and immoderate love the impulsive aesthetic which pushes every matter to excess, and seeks to mislead the ingenuous with mirages of an art that is as impossible as it is fleeting.

But, by heaven, there are men in Italy who possess as much imaginative power as they do vigorous good sense. You, dear Papini, no doubt had your eye on this rabble of young monkeys when you wrote your article in *Tempo*. But in my opinion you slipped up on one thing which could nourish misunderstandings and lead to serious trouble, at least between you and me.

I will not deny that a patient and meticulous study of reality, if it is well directed, cannot but have some result. The same brush manipulated by a very skilled hand, and guided by a watchful eye, attentive and ingenuous, can capture well the impressions of light and shade, and with variety of shades give the illusion of things seen in a mirror. But, for Heaven's sake, don't drag up the moribund issue of 'life-like art'. You might remember the words of Raphael: 'I use certain ideas that come into my head. I don't know if this contains any artistic excellence, but I toil to achieve it.' And if you say to me that this is Platonism, 'irrelevant to modernity, I could remind you of the words of Baudelaire – which you too believe – and convince you that this way of understanding the function of art is valid for all epochs. Here are the words of the great poet which even in their form reaffirm the same thing:

'*En fait, tous les bons et vrais dessinateurs dessinent d'après l'image écrite dans leur cerveau, et non d'après la nature.*' 'In fact all great and true draughtsmen draw from an image written in their brain and not from nature.'

Now when I talk of tradition I mean to reaffirm ancient and universal principles, true for all times, climates and latitudes, and I do not do so out of a macabre fancy for reincarnation. You, dear Papini, know how much I too detest those bloodless products of an art without movement, without warmth and without life, borrowed from the museums, and when I affirm that the modern painter needs more intense study and finer taste and more exquisite judgment, you know what I mean.

Let the barometer of Italian art show stormy weather. The tumult will pass and be succeeded by calm. Let us not forget that certain infantile paradoxes engender more evil than is believed. If our friend Spadini, whose praises you sing, has qualities, he owes them to his temperament and not to his myopia. To say otherwise is to maintain that migraine and colds favour thought.

Justice is not a pleasure. Let the brutes be brutish, and let us rather confess that we too have nourished many heresies. If we have never given in to Lady Industry, we confess that we are not indifferent to the attractions of Sir Progress. First we must conquer in ourselves the heresies bred of passion, since before we can make demands of others, we must first be severe on ourselves.

Even if no glory, no esteem, no memory remains of us, we will endeavour to represent in our minds the dispositions of the souls of those who in the silence were able to give us that sound, restorative art that constitutes one of our greatest glories. What does it matter if our words seem dry: the vein of imagination and rediscovery is not dry, even if the most gifted doctors of art show impatience and make speeches fit only to give vent to an infinite series of personal opinions.

He who works for the recovery of the honesty that is essential and indispensable for the nourishment of art needs very different support. How noxious is the constant drip-drip of conjecture, dear Papini! These are really authentic misdeeds that only a sharp jerk on the reins of reality can contain. Ah, the Italian fantasies of artistic cosmopolitanism and of 'universal art'! What is meant is 'universal confusion'.

Everyone says that we are a nation fed on vain hopes and you, dear friend, accredit this defamatory legend. Italy is anything but the land of vague ideas and coarse approximations, and not only for us, but for all the world, situations are never completely alive or completely dead. This way of understanding art is only justified in those periods of transition in which every criterion is lost. Only when the breath of every song is extinguished do men seek the shadows rather than the light. What does it matter if the names of mere puppeteers dance on everyone's lips like corks on the crest of a wave? Amusing comparisons are idle in our case. The work dictates life, customs, and character to us and also tells us whether he who created it was concerned with the true or the false, with toil or intrigue. Must we then say that, with our continual talk of art, we have given life to the most contrary schools, and to the most shapeless expressions? We have only just emerged from a cruel Babylon, and feel the joy that comes after a dangerous rescue. And it is almost through our very surprise, characteristic of true youth, for which desire, deliberation and action form, so to speak, one sole faculty, that we feel ourselves saved. As we said, as far as we are concerned the vein of research has not dried up, but what is being done in art is not completely Italian. And for this reason it seems to us legitimate to claim that the painter who carries out his researches in the true Italian manner, and with purified judgment, should receive much greater support and material assistance.

Our exhibitions may not teach many things, but they will certainly have already taught one thing, if nothing else, to intelligent art-lovers. In some works there is a manifest indication of a greater control of reality and of method. We do not love geometric confusion; on the contrary, we seek to give to our canvases the expression of a plastic reality as simple and mysterious as an act of nature. It needs must follow that we pursue our track with the certainty of attaining the great constructive values of our race: hence, even if we could, without exaggeration, be said to have almost all of profiteering and materialistic modern society, besides the usual blockheads, up in arms against us, it would still not be legitimate to demand that our poetic faculty, so rich in pleasure, should give place to defensive feelings.

We desire that in painting the particular effects of drawing should contain exactly the same happiness that the Italians usually show in colour. Not plastic reality in its initial state, but an image of the form so brightly lit that it arrests reality itself. Without this structural imperative, spiritual liberty cannot be regained, and our independence of the physical world becomes nothing but a vain and pretentious word. For it is necessary for the painter to think continually of the *essence*, which is the means of achieving true architectural austerity. This is the second reality; this is metaphysical painting; this is the promise of all our great labour.

As has been seen, our painting does not place its aim beyond the planet on which we live. But it seems that the critics did not understand this intention when they offered me a tempting invitation to life. Apart from impressionist misunderstanding which survives and repeats itself here too, I do not see why I should exclude a part of the visible. Perhaps because drawing instruments, manikins, copper fish, biscuits and geographical maps are less worthy of study than the apples, bottles and pipes that made Paul Cézanne a great painter?

That is the gross error into which, perhaps due to over-hasty writing, the critic of one of our official newspapers fell. This is what he wrote:

'I am sure that Carrà blindly believes he is doing his duty. His use of paint is too splendid to permit one to suspect him of the base deception which is evident and ridiculous in the work of many others who surround him in this exhibition. He shows, too, a scientific sympathy for all the marvellous toil of the primitives. But he forgets that those great painters were working within their reality, and to create works of art it is necessary to have one's "own" reality.

'It is all too true that we live in a time of such pictorial filth and of such easy roguery that one wishes *never to go into the open air and to hide oneself in the greyness of rooms crowded with dumb objects, characters of an unreal life, terrible witnesses of our solitary madness.* But one needs courage to take things as they come, for one cannot beat one's own destiny. So out, out from the walls of the house, into the air, the sun, out into the midst of the crowd, into life, friend Carrà.

'Sometimes one catches glimpses of flowers flooded with colour, and joys inserted among the stupid crowds under the great sky that envelops our miserable mortality, which make it worthwhile to live in a more carefree way.'

The same invitation was offered to me by the young director of the Florentine *Centone*, who dressed me up in black pessimistic veils like the astronomers portrayed in antique German engravings, and put a starry magician's hat on my head, then flung at me an endless funeral oration, pregnant with friendly regrets.

For these people 'metaphysical art' means sick and evil air from the north, though they do not realize that this is the greatest prejudice engendered by Positivism, which the same people say is the enemy of every authentic art.

Mystery of mysteries! For the duration of our miserable life-span we really will devote ourselves to a carefree life!

'Great debauchees have been seen to throw all their luxury out of the window and turn to asceticism and bareness in search of bitter, unknown joys.' Again, these words by Baudelaire are perhaps a warning for our idle contemporaries!

'Ouch, I've got a toothache,' the painter Henri Rousseau used to murmur every time someone spoke to him about writers on art.

But why not admit that there are also exceptions among those who write about art? Ardengo Soffici, Alberto Savinio, Raffaello Franchi, Giuseppe Raimondi, Roberto

Longhi, Giovanni Papini, Théo van Doesburg, Mario Recchi, Mario Broglio, Roberto Melli, Aurelio E. Saffi and Goffredo Bellonci have all written courteous words about our labours.

These men should be considered the heralds of a new criticism, giving as they do a new voice, new energy and new thought to pictorial studies.

1918; published in *Pittura Metafisica*, Florence 1919

## Theories as Instrument of Knowledge

Having discovered the interdependence and connections that exist between the means and the object created, let us now pass on to observe with complete open-mindedness some of the propositions made by current artistic theories.

Impressionists, Fauves, Cubists, Simultaneists, Orpheists, Expressionists and all the modern species and subspecies tended to create purely contingent methodologies, or at the most to a hypothetical recognition of the general character of reality.

As we have seen, the discrepancies of opinions concern differences of essential relationships. The above-mentioned schools held for certain, in the manner of the earliest naturalists, that every mental concept is born of the sensation, and is contained in it. Now let us see what this intentional and sensory theory managed to achieve. We will not be amazed if within this concept of materialist ideology there are found the concomitant reasons for the weakness and creative superficiality of contemporary artists.

But we do not forget that if we understand art, we owe it to a different sort of mental process which does not merely consist of drifting with the current of sensations. Hence it follows that we instinctively undergo that processing of knowledge that precedes knowledge itself – which the moderns define as intuition – to proceed towards the metaphysic that enables us to find ourselves on a later plane, in a moment of knowledge wider than the previous one. Connected one to the other, these moments constitute the necessary corollary for the aesthetic idea; like concentric circles in water disturbed by a stone, the ripples of these moments distend in the most unexpected directions, with greater or lesser density.

The drawing precedes the work on a summary basis, susceptible to modification, hence it is understandable that it leaves obscurity and doubt, but it is linked gradually to the informing principle, which is immutable in its imaginative essence. The spirit determines the concrete reality. Our obstinate demand is to succeed in making the drawing precede the reconstruction of the picture, which happens architectonically and not by chance, like the sum of raw facts put in order. First the general solution by deduction, and after this the solution of the details. Once the Principle has been clarified one works coherently from the start. Once the law has been discovered, it can be applied to individual cases. Not that this means that credit should be given to the fatuous literary precepts of the past.

This war between doctrine and art derives from the fact that the artist, wishing to convince a considerable number of ordinary men, does not act according to his natural impulses, but according to mediated interests.

He who is over thirty years old and is over-anxious to temper, sharpen, reclean and correct the errings of genius will confirm that he can no longer use the instruments that he has constructed with excessive haste, as has happened to many very great talents, who should be pointed out to everyone as examples, to prevent them falling into the same error. And so I again find myself, without realizing it, concerned with the passions of men and the study of the times. Our Italians, so knowledgeable in many civilized matters, show, where the real and principal aim of art is concerned, that if they feel little they know little or nothing.

From this it could be concluded that the deduction we make is not always one which is able to suggest to us the typical and most correct form of expression. Nevertheless, through the very difficulty we encounter in this operation, it often happens that philosophizing on works of art becomes an enticing artifice, and a sophistical way of hiding our own oscillating position from other people's eyes.

In fact, if one examines closely the methods used by the moderns, though we recognize that they seek concision, and have made every attempt to eliminate elements of redundancy, we must conclude that they often abandon themselves to the artifices of eloquence with the intention of passing off their own mere opinions as actual proof.

Under this aspect, the syllogisms employed by them come to be considered in their own right, detached from the selective process of felt emotions; this involves a deep contempt for truth, which is more concerned with itself than with their elaboration.

But all this cannot, by force of logic, exhaust the question, all the more so since some people maintain, with disingenuous arguments, that any 'rule' expresses nothing but the consistent coexistence of certain effects with certain others, and that therefore, this too is always susceptible to modification by our interpretation of artistic phenomena.

The rule transcends individual facts because it is little affected by the verification or non-verification of the facts it affirms. Hence the issue is not that such or such a fact happened or did not, but only which are the facts by which it is accompanied when it happens (or would be accompanied if it did happen).

To better clarify our concept we should note whether the 'will' can or cannot contribute towards the determination of the direction of the artistic phenomenon, or whether the 'will' is in its turn determined by circumstances.

A great number of writers have answered this question, but hardly ever in an exhaustive or persuasive way.

Laforgue, like an excellent impressionist, instead of resolving the problem, annuls it with this famous sentence: 'The unconscious blows where it will.' But, if these questions about determining circumstances are resolved in this way, we have fled so far from the oppressions of the old aesthetic which puzzled over objective absolute beauty and ill-served any expressive intent, that with the hasty formula of the impressionists we fell out of the frying pan into the fire. Therefore, to the reader our propositions will seem idle, even if he takes into account the continual lies told by artists who, in order to demonstrate the sincerity, soundness and excellence of their works, pretend to be 'inspired' at every opportunity, and in the manner accredited by spiritual mediums, work only according to the movements of the constellations.

They wanted to overturn artistic values, which is unnecessary; instead of the bubbling of a spring, out of absolute 'liberty' there sprang thorns and nettles, and there was born the greatest aesthetic swindle of our time. For whereas the painters of old were used to exalting magic with the firm intention of getting their own genuine discoveries accepted, these modern conjurors try merely to exploit prejudice as best they can.

Now I would like to know how many artists there are today who know how to renounce charlatanism? What would be left of their work if they did?

But there are also those who believe that they can give an affirmative answer to these problems with the slogan of 'the absolute domination of our will', and all its effect on art. These people are even more deceitful, for with their false and subtle reasoning, they aim to resolve everything completely, without any contact with contingent reality.

If we are to return to objects, in order not to lose ourselves in the whims of the romantic 'subjectivism' of the impressionists, if we accept all the conditions necessary for the production of a given effect, it is not irrelevant to insist on the correlation of the aesthetic and moral experience of art.

We believe that only a spirit saturated with historicism will possess the necessary awareness, and will be able to turn to the future with real profit. And since the sensibility confirms the meaning of brushstrokes, hierarchies become genuine and fresh. The value of contemporary art will be to rethink life with a new metaphysical co-ordination. In this way, and only in this way, an excellent painter will be able to merge all the conditions which must flow in harmony to insure the verification of those ideals which alone make great the man who serves them.

For the painter, the forms and colours, or rather, the orderly movement of material, represent the very soul of his activity.

Everything created by man must of necessity be created with a reason, without which nothing at all would happen, and in the creation of art the brain makes use of necessary and inevitable motivations as auxiliaries for the manifestation of the beautiful.

The study of the reasons that make a form pleasant or painful is an activity more suited to the critic.

The great difficulty in rendering in words the tranquil feeling enclosed in a masterpiece (and one should concentrate only on masterpieces) always makes us doubt the quality of our reasoning.

1918; published in *Pittura Metafisica,* Florence 1919

## The Quadrant of the Spirit

### I

I am well aware of the unimportance of vain philosophizing, but people will always be drawn to attribute to us qualities beyond our scope.

I am well aware that only for brief moments is it granted to me to lose myself in my work, but this thought provokes the opposite feeling to that which people imagine. Since I now find myself indivisible from my consciousness, the saying is confirmed that to conquer art coldness, rather than bigotry or untamed heat, is necessary.

Behold, the colours already flow en masse to the initial limits of the new architectural essentials which press upon the surfaces of the canvas.

The painter-poet feels that what is true, immutable and essential stems from the unseen. His elation is not transitory, because it is not of a physical order, even if the faculties of the senses are his accessory instruments. He feels himself to be a plastic microcosm in indirect contact with everything.

The very material itself has only that degree of existence which is implied in the degree of responsibility that is in him.

And so I, in this somnambulant navigation, abandon myself to the infinite element of eternity that is in me, through which I feel a relationship with my truer self, and seek to penetrate the hidden intimacy of ordinary objects, which are the last to be conquered. I feel that is not I who exist in time, but that time is in me. I can also acknowledge that it is not for me to revolve the mystery of art in an absolute way, although at times I almost believe that I am about to lay my hands on divinity: even though, apart from being blameworthy, this act demonstrates an unpardonable frivolity.

I feel myself to be a law and not merely a simple meeting place of elements, as the naturalists would have me believe, holding that all art can be reduced to things executed with manual skill. Thus it happens that I demand all, and not a conditional part, of every inner tremor. Because I make no additions, the distinctive criterion of reality makes itself manifest in me, indivisible and fundamental; I immediately objectivize the idea that creates the form, and to every external object I give a value that is not relative.

### II

A very vexed question is that of art getting the uppermost of man.

It seems that my soul moves in a material unknown or lost in a whirlpool of sacred agony. It is knowledge! It is a sweet dream that dissolves misery and enlarges my individuality in relation to objects. The periodicity of the times, their beginnings, and their continuation, are also enlarged. At this moment I feel estranged from social institutions.

Below me I see Human Society.

Ethics, too, are submerged.

The universe appears entirely in signs and all at the same distance as if printed like a town plan.

And yet I see the limit that is still distant, very distant, and the way to God is still long.

Here I am, doubtful of attaining that absolute intensity of expression that not long since I yearned for, together with that degree of imperfect perfection which yet achieves an organism that is alive in its own right.

The two are not yet made one – that one that is no longer me and is no longer nature.

Alas! now I see that I have been the blind man who destroyed life's magic when he regained his sight. My idea runs the risk of being overturned if it goes beyond my capacity.

I have believed and sworn by the deceiving concept of my mind. Fugitive delight: how my enthusiasm has waned.

It is an illusion that I can halt the immortal part of myself. It is still and always my own ravaged being.

Vain bodies and vain planes smoothed into cubes. My numeratory segments pair abstract and detached stylistic manias, cold, dead and clumsy are these images that I believed constructed in the spiritual centre of time and all times.

Far from frenzied seeking, I felt so secure in the shadow of my work. I felt I had arrived at that point close to happiness which is dear to us above all else.

Oh, the terrifying Beauty that leads to the arbitrary paradises of the Unique God.

### III

In my soul there resounds a command. Here I am again to summon my heavy nostalgia that miraculously survives. And I say: leave the ohs!, the ahs!, the alases! Here I am to muse upon the solid geometry of objects. Will I achieve an ultimate song if a mere nothing sends me into raptures, if a mere nothing sets my heart atremble?

This consideration is here as a parenthesis, a comment upon my own inner drama.

### IV

Natural brevity, intimate and precise in grain and porosity, primordial calls of iridescent solidity, are welcomed by my magnetic instinct.

The sphere indicates: sight is no longer animal.

The cruising of the winds and the wheels of the ultrasensory Fates have come to a halt at the black sea which sleeps perhaps beyond the low level, ashy and striped.

Leaping in its vertical planes the metaphysical house of the Milanese proletariat encloses an immense silence.

Because the curve of the earth has grown rigid the antenna of Marconi's telegraph murmurs the syllables of the legends that return every spring.

This is the poetry of this great and mathematical hour!

The vast sky flattened in the intense tone of slate.

The struggle is about to be resolved as in the year one.

The electric man surges upward in the guise of an upturned cone.

His chest is the shape of an hour-glass, and joy of circular, mobile planes of polychrome tin that make us consider reality as if seen through concave and convex mirrors. On his chest and abdomen are piercing volumes and on his shoulders black studded emblems shot with white light.

On the same plane, but further back, rises the archaic statue of my childhood, (anonymous and timid lover, or angel without wings?) In his hand a tennis racquet and ball like his rubber sister on the wall in front of me.

Still further back, and to the right, can be glimpsed the funeral cippus that perhaps bears an inscription in Latin which for us Italians sounds as sweet as Provençal for a Frenchman.

At the same distance, and parallel, immobile and spectral, is the enormous overthrown copper fish, resting on two primitive iron bars. (Could it have escaped from a museum?)

The shadows fall piercing and black on the grey floor. This is the drama of the apparitions.

Published in *Valori Plastici* (Rome), 15 November 1918

## The Compass-Rose of Will

Obliquity of the north on the mobile confines of ash
Bewildered nudity in the cruel canals of the rectilinear silences of this leaden road
Rubber solitude that repulses me
Poor road you too have never heard the beating of the hammers of Dawn
Tremors of roseate clearness reflecting the voluptuously nestling glories of the iris
   in the hot shadow between sheets of magnetized platinum
Where are the echoes of Babylon inserted one day into the algebraic slate of the skies
   of a skirt
The passion of my dusty childhood down there bewildered at the edge of the ravine
Who was it who threw my destiny into the deep tufa well
Giotto Paolo Uccello
Poor driver amidst the opaque vapours of dreams
When will we fly

When will we fly

Never as now have you seen my splinters of gold shining on the repellent body of
Buddha abandoned there on the red divans of the night cafés of Europe

On the flat moor of Lombardy a new poster grates out its mechanical nightingale's
hymn in the diagrams of the fanfares of Tortum lake

On the banner of my martyr's white are coupled black spheres

Marine silences

The Rose of Will is borne on the neighing of the Resegone beyond the tragic constellations that appear in the skies of the Fatherlands in the vortex of an overturned abyss.

Do not press too hard upon my heart

Spirit bewildered by excessive faith

I stretch out upon the flat moor and close my eyes on the day's resonant tin.

Published in *La Voce* (Florence), 15 December 1915

## Christian Night

Along the absurd roads of terrestrial theology I have cursed the stability of anarchy

The majestic alcoves of the world already know the magnetism of my footsteps and of
my barbaric roars

I fade away into the brackish odours and the rubber of oriental roadways after drinking a toast with General Booth in the taverns of Whitechapel

That evening for the first time I saw disappearing behind my squat figure of an innocent sleepwalker the closed orders the spring frontiers and the hierarchy of the
spirit

I too move every morning at the break of dawn on the mute plain of the infinite

My Destiny a hundred times crucified awaits resurrection

O Night, why disappear before Easter resounds throughout the streets of the Christian
City the song of the mystic pilgrim dug out down there between the strata of
rock and your high sidereal sky

Smitten and bent the enflamed passion seems mystical to the spirit that re-finds its
faith

But the barbaric nocturnal Idols no longer assault with their beautiful autocratic eyes
my childhood far away on the black clouds of mythologies that have fled with their
artificial paradises

O Night, all strewn with golden stars like the madonnas of my ancient brothers my
millenarian body crumbles against the steel pavements of this cruel Enemy City

Published in *La Voce* (Florence), 31 January 1916

**Orientalism**

## THE DRUNKEN GENTLEMAN

SOLILOQUY        ANALYSES AND SYNTHESES        MONOLOGUE
critic                    OF                      sung
MY RECENT PICTURE

After the first flight I noticed immediately that elision of particularities[1] signified that the unknown syllogism[2] presides over the emptied measure, so that the particularities appeared as if overturned into an opacity both negative and hopeless

But a closer examination convinced me that the particularities, like spiders, continued with the patient elaboration of their sensitive tissue penetrating my heart with their so sweet rustling

Heart, curious, ironic heart, your deceitful beatitudes would have it that divine beauty resides in the sidereal irreality of sentiment –

Meanwhile the conscience fluctuated from North to South in the blossoming discomfort that overran the last hope. In vain I thought of the formal imperfections that are apparent in even the most beautiful women, in vain I thought of nature and her transient joys, of the excessive wine-like colours of the marvellous autumn sunsets in postcardlike shades of violet, of spring dawns, in vain I sought out the realized parts of the parallelogram and savoured them with the refined pleasure of the Sybarite, in vain I drank the poison of deceit

The syllogism and interrogation of the logics became more inexorable than life more inexorable than the shadow in the blind man's sunken eye

I had therefore to deny sentiment as I had previously denied the arbitrary presupposition of the celestial theory

And flying up with improvised medleys of colour reducing everything to a skeleton I threw myself upon the last astral glowworms

I was forced to seek beyond that point to dig deeper if I wanted a more lasting contentment

Particularities seemed too much conditioned by themselves and too transient

Syllogizing too wary and diffident

Then it seemed too that the extreme degree of knowledge rests upon the illusory problem of an unattainable unique sonority

It was total failure in place of total glory and I was the man battened to the swamp to clarify to what extent the sky excels in purity the puddle that reflects it

I know that the celestial theory again became estranged from the beauty I saw floating in ephemeral infinity

Suffocated by the hostile opacity I asked for a little air

The Milanese midday hung oily over the city sunk in an oppressive vapour like that of a painting by Carrière

79

[1] Word used for sensation.        [2] Word used for concept.

The subject broken down into its essential motifs is thrown into liberty in the black
and pink toned spatiality

The composition becomes as limpid and sonorous as music on a summer morning

The four tones leadgreyblue Pink White Black like a bunch of ripe grapes project
on to the spherical surface of the composition various reflections of infinite sweetness infinite variety in the unity of four numbers

It is the celestial theory that makes the mute vortex of reality drowsy and changes its
song

It bites into hearts to resolve itself in the crimson of their blood and then to languish
in Nirvana in this haze of pinkish ochre

In the magic of its acrid porosity is incised the semblance of the human male the bottle
laden with its conical form encloses sinuous shading ploughed with austerity in
definitive lines of lyrical deformation

The feminine white-gloved hand in the real convexity stands out clearly against the
varied pink background and with the white of the ocular globe eyepiece of the young
drunkard links the foremost plane of the living parallelogram with the spatial
profundity of the construction conscience returned limpid and sonorous like music
on a summer morning

The terrible logics turned towards the starry heavens migrate slowly from an already
surpassed historical space on the axis of method I saw the five parallels

To insert oneself into one of these signifies to make one's heart palpitate with everything more life another life

enchantment for a beauty that spiritualizes the breakable quadrant of material

Spatiality was completely penetrated by the substance of a light made solid of forms
that perspire in the solar rhythms of futurist orientalism

Here there will be no more tears and no more laughter

The tragic wheeling of the universe is purified in arrested reality

The art of midday is liberated beyond an already surpassed historical space

For nothing my beautiful bliss

What does it matter if we shall not have our Abu-Bekr

Corporeal beauty is spiritualized

Published in *La Voce* (Florence), 30 June 1916

## Evening

Phantoms who walk
in the shade, under the trees.
Phantoms who touch things
with a tender gesture of benediction.

Military hospital, April 1917 (unpublished)

## The Time is Ripe for Questions

The time is ripe for questions,
Singer stabbed in a *bal-musette*!
I have thrown the glass glove to the ground,
I am an acrobat without an audience.
It is night
My soul dances
Sweetly filters the melancholy
of popular songs.

May 1917 (unpublished)

## Fragment

Unsaluted youth your innocence
Provokes madness in the iron wire sleepwalker
On the rectangular canvas
Twilight of tacit adoration
On the pedestal of Pallas the female puppet
Tinted flesh pink
I am the central axis of the white cabin
Stripped of joy my majesty reposes
Behold, my spirit frees itself
I am a granite ball on the pilaster in which the iron lance imbeds itself
With my anatomic hand I coat the glass rotundity
I am the manikin in a lemon shirt on a metaphysical
Penny farthing bicycle for new races in the third rate cycle tracks
Ecce panis angelorum on the hexogram of a phantomatic figure
Soon I will fly up with the low flight of the black cuckoo
Articulated toy held by the plumb line
They will see me ascend the Eiffel Tower by lift
Calm Piedmontese engineer
I have made svelte the hermetic body with paradoxical tattoos
With a fairy rubber glove
On the columns are coats-of-arms of coloured cardboard
Departures for the third magnetic pole begin
The door has opened wide on new metaphysical halls
Up with the flags!
Haul up! Haul up!
Poetry has the shallow breath of a doll
The cuckoo huddles on the black pine
Singing the refrain of my solitude.

Villa Seminario, May 1917; published in *Antologia della Diana,* Naples 1918

## Rainbow of Enamelled Tin

*For my friend Savinio*

Today the spectral grace blossoms from you.

The block of Cantofermo resounds under the white vaults of April.

I know that all your strength lies in those eyes precious with magic.

On a thousand and one starlit nights with you, Savinio, I have met the guardian of the all-powerful monarch, but my opacity did not disappear under his mechanized eyes, even though in me he recognized the vertical clarity of his native Allobroges.

I have breathed in the atmosphere of fierce music. In the sweetest geometries I saw all the possibilities open out, all the promises scarcely caressed.

I have lived in the triumphal throbbing of this moment 1917 so as not to lose myself in the crowded shadows of the fearful poles.

Citizens of the subordinate streets I have captured the profound rhythm of messianic plastic stillness that still breathes the simplified words of legend.

In the glassy speech of the local ruffians I have found again the enchantment of a new Don Quixote the Martyr. I have offered my absurd noon a flash of a green terraced garden.

Captain, see how many intertwined rainbows there are.

I beat my drum with the sun.

In the many-meaninged squares of Europe.

And so the re-established law warms the work that remains silent on the adventurous quadrant of modern mathematics.

O Savinio we will nourish logical explorations and our fullness will appear in shop windows with the imitation fish and birds of zinc and rubber.

Our songs, like multicoloured Eiffel Towers, vibrate against the skeletal reality of a flattened sky.

In the shadow of a Jewish café we unite with the Negro Age of vast, unexpected splendours.

Here in the Worbas the young wear on their sleeves a rainbow of enamelled tin the dogs have the constricted gait of domesticated bears and the decapitated manikins in the ghetto make platonic love with the stars of Verdi's night.

Infantile symbol of Lazarus alive in the medium's reality of four hotel walls, but when the hour of the people arrives and the habitual ornaments of cubic melodrama are thrown down I will rise to 6,000 metres.

With a fresh whirring of the propeller, O Savinio, we will nourish our logical explosions.

And our fullness will soon appear in shop windows with the imitation fish and birds of zinc and rubber.

1917

## Enigmas

One flash of beauty and we will forget whether our life is secure or not
Let us make contact with new myths
The great interrogatives
The obscure pretexts
The noble lies
The great names that have flowered through the centuries!
They say that the will of prophets can melt enigmas
But the gravest sin is still to make love
With necrophiles.
Friends do not think me foolish
If I confess to feeling detached from whatsoever form of wisdom
I prefer to devote myself to problems which have a playful inclination.

Milan 1918 (unpublished)

## The Return of Tobias

'We will soon see our corpses dressed in terrifying black tail coats playing cards at the surgeon's white waxed table.'
It was cold December and Tobias returned to his father's house with few illusions in his heart and in his eye a secret sweetness full of shadows and eternity.
When Tobias entered the city the four gates closed on the dawn landscape.
'City that has no beggars! Welcome the mendicant of the spirit.'
So spoke Tobias as he entered his father's city.
Since his hallucinatory vision was returning, Tobias attempted to persuade himself that nothing evil would befall him.
Because life, his life, quivered around him with the vibration of the elements.
Because his spirit was diffused in a beginning secretly initiated by his destiny.
Because his body appeared diffused in that fear-filled reality like a figuration in the glass of an agitated aquarium.
It was the first time that this had happened. Tobias shivered.
Quite different were the defences the ghost would have liked to assume at that moment, if reason, divine reason, had sustained him a little.
Did Tobias feel himself to be a useless molecular group lost in a totality of vibrating points?
'O purity! O madness!'
His heart had grown heavy. The very stuff of his body mineralized under the fury of a God who raged against the weight, velocity and force of the elements.
'O purity! O madness!'
Tobias felt he had reached the point at which even deep love of life seemed to be great folly.

Tobias returned to his father's house with the smells of the laboratories of America in his soul, and repeated continually to himself that there they would soon conquer chemically the strength of the saints of old and would devise a punishment for all sins.

(At that moment the clock on the tower confirmed the hour of the evangelical age.)

Then Tobias turned to the west and said: 'Welcome to your wisdom. The respite will not be long. Never again, never again!'

The whirling wind carried his words away. Then Tobias felt himself almost redeemed from every punitive idea.

On arriving at the red barracks Tobias remembered the embrace of the drunks endured in the taverns of America and said, 'On the doors of the houses of Europe I see, I see the palm of zinc.'

Then continuing on his way, from the hangars he heard the spinning of propellers. And he said: 'There are our animated machines for new metaphysical journeys; this proves that we have entered the reign of the new astrology.'

Arriving at the Polytechnic the plaster Progress (voltaic battery and cog-wheel) greeted him joyfully. Tobias answered: 'Carry on with your calculation, longer than that which preceded it. Ephemeral buffoon of the fantastic world!'

Tobias, although he was an open-minded man, felt slightly perturbed. Then he walked and walked and arrived at his father's house. He saw that the door was open and was not surprised by this. He entered. He saw the room in the light of the magnesium lamp.

The fantastic essence of that reality was full of a silent gravity that imparted to the objects (papier-mâché globes of the world, thermometers, magnetometers, blackboards, three electric marionettes) a spectral, phantomatic, aberrant feeling.

Tobias felt that these old objects were watching him, watching him.

The stereoscopic silence that his paintings had in common with the primitive images of divinity, now mouthed the ironic enchantments of Satan.

In vain, in vain, Tobias tried to convince himself that all maledictions are confined by the limits of the sky.

Geometric expansion. School assembly hall stupefied in the vertical spirit of silence!

Perhaps there is an imperative command that one must accept like a preparatory affirmation of a higher purity? Why this organic inability to formulate an act of will which will rouse men's minds?

That silence, that silence perhaps desired the name of its imminent Pharaonic obscurity?

It was a midday nightmare

Tobias felt his bones liquefy.

'O purity! O madness!'

His spirit grated in his throat.

That silence had a unique rhythm, like a mineral hum, monotonous, persistent, paradoxical.

With a desperate effort Tobias rushed into the next room.

The corpses of his friends – supreme delicacy of wax – in their terrifying black tail coats were playing cards at the white waxed table. In front of the table was an empty chair.

Then Tobias understood that his destiny was fulfilled. The bells of the city were pealing and the people came and said:

'Who would ever have imagined such a wretched death?'

'Poor man, he was still so young.'

'He was rich and could have been happy.'

'How did he fall into such despair?'

'Find out whether he had gone mad.'

'Oh, that's what they said.'

'We knew it too.'

'In that case his possessions should, by law, be divided among the people!'

## POSTSCRIPT

His longing for virtue led Tobias, from his childhood, to rave against the extreme baseness of humanity; but as his knowledge increased it seemed right to him to restore a considerable amount of primitive wildness, and in his dealings with men to assume that airy indulgence that was later to characterize the whole of his work.

His ideas on this subject can be partly understood from these lines that were found among his papers:

'The *a priori* synthesis and the categorical imperative are not to be confused with the sighs of the blinded chaffinch, but to me it seems equally true that from the romanticism of the master of Königsberg stems a large part of the philosophical disorder that troubles our contemporary culture.'

And at another point he wrote:

'Immanuel Kant's caterpillar-man destroys the world with his egoistic individuality. I favour a doctrine that affirms the harmony between nature and man, and only in the recovery of harmony do I see any motive for overcoming our lamented spiritual disorder.'

And again: 'All modern philosophy is reduced to the manifestation of pride, but the uselessness of trumpeting along the road of pride can be seen from the present state of dark desperation.'

In substance, Tobias envisaged the salvation of man solely as a concrete agreement of the infinite pluralities that form the world, and held that only in this agreement could man find again the repose and peace essential to him.

He loved to repeat that the concept of the absolute that we create is born of the fact that without this we would be unable to conceive of a continued existence; he also said that the idea of values endows events with the expression of eternity, and that the judgment we formulate on these makes them actual, even if the events took place in remote times and places. So that value, time and judgment remain the same.

But if Tobias loved the intricacies of philosophical terminology, his passion for the use of language soon led him to acquire a limpid and cordial style, rich in colour and skilful pauses. But Tobias' most remarkable inclination is to be found in painting in which he achieved the supreme expression of his personality. A profound understander of all the artifices and resources that concur to condense in a work the finest and most acute feelings we conceive towards reality, he was opposed to all the theories put in circulation in Europe by cosmopolitan and esperantist intellectualism, seeing these as cleverly disguised deceptions. In other words, Tobias wanted an art that was the expression of an authentic human spirituality, simple, pure forms full of poetic reality, saturated with transcendence and dreams. But people, intoxicated with the theories then in vogue, failed to see the high truth expressed in his pictorial work and continued to ostracize him.

But this did not make Tobias change his mind, and to the last he followed his path undeterred. To those who chid him amicably for his obstinate intransigence he replied with Leopardi's words: 'If the world reproves us for our perseverance, we will show ourselves to be all the more firm and imperturbable in our pursuit, disregarding such voices, since those who are initially condemned or seem strange, will eventually be considered reasonable and regular; because the world which never believes that he who does not give in is wrong, will ultimately condemn itself and absolve us.

'Hence it happens, and is well known, that the weak live according to the will of the world, and the strong according to their own will.'

The day will come, Tobias, when men, liberated from the bonds of deceit, will turn their eyes towards the cold, evangelical morning of your return, and, acknowledging their error, will manifest their gratitude towards your persevering intellectual heroism.

Milan, February 1918

# Giorgio de Chirico

## On Metaphysical Art

We should keep constant control of our thoughts and of all the images that present themselves to our minds even when we are in a state of wakefulness, but which also have a close relationship with those we see in dreams. It is curious that in dreams no image, however strange it may be, ever strikes us because of its metaphysical strength; and therefore we flee from seeking a source of inspiration in the dream – the methods of people like Thomas de Quincey do not tempt us. Yet the dream is an extremely strange phenomenon and an inexplicable mystery; even more inexplicable is the mystery and appearance that our mind confers on certain objects and on certain aspects of life. Psychically speaking, the fact of discovering the mysterious aspects of objects could be described as a symptom of cerebral abnormality akin to certain forms of madness. I believe that every person can undergo such abnormal moments, and that this is all the more fruitful when made manifest in an individual gifted with creative talent and clairvoyance. Art is the fatal net that catches these strange moments in flight, like mysterious butterflies, unnoticed by the innocence and distraction of ordinary men.

Joyful but involuntary moments of the metaphysical can be observed both in painters and writers, and speaking of writers I would like to remember here an old French provincial who we will call, for clarity's sake, the armchair explorer. I refer to Jules Verne, who wrote travel and adventure novels, and who is considered to be a writer for children.

But who was more gifted than he in capturing the metaphysical element of a city like London, with its houses, streets, clubs, squares and open spaces; the ghostliness of a Sunday afternoon in London, the melancholy of a man, a real walking phantom, as Phileas Fogg appears in *Around the World in Eighty Days*?

The work of Jules Verne is full of these joyous and most consoling moments; I still remember the description of the departure of a steamship from Liverpool in his novel *The Floating City*.

### NEW ART

The restless and complicated state of the new art is not due to the whim of Destiny, neither is it the result of a yearning for novelty or of a sense of opportunism on the part of a few artists, as some people innocently believe. It is rather a fatal state of the human spirit which, held by fixed mathematical laws, ebbs, flows, departs, returns and is reborn like all the elements manifest on our planet. At the beginning of its existence a race loves myths and legends, the unexpected, the monstrous, the inexplicable, and seeks refuge in these. As time goes on and the race matures into a civilization, the primitive images are whittled down and reduced, moulded and clarified according to the needs of the intellect, and a history scattered with the myths of origin is written. A European era like ours, which carries with it the enormous weight of infinite civilizations and the maturity of so many spiritual and fateful periods, produces an art that in certain aspects ressembles that of the restlessness of myth. Such an art arises through the efforts of the few men endowed with particular clearsightedness and sensibility. Naturally such a return brings with it signs of the various antecedent epochs, hence the birth of an art that is enormously complicated and polymorphous in the various aspects of its spiritual values. Therefore, the new art is not a fashion of the moment. Nevertheless it is pointless to believe, like certain deluded and utopian people, that it can redeem and regenerate humanity, or that it can give to humanity a new *feeling* for life, a new *religion*. Humanity is, and will always be, as it has been. It accepts and will increasingly accept this art; the day will come when people will go to museums to look at it and study it. One day they will speak of it with aplomb and naturalness, as they do today of the more or less remote heroes of art, who, already listed and catalogued, have their place and their pedestal in the museums and libraries of the world.

The fact of comprehension is one that disturbs people today, but tomorrow it will do so no longer. To be understood or not is a problem of today. In our work, too, men will one day cease to find the appearance of madness, that is of that madness that they see, since great madness is precisely that which cannot be seen by all, and will always exist and continue to gesticulate behind the inexorable screen of materiality.

### GEOGRAPHICAL FATALITY

From the geographical point of view it was inevitable that the initial conscious manifestation of the metaphysical movement should have been born in Italy. In France this could not have happened. The facile talent and carefully cultivated artistic taste, mingled with the dose of *esprit* (not only in their exaggerated use of the pun) sprinkled on ninety-nine per cent of the inhabitants of Paris suffocates and impedes the development of a prophetic spirit. Our soil, on the other hand, is more propitious to the birth and development of such animals. Our inveterate *gaucherie*, and the continual effort we have to make to get used to a concept of spiritual lightness, bring with them as a direct consequence the weight of our chronic sadness. And yet the result would be that great shepherds can only appear among very similar flocks, just as the most monumental prophets throughout history have sprung from the tribes and races whose destinies are the most miserable. Hellas, aesthetic in art and nature, could not have given birth to a prophet, and Heraclitus, the most profound Greek philosopher I know, meditated on other shores, less happy because closer to the hell of the desert.

### MADNESS AND ART

That madness is a phenomenon inherent in every profound manifestation of art is self-evident.

Schopenhauer defines as mad the man who has lost his memory. A definition full of acumen since that which forms the logic of our normal acts and of our normal life is indeed a continuous string of memories of relationships between objects and ourselves and vice versa.

Let us take an example: I enter a room and see a man seated on a chair, hanging from the ceiling I see a cage with a canary in it, on a wall I notice pictures, and on the shelves, books. All this strikes me, but does not amaze me, since the chain of memories that links one thing to another explains the logic of what I see. But let us suppose that for a moment and for reasons that are inexplicable and independent of my will, the thread of this chain is broken, who knows how I would see the seated man, the cage, the pictures, the bookshelves; who knows what terror and perhaps what sweetness and consolation I would feel when contemplating that scene.

But the scene would not have changed, it would be I who would see it from a different angle. And here we have arrived at the metaphysical aspect of things. One can deduce and conclude that every object has two aspects: one current one which we see nearly always and which is seen by men in general, and the other which is spectral and metaphysical and seen only by rare individuals in moments of clairvoyance and metaphysical abstraction, just as certain hidden bodies formed of materials that are impenetrable to the sun's rays only appear under the power of artificial lights, which could, for example, be X-rays.

For some time, however, I have been inclined to believe that objects can possess other aspects apart from the two cited above: these are the third, fourth and fifth aspects, all different from the first, but closely related to the second, or metaphysical aspect.

## THE ETERNAL SIGNS

I remember the strange and profound impression made upon me as a child by a plate in an old book that bore the title 'The World before the Flood'.

The plate represented a landscape of the Tertiary period. Man was not yet present. I have often meditated upon the strange phenomenon of this absence of human beings in its metaphysical aspect. Every profound work of art contains two solitudes: one could be called 'plastic solitude', and is that contemplative beatitude offered to us by genius in construction and formal combination (materials and elements that are dead/alive or alive/dead; the second is the life of the *nature morte*, still-life captured not in the sense of pictorial subject, but of the spectral aspect which could just as well belong to a supposedly living figure). The second solitude is that of signs, an eminently metaphysical solitude and one which excludes a priori every logical possibility of visual or psychic education.

There are paintings by Böcklin, Claude Lorrain and Poussin which are inhabited by human figures, but which, in spite of this, bear a close relationship with the landscape of the Tertiary. Absence of humanity in man. Some of Ingres's portraits achieve this too. It should, however, be observed that in the works cited above (except perhaps in a few paintings by Böcklin), only the first solitude exists: plastic solitude. Only in the new Italian metaphysical painting does the second solitude appear: solitude of signs, or the metaphysical.

The appearance of a metaphysical work of art is serene; it gives the impression, however, that something new must happen amidst this same serenity, and that other signs apart from those already apparent are about to enter the rectangle of the canvas. Such is the revealing symptom of the *inhabited depth*. For this reason the flat surface of a perfectly calm ocean disturbs us, not so much because of the idea of the measurable distance between us and the sea bed, but more because of all the elements of the unknown hidden in that depth. Otherwise we would feel only a vertiginous sensation similar to that experienced at a great height.

METAPHYSICAL AESTHETIC

In the construction of cities, in the architectural forms of houses, in squares and gardens and public walks, in gateways and railway stations etc., are contained the initial foundations of a great metaphysical aesthetic. The Greeks possessed certain scruples in such constructions, guided as they were by their philosophical aesthetic; porticoes, shadowed walks, and terraces were erected like theatre seats in front of the great spectacles of nature (Homer, Aeschylus): the tragedy of serenity. In Italy we have modern and admirable examples of such constructions. Where Italy is concerned, for me the psychological origins remain obscure. I have meditated at length upon this problem of the metaphysics of Italian architecture and all my painting of the years 1910, 1911, 1912, 1913 and 1914 is concerned with this problem. Perhaps the day will come when such an aesthetic, which up to now has been left to the whims of chance, will become a law and a necessity for the upper classes and the directors of public concerns. Then perhaps we will be able to avoid the horror of finding ourselves placed in front of certain monstrous apotheoses of bad taste and pervading imbecility, like the gleaming white monument to the Great King [Victor Emmanuel] in Rome, otherwise known as the Altar of the Fatherland, which is to architectural sense as the odes and orations of Tirteo Calvo are to poetic sense.

Schopenhauer, who knew a great deal about such matters, advised his countrymen not to place statues of their famous men on columns and pedestals of excessive height, but to place them on low platforms 'like those they use in Italy' he said, 'where every marble man seems to be on a level with the passers by and to walk with them.'

The imbecilic man, that is, the a-metaphysical man, inclines by instinct towards an appearance of mass and height, towards a sort of architectural Wagnerianism. This is a matter of innocence; they are men who are unacquainted with the terribleness of lines and angles, they are drawn towards the infinite, and in this they reveal their limited psyche enclosed as it is within the same sphere as the feminine and infantile psyche. But we who know the signs of the metaphysical alphabet are aware of the joy and the solitude enclosed by a portico, the corner of a street, or even in a room, on the surface of a table, between the sides of a box.

The limits of these signs constitute for us a sort of moral and aesthetic code of representation, and more than this, with clairvoyance we construct in painting a new metaphysical psychology of objects.

The absolute consciousness of the space that an object in a painting must occupy, and the awareness of the space that divides objects, establishes a new astronomy of objects attached to the planet by the fatal law of gravity. The minutely accurate and prudently weighed use of surfaces and volumes constitutes the canon of the metaphysical aesthetic. At this point one should remember some of Otto Weininger's profound reflections on metaphysical geometry: 'As an ornament the arc of the circle can be beautiful: this does not signify the perfect completion which no longer lends itself to criticism, like the snake of Midgard that encircles the world. In the arc there is still an element of incompletion that needs to be and is capable of being fulfilled – *it can still be anticipated.* For this reason the ring too is always the symbol of something non-moral or anti-moral.' (This thought clarified for me the eminently metaphysical impression that porticoes and arched openings in general have always made upon me.) Symbols of a superior reality are often to be seen in geometric forms. For example the triangle has served from antiquity, as indeed it still does today in the theosophists' doctrine, as a mystical and magical symbol, and it certainly often awakens a sense of uneasiness and even of fear in the onlooker, even if he is ignorant of this tradition. (In like manner the square has always obsessed my mind. I always saw squares rising like mysterious stars behind every one of my pictorial representations).

Starting from such principles we can cast our eyes upon the world around us without falling back into the sins of our predecessors.

We can still attempt all aesthetics, including the appearance of the human figure, since through working and meditating upon such problems, facile and deceitful illusions are no longer possible. Friends of a new knowledge, of new *philosophies*, we can at last smile with sweetness upon the charms of our art.

Published in *Valori Plastici* (Rome), April–May 1919

## Impressionism

To talk again of impressionism in October 1919 might seem to be retrograde chit-chat, and yet perhaps this phenomenon has not yet been defined in its true psychological essence.

The greatest manifestations of impressionism in the plastic arts are to be observed amongst the least philosophical races and in transitory eras, between one period of metaphysical effort and another.

After the great maturity of the Hellenistic Greeks (an eminently philosophical race), the apex of their classicism being passed (Phideas, Praxiteles), Asiatic art rises (the *Laocoön*).

The Japanese, Chinese and Russians are the peoples most inclined towards impressionism, precisely because in art they always find themselves far from metaphysical reality and strongly attracted by materialistic reveries.

The most antiphilosophical European race, the English, is precisely that which fathered the most significant impressionist, Turner.

Proof of this is this painter's passion for Venice, an eminently metaphysical city which he saw reversed, but so completely reversed that his paintings are of interest for the paradoxical materialism of their interpretation. Turner's Venice can be compared, for example, with Canaletto's Venice.

It has always been commonplace to believe that impressionism is purely French in origin and spirit. The French spirit is too fiercely attached to reality to be truly impressionist. Its reality is certainly not that of an Italian or a German; it is less metaphysical, less lyrical, less warm, but it *is* a reality, and therefore excludes impressionism. Apart from this the French spirit embodies an inveterate cult of grace, in the sense of the French word *joliesse*. To express this cult another is necessary; that of line and of form, which, as everyone knows, are at the antipodes of impressionism. The paintings of Prud'hon, of Watteau and Lancret come to mind. This cult of grace links the French spirit to Greek classicism, even though, where the metaphysical aspect of art is concerned, French art, when compared to that of the Greeks, is on a lower plane, and expresses a grace that is, so to speak, at ground-floor level.

The phenomenon of French impressionism is a phenomenon of disguised exhaustion; hence it lacks profundity, and is no more than an interval in the history of the art of the French people.

The severity and the cult of the antique that animated the great French painters during the Revolution and which subsequently developed throughout the Napoleonic era, died in the art of two notable painters who were significant, but decadent: Delacroix (romanticism), and Courbet (naturalism). As proof of this it should be observed that these two painters had no imitators, while Girodet, David and Ingres were followed by a legion of disciples. After their magnificent efforts there gradually arose an art that was more superficial and less demanding. One could almost say that the French painters felt a need to work less, to desert their studios for the greater delights of the open air. Even though this attitude persists, I repeat that impressionism does not belong to real French art.

Many critics, afflicted with short-sightedness, have placed Cézanne amongst the impressionists. By now it is apparent to all those who see clearly in matters of painting that this descendant of emigrants from Cesena was anything but an impressionist.

I stated at the beginning of this discussion that the Italian and German races are the least disposed to impressionism. It is noticeable, in fact, that in Italy the style was adopted by the least intelligent and cultured painters. It was clumsily confused with the naturalism that descended from Courbet, and so was born this ambiguous, bourgeois, flat, crude and ignorant art, which could for greater clarity be called 'Secessionist'. This still survives in Italy, where it satisfies official and pseudo-academic circles, as well as the educated bourgeoisie.

And so we must conclude that impressionism has never existed in Italy. Let us therefore seek it in other countries.

More significant examples of impressionism are to be found among oriental races: the Chinese, Japanese and Russians. Speaking of the Russians, it is interesting to observe the differences that exist between their impressionism and that of the English. English impressionism is more coloured, less spiritual (if one can speak of the spirit in terms of impressionism) and at the same time more elegant, less hysterical, maintaining a constant level of *chic* and *bon ton*. In Russian impressionism, on the other hand, the forms are more complicated, more stumpy and twisted, tinged, too with the suffering of popular art, and more restless.

When this impressionism was wedded to the more hysterical and depraved impressionism of music a subtler and more frenzied art was born: the Russian ballet.

Where Far Eastern impressionism is concerned, it would be difficult for a European to give judgment. I am inclined to believe, however, that it contains nothing of particular interest for us. Fatality is excluded a priori, as is any sense of eternity in the subject matter and any feeling of beauty.

The greatest damage that impressionism has done to the plastic arts is to have misled pictorial feeling. This was a feeling (unfortunately one must use the past tense) that still existed in Europe up to half a century ago; today it is extinct. The depth of an artist's pictorial feeling depends on his lyrical sense of art, and on the extent of his metaphysical tendencies. It used to be commonplace among European writers on art to attribute inferior pictorial quality to those works that represent spiritual manifestations. The famous phrase *'c'est de la littérature'* is the favourite refrain of critics north of the Alps who support pictorial raggedness. On the contrary, decadence of pictorial feeling and neglect of material begin with the painters who eliminate every spiritual objective from their art. This pictorial feeling that still flowed through the fingers of painters half a century ago has completely disappeared today. In France there are still a few very old men who preserve the remains of the lost gift; I name only Bonnat, Renoir, Jean-Paul Laurens. I should say they 'used to' preserve, since now they too have degenerated, more through the influence of the world around them than through the effects of senile decay.

The spiritual impotence that leads to naturalism inevitably drags painting to the neglect of the work of art, which is no longer considered as a precious, marvellous and miraculous object, but as an unspecified object, satisfying more or less the demands of the admirers of laundry or kitchen art. The present mania for quick execution leads to neglect of the means: use of bad paints and poor canvas, slovenly strokes with unwashed brushes on canvas already encrusted with paint, tones impastoed on palettes that are never scraped clean, ignorance and complete negligence in the use of paint. There are individuals today who call themselves painters and who waste tons of paint without succeeding in obtaining even one square centimetre of pictorial material. They paint canvases on which the clots and crusts have the appearance of walls destined for use as public urinals, which, through the providence of a public health inspector, have been covered with several buckets of lime. On the other hand, one sees surfaces so weak in material that the grain of the canvas appears under the layer of paint.

Humanity can go astray in certain ways without necessarily degrading itself. Hence the women of today have gone astray, where their relationships with men are concerned, in that they have lost their beard-sense. But in painting it is another kettle of fish. The terrible problem of painting (the most difficult of all arts) cannot be resolved by chit-chat and superficiality. The guilt of the naturalists, of the Courbets and Manets and of the impressionists falls again on the heads of all the painters of today's generation. And if there are a very few (in Italy there are four of us at the moment) who assess the situation lucidly and who draw away in disgust from the slovenliness of modern painting to persist in the realization of their great interior dream, these painters must labour a hundred times more to make their voices heard than they would have laboured in less degenerate times.

Published in *Valori Plastici* (Rome), June–October 1919

## The Architectonic Sense in Ancient Painting

Among the many senses that modern painters have mislaid must be included the architectonic sense. The construction accompanying the human figure, whether alone or in a group, the episodes of life and historical drama, were of great concern for the painters of old, who applied themselves with a loving or severe spirit, studying and perfecting the laws of perspective.

The architectonic sense in man's intellectual manifestations goes back through the centuries to remote eras. By the time of the Greeks there existed a great cult of architecture and the arrangement of the places in which poets, philosophers, orators, warriors and politicians were to meet, men whose intellectual possibilities surpassed those of common men.

The Greeks loved colonnades, under which they could walk discussing and philosophizing, sheltered from the rain and from the fierce rays of the Attic sun, and at the same time enjoy the spectacle offered by the harmonious lines of the mountains, the ridges of Hymettus sloping towards the sea that opened out below into the gulf of Falerus.

The landscape, enclosed between two columns as in a square or the rectangle of a window, acquires greater metaphysical value, since it is solidified and isolated by the space that surrounds it. Architecture completes nature. This marks a step forward in the progress of the human intellect in the field of metaphysical discoveries.

The primitive poet, Homer, for example, who sings of infinite space, the resounding sea and the abysses of the sky fertile with gods, and the forests and the great free planes as yet ungeometricized by builders, that poet, I say is less advanced in lyrical profundity than the tragedian who on a limited and enclosed platform, manipulates the few characters of a tragedy, around whom, close-packed by the lines of construction, those same images of which, in their free state, the primitive poet sang, rise up with greater profundity and with a more surprising lyricism.

The architectonic sense is apparent among [the Italian] primitive painters. The figures often seem to be enclosed in the squares of doors, windows, surmounted by arches and vaults. In this respect these painters were also helped by the fact that the saints they represented were nearly always imagined in the solemnity of their moments of ecstasy and prayer in the temples or near human habitations.

The Christian spirit is much closer than the pagan one to the constructive and architectonic sense, especially since the Christian spirit nearly always flees from the vast poetry of nature in its changing and eternal aspects; following the line of the Semitic spirit, it rises to the arcane joys of mysticism and of the metaphysical, in stripped and geometric surroundings in which the architectonic sense is born and develops more easily than in free nature. Nature herself is seen by the ancient painter through the eyes of the architect or builder. He saw the sky like a cupola or vault, and in it he felt the solidity of the cupola or vault. As happens in the life of man when primitive images and childhood sensations become profound thoughts with the passing of the years, so the first images of the primitive craftsmen, solidly architectonic and sculptural, were developed by the painters who followed with that magnificent sense of solidity and equilibrium that so severely characterizes great Italian painting. The clear horizons that the youthful Perugino saw opening before him behind the dark houses and hills of Muiano, the solid magnificence of the skies he painted later between the arches of the vaults that rise up behind his arrow-pierced St Sebastian, are metaphysical in the style of Phidias. And this element appears again in the triptych of Santa Maria Maddalena dei Pazzi, in which the vaults merge into infinity and penetrate the high and distant sky over the deserted Umbrian landscape in which the tragedy of the Crucifixion takes place.

In the work of Giotto, too, the architectonic sense creates great metaphysical spaces. All the openings (doors, arcades, windows) that accompany his figures portend the cosmic mystery. The square of sky outlined by a window is a second drama inserted into that enacted by the figures. Indeed, more than one disturbing question comes to mind when the eye meets that blue or greenish sky, enclosed by the lines of geometricized stone: What lies beyond? Perhaps that sky lies over a deserted sea or a populated city? Or perhaps it stretches over a great expanse of free and restless nature, wooded mountains, dark valleys, and planes gouged out by rivers? And the perspectives of the buildings rise full of mystery and foreboding, the angles conceal secrets, and the work of art is no longer a dry episode, a scene limited by the acts of the figures represented, but is the entire cosmic and vital drama which envelops man and constricts him within its spirals, in which past and future are confused, in which the enigmas of existence, sanctified by the breath of art, strip off the tangled and fearful aspects that man imagines beyond art to restore the eternal, tranquil and consoling aspect of the structures that are created by genius.

Among the French, Nicolas Poussin and Claude Lorrain possessed this architectonic sense more profoundly than any others. In Poussin this sense is so inherent that even in his simple landscapes his powerfully constructive spirit is always apparent. In this way the trees, plants, mountains and horizons extend, overshadow, sustain and complete each other in turn, fused and completed at the same time by the surrounding air, as happens with the various parts of a building which, whilst concurring one with another, form the mass of the construction and are themselves restrained and completed by the lines of the surrounding buildings, by the streets and squares that are near them. In some paintings, like the *Rape of the Sabines*, Poussin achieved the highest level of balance and architectonic power. In this inspired composition the bodies, like statues, seem to be married to the cubes of stone, they rise up like caryatids to support the corners. In spite of the movement of the battle, the figures have that sense of stability and immobility without which a work never achieves the level of great art. And in another painting in the Louvre, *The Blind Men of Jericho*, the figures in the foreground, Christ touching the eyes of the kneeling blind men, seem to be a prolongation of the architecture, which, with biblical serenity and solidity, stretches in regular harmonious and balanced masses to the clear and distant horizon.

A magnificent example of the metaphysical nature of architectonic construction is offered by another painting by the Franco-Roman master: *Theseus Discovering his Father's Sword*. Here the man is in the middle distance, and idyllic Nature, the leafy trees, the water, the mountains, and the lofty, awesomely serene sky that acquires an appearance of surprising stability and distance in the embrace of the vaults and arches, in the frame of the columns and the buildings receding according to the immutable and exact laws of divine perspective. When architectonic representation is lacking in a work by Poussin, or is to be found on a secondary plane, as in the landscape in the Prado in Madrid, then it is the trees that acquire the appearance of constructions, of scaffolding, of skeletons and anatomy. The trunks, and branches, studied like human bodies, make one think of certain nudes by antique sculptors, or of certain perfectly muscled limbs. Others with their complicated and at times painful writhings bring to mind this sad line from Dante's Divine Comedy: '*Uomini fummo, ed or sem fatti sterpi*'; 'Once we were men and now we have become brushwood.' The masses of foliage, thrown into chiaroscuro by the tranquil light, rise up with the festive solemnity of Corinthian capitals.

With his harbour views, Claude provides a prelude to the emotions of romanticism: the classical magnificence of his palaces surmounted by statues in thoughtful attitudes – muses confined in severe tunics, weary warriors leaning on their lances – staring out with eyes of stone towards the sea, distant and dark, on which, making towards the calm of the port, sail vessels laden with arms and merchandise and fruit matured in distant countries. One thinks of the princes, philosophers and poets who dwell in those palaces, and, further away, in the heavy towers, prisons or fortresses, places of suffering and of melancholy.

He loved harbours, and rendered in architecture their remote and mournful lyricism. His genius could arrange a row of columns, a rampart, or a portico so that its mass concealed a part of life and Nature which yet could be vaguely felt because of the masts, the banners, the limp or swollen sails which rose up behind the buildings. These buildings as they expand in another direction, unfold distant horizons and deserts, or inhabited countryside, thus rewarding the onlooker with that happy shiver of surprise and curiosity that is one of the truest signs of genius in a work of art.

Published in *Valori Plastici* (Rome), May–June 1920

# Max Klinger

PRELIMINARY REFLECTIONS

Germany is situated in the middle of Europe. Such a fate places a barrier between her and the Mediterranean and Eastern countries. Whilst Italy and France stretch out so that with the extreme boundaries of their territory one almost touches Greece and the other Africa, Germany cannot feel the spirit of these countries or receive the torrid or refreshing gusts that blow from them except across the forests and mountains that encompass her in the south and the east. In the course of this study we will see whether this factor can have a beneficial or harmful influence on the intellectual manifestations of a country and on the work of her best artists.

Meanwhile, we can begin by observing to what extent the influence exerted by Greece first on the Romans, and later on the Italians of the Renaissance, was more a formal influence than a spiritual one. In fact, as far as I know, there has been no Italian philosopher, poet, painter or sculptor who has been disturbed by the mystery of Greece. This is not intended as a reproof for my contemporaries, who, to compensate for this, have been and still are disturbed (as far as my contemporaries are concerned I would like at least to hope that this is true) by other mysteries, mysteries of our own land and of our race, which are by no means inferior to those that can arise from the art, thought, and appearance of the Hellenic peninsula.

France cannot boast of such a substitute for her lack of comprehension of the Greek spirit. She, on the other hand, nurtures an immense sympathy for the Orient, in which there is little or nothing to understand, and loves it for its confused variety. Her poets, writers and painters cannot refrain from describing and representing the magnificence and sumptuousness of Morocco, Arabia, Egypt, and of Asian and European Turkey. Some of her philosophers even consecrate a considerable part of their activity to the study of Oriental legends, and reading these one gets the impression that they go into ecstasy every time the opportunity presents itself for writing the oily and complicated fat name of a famous sultana or of a celebrated eunuch. So we see François-Marie Arouet [Voltaire], the horrid philosopher of Ferney, in his *Vision of Babouc* stitching together all his acid, sarcastic criticisms of French society and the city of Paris with allusions derived from copious descriptions of the individuals, society and country of the Asian Orient. Or, in his *Zadig,* he brings to life the pomp of Persian legends; or, in his *Babarek and the Fakirs,* he daydreams of India. Not to mention the Oriental influence on painters of genius like Delacroix, or mediocre ones like Benjamin Constant, or the stupid novels of the Turcophile Pierre Loti.

Where Germany is concerned, the fact of having this powerful barrier between her and the Mediterranean and Oriental worlds, means that when her men of genius want to look deeply into these worlds, they have to lean out like prisoners between the bars of high windows. They have to toil and struggle and put into violent motion all the complicated mechanisms of thought and imagination. The result of this distance and of this effort is a greater and more profound comprehension of what they desire to see and understand. This phenomenon is similar to the case of a man of genius who is usually better observed and understood by a person who is distantly acquainted with him than by his relations and intimate friends. Again, one can quote the example of the landscape that reveals the spirit of its lines only to the man who surveys it from a certain distance.

## THE MYTHICAL-HELLENIC SENSE

When one looks at the work of Max Klinger, especially his etchings, one is immediately struck by the strange and fantastic way in which he represents the Greek myth. The spirit contained by many of his compositions surprises because before seeing it one did not suspect its existence in Greek art, whereas after seeing Klinger's work one is aware of origin. This demonstrates his genius; his work, although very fantastic, and rich in images which, for those little acquainted with metaphysical subtlety, might at first seem paradoxical and senseless, is nevertheless always based on a foundation of clear reality, powerfully felt, and never wanders into delirium and obscure ravings.

Take, for example, the etching of the series *Brahmsphantasie* that represents *The Seizing of Prometheus*. There is no trace in this work of the cloudily and mistily fantastic. Above a stretch of sea, covered by a wide net of foam, Prometheus, held up by Mercury and the eagle of Jove, is being carried off bodily, like a wounded or sick man. In the group the real struggle of those three beings is apparent. The movement of the eagle, forced to fly against the wind and carrying a great weight, is expressed with extraordinary shrewdness of observation. So too is Mercury who seems like a flying phantom, and who, in order to prevent his winged hat from being carried away by the wind, has grasped the chin-strap between his teeth, and supports Prometheus under his knees. Prometheus clings desperately to the eagle, whilst the leaves of his laurel crown, given to him by men as reward for the stealing of the divine fire, fall one by one.

To render the scene even more real, Klinger places the group at the level of the spectator, so that the onlooker can participate in the emotion of that strange flight.

The genius of this composition is clearly demonstrated by the fact that the spectator receives the impression of a scene that is really happening. It is somewhat the same phenomenon as Arnold Böcklin's *Centaur at the Blacksmith's*, which, for a moment, makes one think that centaurs really existed once and that even today, whilst walking down a street or entering a square, one could come across a survivor of the species.

Perhaps it was the influence of Böcklin that encouraged Klinger to develop this curious feeling for mythological beings in numerous etchings. Centaurs, fauns, tritons are represented not only in the midst of deserted nature, or in the company of gods and demi-gods, as artists have always shown them, but in the company of men, in a surprisingly *natural reality* which, when seen for the first time, gives the impression, as I said before, that these beings really existed.

Among the principal etchings by Klinger that contain this feeling is *The Centaur and the Washerwoman.* A centaur, having approached the first houses of a village, has taken up the position of a classical statue, and leaning against a rock, is talking calmly with two washerwomen who are rinsing clothes on the bank of a stream.

Another etching bears the title: *The Fleeing Centaur.* In a field of corn near the outlying houses of a hamlet, a great centaur flees, using his bow like a Parthian. He is pursued by men bent over the necks of their galloping horses, and one of the horses rears up, struck in the throat by an arrow.

As for landscape, Klinger nearly always portrays coasts, gulfs and islands, with pines bent over rocks that overhang the sea.

His landscapes contain a profound lyrical and philosophical feeling akin to that generated by the thoughts of some of the Greek philosophers of Asia Minor, and by some of the thinkers and poets of Hellenistic Greece. A feeling of sweet and Mediterranean tranquillity: happy figures stretched out on the sea shore in the shadow of the pines, in the light of a sun that does not burn. A barely susceptible sense of *ennui* that breathes over everything: over water, earth, plants, over men and animals. A profound feeling of a distant horizon, but not an awesome one, the nostalgic feeling of the peace that follows a great effort.

For the reasons mentioned above the spirit of Klinger's landscapes is in contrast with those of Böcklin, who felt the tragedy of a more northern and continental landscape, and evoked remoter visions in obscure, disturbing epochs, sacred places, exposed to northern winds under the influence of the demons of the North: the prophetic oak trees of Dodona (*The Sanctuary of Hercules*), the savage mountains of Thessaly, inhabited by ferocious centaurs, and dark cypresses bent and tormented by the sea winds (*The Island of the Dead, The Villa on the Seashore*).

But Klinger, who possessed a more complicated, albeit less classical spirit than Böcklin, often unites scenes of contemporary life and ancient visions in a single work, thereby achieving a highly effective dream reality.

The etching entitled *Agreement,* also one of the *Brahmsphantasie* series, provides an example: on a scaffold washed by currents and foam, a pianist dressed in black sits at a piano and plays just as if he was in the calm and sleepy atmosphere of a concert hall. Near him sits a woman. Behind these two people fall the folds of a curtain, that hides the mysterious horizon. Below, in the water, a triton struggles to hold an enormous harp which the wind beats against his forehead, and seaborne women play that harp. On the sea a swift boat, a sort of cutter, bent by the force of the wind, sails towards a mysterious place, a stretch of dark and calm sea enclosed like a high rock pool, cut off from winds and tempests; and in the depths of this is the glistening of the marble of a villa.

To render this so paradoxically lyrical scene even more real, Klinger has placed near the pianist a wooden ladder similar to those leading up into bathing-machines, and the lower rungs of this ladder are submerged in the water. The *idea* of this ladder is a stroke of extraordinary genius. Going back to my childhood memories I remember that the ladders of bathing-machines always disturbed me and gave me a great sense of dismay. Those few rungs covered in seaweed and fungus and immersed at least a metre in the water seemed to me to go down for leagues and leagues, to the heart of the ocean's shadows. I felt the same emotion again when I saw this etching by Klinger. In this, however, the ladder has another meaning: it unites the real and unreal scenes, and since they are both expressed with the same means, and the unreal is not misty and confused, which is how certain painters treat compositions containing unreal sections (one thinks of Detaille's *Dream*), it seems that when the pianist leaves his instrument he can descend into the sea, and that when the marine creatures climb up the ladder they can sit on the scaffolding.

It is a dream and at the same time, reality. To the man who contemplates it, it seems to be a scene already experienced, though it is impossible to remember when or where.

Through its profundity and metaphysical feeling this vision of Klinger could be compared in literature with Thomas de Quincey's tale of a very strange dream in which, as he narrates, he found himself in the hall of a festively-lit palace in which historic ladies and gentlemen were dancing, when all of a sudden a mysterious voice cried out *consul romanus* and the consul appeared with his legions and clapped his hands three times. At that signal the dancing company vanished, whilst around the consul insignias and standards were raised, and the terrifying 'Hurrah' of the legions rang out.

Not many men are capable of creating and expressing such images with such clarity, and it is easy to understand why Klinger's etchings are still not understood by the majority of people, and do not arouse the uproar that is sometimes caused by the works of certain painters who attempt to transform their deficiency and impotence into genius.

THE MODERN-ROMANTIC SENSE

From modern life, from this continual development of activities, from machines and constructions, and the comfort of present-day progress, Klinger extracts the romantic sense in its strangest and most profound aspects. What is this romanticism of modern life?

It is the breath of nostalgia that passes over European metropolises, over streets black with crowds, over city centres rumbling with activity, and suburbs where the geometry of factories and workshops reigns; over the estates immobile like cubic arches of stone and cement, immobile in the middle of the sea of houses and buildings, pressing to their hard flanks the hopes and sorrows of colourless, day-to-day life. And the upper-class villa in the suffocating stupor of a spring morning, or in the moonlit calm of a summer night, with all the blinds lowered behind the trees of the park, and its gate of wrought iron. And the nostalgia of railway stations, of arrivals and departures, the melancholy of seaports, with transatlantic liners which cast off their

o Giorgio de Chirico, photographed by Man Ray

41 Signora Gemma de Chirico with her sons Giorgio and Andrea (Alberto Savinio)

42 ARNOLD BÖCKLIN *Triton and Mermaids*

43 GIORGIO DE CHIRICO
*The Dying Centaur* 1909

44 GIORGIO DE CHIRICO
*Seascape with Mermaid* 1909

45 GIORGIO DE CHIRICO
*The Convent on the Mountain* 1909

ARNOLD BÖCKLIN *Odysseus and Calypso* 1881–83

48 Group of *Garibaldini*, with Giorgio de Chirico and Alberto Savinio as children

GIORGIO DE CHIRICO *The Enigma of the Oracle* 1910

GIORGIO DE CHIRICO
*Melancholy of a Beautiful Afternoon* 1913

50 GIORGIO DE CHIRICO *Portrait of
Andrea de Chirico* (Alberto Savinio) 1910

52 GIORGIO DE CHIRICO *Self-portrait (What shall I love if not the Enigma?)* 1911

53 GIORGIO DE CHIRICO *Nude (Study)* 1911–12

51 GIORGIO DE CHIRICO *The Tower* 1911–12

54 GIORGIO DE CHIRICO *Meditation of an Early Morning* 1912

55 GIORGIO DE CHIRICO *The Great Tower* 1913

56 GIORGIO DE CHIRICO *The Enigma of the Hour* 1912

GIORGIO DE CHIRICO *Drawing* 1913

58 GIORGIO DE CHIRICO *The Delights of the Poet* 1913

59 GIORGIO DE CHIRICO
*Melancholy* 1912( ?)

GIORGIO DE CHIRICO
*The Song of Love* 1913

61 GIORGIO DE CHIRICO *The Square* 1913

62 GIORGIO DE CHIRICO
*The Uncertainty of the Poet* 1913

63 GIORGIO DE CHIRICO
*Self-portrait*
1913

65
GIORGIO DE CHIRICO
*The Chimney* 1913

64 GIORGIO DE CHIRICO *The Pink Tower* 1913

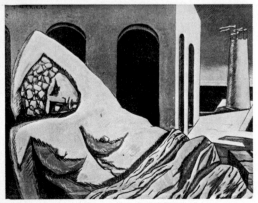

66 GIORGIO DE CHIRICO *The Silent Statue* 1913

67
GIORGIO DE CHIRICO
*Nostalgia of the Infinite*
1913/14

68 GIORGIO DE CHIRICO *The Dream Transformed* 1913

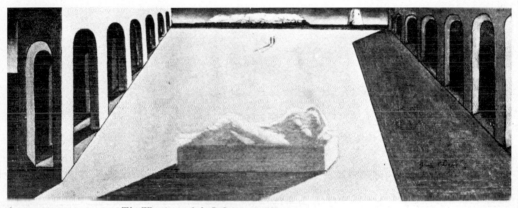

69 GIORGIO DE CHIRICO *The Weariness of the Infinite* 1913(?)

70 GIORGIO DE CHIRICO *The Anxious Journey* 1913

72 GIORGIO DE CHIRICO *Ariadne* 1913

71 GIORGIO DE CHIRICO
*Ariadne's Afternoon* 1913

73 GIORGIO DE CHIRICO *The Joys and Enigmas of a Strange Hour* 1913

74 GIORGIO DE CHIRICO *The Poet's Recompense* 1913

75 GIORGIO DE CHIRICO *Ariadne* c. 1913

GIORGIO DE CHIRICO *I will be
ere . . . The Glass Dog* 1914

77 GIORGIO DE CHIRICO *Gare Montparnasse
(The Melancholy of Departure)* 1914

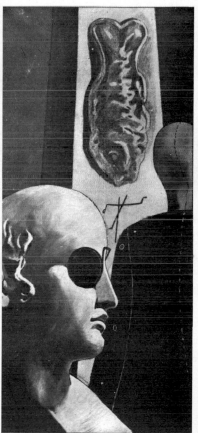

GIORGIO DE CHIRICO
*he Child's Brain* 1914

79 ANDRÉ BRETON
*The Reawakening of the
Child's Brain* 1950

GIORGIO DE CHIRICO
*emory of Italy c.* 1914

81 GIORGIO DE CHIRICO *Portrait
of Guillaume Apollinaire* 1914

82 GIORGIO DE CHIRICO
*The Dream of the Poet* 1914

85 GIORGIO DE CHIRICO
*The Evil Genius of a King* 1914–1

83 GIORGIO DE CHIRICO
*The Philosopher's Outing* 1914

84 GIORGIO DE CHIRICO
*The Endless Journey* 1914

86 GIORGIO DE CHIRICO
*The Sailors' Barracks* 1914

88 GIORGIO DE CHIRICO *The Great Tower* 1914

87 GIORGIO DE CHIRICO
*The General's Illness* 1914–15

GIORGIO DE CHIRICO *The Enigma of Fatality* 1914

90 GIORGIO DE CHIRICO *The Enigma of a Day* 1914

GIORGIO DE CHIRICO *Mystery and Melancholy of Street* 1914

92 GIORGIO DE CHIRICO *The Scholar's Serenity* 1914

93 GIORGIO DE CHIRICO
*The Poet's Departure* 1914

94 GIORGIO DE CHIRICO
*The Day of the Fête* 1914

95 GIORGIO DE CHIRICO *A Span of Black Barbed Wire*

96 GIORGIO DE CHIRICO
*The Destiny of a Poet* 1914

97 GIORGIO DE CHIRICO *Still-life: Turin, Spring* 1914

98 GIORGIO DE CHIRICO *The Philosopher's Conquest* 1914

GIORGIO DE CHIRICO *Melancholy of Turin* 1915

100 GIORGIO DE CHIRICO
*The Poet's Torment* 1914

101 GIORGIO DE CHIRICO
*The Anguish of Departure* 1914

2 GIORGIO DE CHIRICO
*e Fatal Light* 1915

103 GIORGIO DE CHIRICO
*The Philosopher and the Poet*
1915(?)

104 GIORGIO DE CHIRICO
*The Philosopher and the Poet* 1915(?)

105 GIORGIO DE CHIRICO
*The Soothsayer* 1915

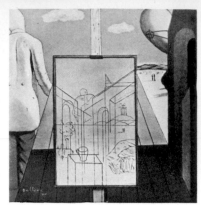

106 GIORGIO DE CHIRICO
*The Double Dream of Spring* 1915

107 GIORGIO DE CHIRICO
*A Girl's Pastimes* 1915

108 GIORGIO DE CHIRICO
*The Duet* 1915

109 GIORGIO DE CHIRICO
*The Astronomer (The Anxiety of Life)* 1915

110 GIORGIO DE CHIRICO
*The Sage's Prophecy* 1915

111 GIORGIO DE CHIRICO
*The Inconsistency of the Thinker* 1915

112 GIORGIO DE CHIRICO
*The Prince's Toys* 1914–15

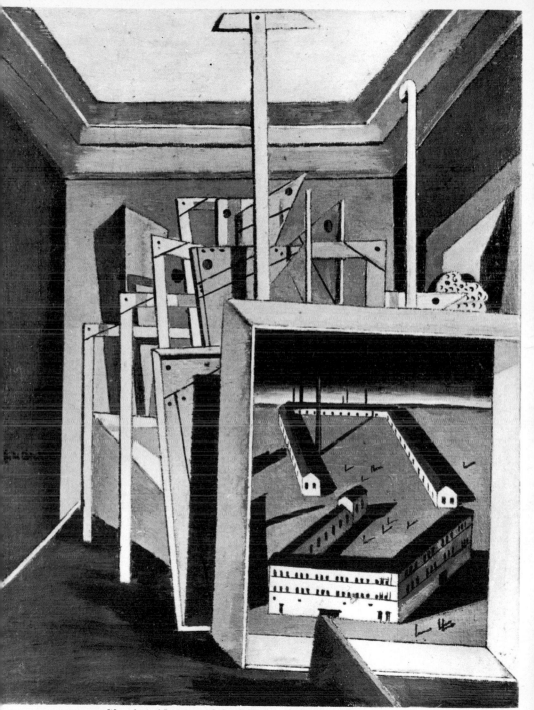

GIORGIO DE CHIRICO *Metaphysical Interior with Small Factory* 1916

114 GIORGIO DE CHIRICO
*The Two Sisters* 1915

115 GIORGIO DE CHIRICO
*The Joy of Return* 1915

116 GIORGIO DE CHIRICO
*The Purity of a Dream* 1915

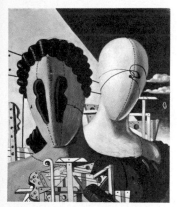

117 GIORGIO DE CHIRICO
*Two Masks* 1916(?)

118 GIORGIO DE CHIRICO
*Hector and Andromache*
1916(?)

119 GIORGIO DE CHIRICO
*Metaphysical Interior I* 1916

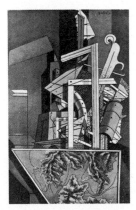

120 GIORGIO DE CHIRICO
*The Melancholy of Departure*
1916

121 GIORGIO DE CHIRICO
*Metaphysical City* 1916(?)

123 GIORGIO DE CHIRICO
*War* 1916

124 GIORGIO DE CHIRICO
*The Language of a Child* 1916(?)

GIORGIO DE CHIRICO *Grief* 1916

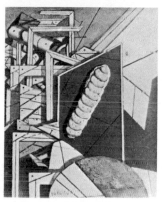

125 GIORGIO DE CHIRICO
*The Engineer's Homesickness* 1916

126 GIORGIO DE CHIRICO
*Metaphysical Still-life* 1916

ORGIO DE CHIRICO
*ical Still-life* 1918

128 GIORGIO DE CHIRICO
*Politics* 1916

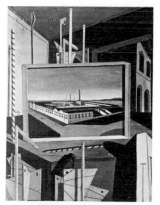

129 GIORGIO DE CHIRICO
*Metaphysical Interior with
Large Factory* 1916

130 GIORGIO DE CHIRICO *Death of a Spirit*
1916

131 GIORGIO DE CHIRICO *The Faithful Serv*
1916

132 GIORGIO DE CHIRICO
*The Temperate Afternoon* 1916

133 GIORGIO DE CHIRICO *Greet-ings from a Distant Friend* 1916

134 GIORGIO DE CHIRICO
*The Sage's Revolt* 1916

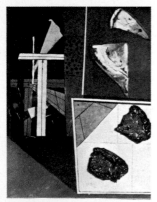

135 GIORGIO DE CHIRICO
*Metaphysical Interior* 1917

136 GIORGIO DE CHIRICO
*Metaphysical Interior* 1917

137 GIORGIO DE CHIRICO
*Great Metaphysical Interior* 19

138 GIORGIO DE CHIRICO *The Disquieting Muses* 1917

139 GIORGIO DE CHIRICO
*The Disquieting Muses* 1924

140 GIORGIO DE CHIRICO
*The Disquieting Muses* 1947(?)

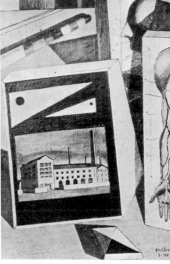

141 GIORGIO DE CHIRICO
*A Scholar's Toys* 1917

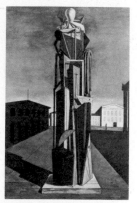

143 GIORGIO DE CHIRICO
*Metaphysical Interior with
Biscuit and Cigarette Holder*
1917

142 GIORGIO DE CHIRICO
*The Great Metaphysician*
1917

144 GIORGIO DE CHIRICO
*Evangelical Still-life* 1917

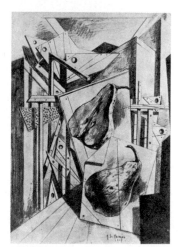

145 GIORGIO DE CHIRICO
*Metaphysical Interior*

146 GIORGIO DE CHIRICO
*Troubadour* 1917

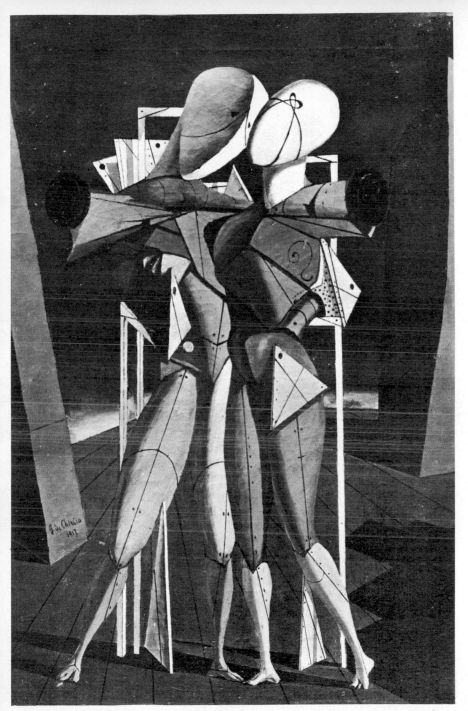

147 GIORGIO DE CHIRICO *Hector and Andromache* 1917

148 GIORGIO DE CHIRICO *Meta-physical Interior with Waterfall* 1918

149 GIORGIO DE CHIRICO *Hector and Andromache* 1918(?)

150 GIORGIO DE CHIRICO *Hermetic Melancholy* 1919

151 GIORGIO DE CHIRICO *Still-life with Salami* 1919

152 GIORGIO DE CHIRICO *The Sacred Fish* 1919

153 GIORGIO DE CHIRICO *Lucretia* 1921

154 GIORGIO DE CHIRICO *The Return of the Prodigal Son* 1922

155 GIORGIO DE CHIRICO *Hector and Andromache* 1924

157 GIORGIO DE CHIRICO
*The Poet and his Muse* c. 1925(?)

5 GIORGIO DE CHIRICO *Memories of the Iliad* 1924

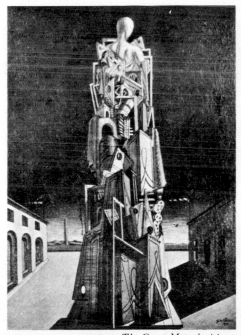

8 GIORGIO DE CHIRICO
*e Contemplation of the*
*inite* 1925

159 GIORGIO DE CHIRICO *The Great Metaphysician*
c. 1925(?)

160 GIORGIO DE CHIRICO *Day and Night* 1925

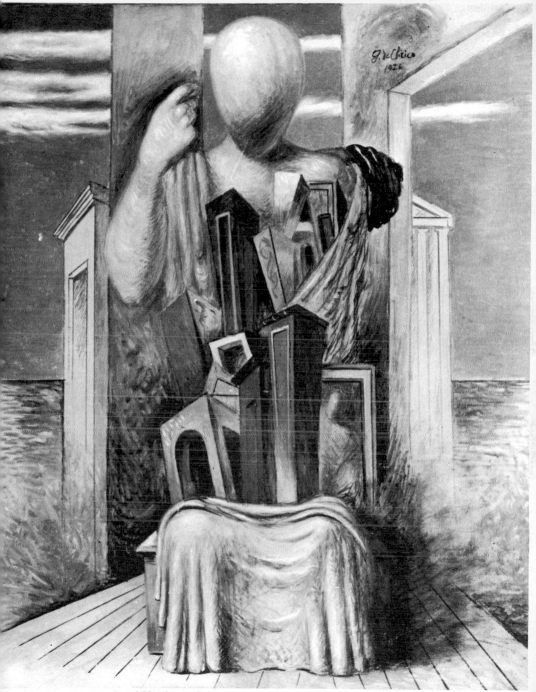

I GIORGIO DE CHIRICO *Seated Manikin* 1926

162 GIORGIO DE CHIRICO *The Archaeologists* 1926

163 GIORGIO DE CHIRICO *Interior in a Valley* 1927

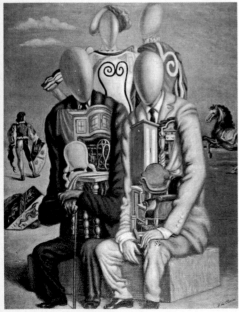

164 GIORGIO DE CHIRICO
*The Gentleman in City Clothes*

165 GIORGIO DE CHIRICO *Lion and Gladiators* 1927

166 GIORGIO DE CHIRICO *Furniture in the Valley* c. 1927

167 GIORGIO DE CHIRICO *Furniture in the Valley* 1927

168 GIORGIO DE CHIRICO *Victory* 1928

169 GIORGIO DE CHIRICO
*Warriors Resting* 1929

70 GIORGIO DE CHIRICO *The Constructors of Trophies* 1928

171 GIORGIO DE CHIRICO
*Warriors* 1928

172 GIORGIO DE CHIRICO *Horse and Gladiators* 1930

173 GIORGIO DE CHIRICO *The Boat*

174 GIORGIO DE CHIRICO *Gladiators* 1931

GIORGIO DE CHIRICO *The Mysterious Swimmer*

176 GIORGIO DE CHIRICO *The Dioscuri* 1934

177 Giorgio de Chirico

moorings and sail at night on the black waters, illuminated like festive cities – Klinger feels this *modern drama* deeply and in more than one work he expresses it with supreme skill. In the etching entitled: *Caught in the Act,* we see this nostalgic aspect of the villa, mentioned above, completed by the element of spectral drama that is also to be found in certain successful cinematographic scenes: it is a moonlit night, and the outside of a villa is visible. From behind the pillars of a window on the second floor a man, the husband, has shot at the adulterous couple on the balcony below. He still holds the smoking gun. A few pigeons, awakened by the shot, wheel confusedly overhead, white against the black sky like birds in Japanese paintings.

The lover who has been shot is stretched out on the boards of the balcony; all that can be seen of him is a leg and the edge of his jacket, the rest of the body being hidden by a plinth on which stands a great vase decorated with reliefs of tendrils.

The woman, consumed by fear, hides herself, pressing her hands over her ears in the anguished expectation of a second shot. Plants and the large leaves of the trees around augment the strangely tragic power of this scene. It is one of Klinger's most beautiful images. As I have already said, it possesses the dramatic sense of certain moments in the cinema in which people inhabiting tragedy and modern life appear frozen in the spectrality of a moment, scenes that are terrible and real.

In the series of etchings called *Paraphrase on the Finding of a Glove,* to the sense of the modern romantic Klinger adds the fantasy of a dreamer and of a narrator, shadowy and infinitely melancholy. This series is autobiographic, the unfolding of an episode in his life. One evening at a roller-skating rink, Klinger, who is among the skaters, finds the glove of a woman on the ice. He picks it up and keeps it. That is the first etching. Around the finding of this glove the artist builds up a wonderful tale of marvellously lyrical fantasy. In the second etching, entitled *The Dream,* he is sitting up in bed, his face hidden in his hands. The glove lies on the bedside table near a lighted candle, and in the background the wall has opened, like the curtains of a stage, to reveal a distant and nostalgic spring landscape. Other visions follow in subsequent etchings. The spring landscape is transformed into a storm-swollen sea; the white horses reach the bed and seize the glove and the dreamer dreams that he is on the high sea, alone in a barge beaten by the waves, and with a hook he anxiously attempts to retrieve the glove as it floats on the foaming water.

Then the glove appears again, grown to enormous proportions. It has become a strange symbol of mysterious and disturbing love, and glides over the water in triumph in a shell pulled by agile marine horses whose reins it manipulates by pressing together its long, empty leather fingers. In the following etching the glove lies on a smooth rock that rises up like a tomb on the sea shore. Great antique lamps burn at the sides, and the waves come covered in roses that they throw at the foot of the rock.

But now the dream becomes agitated and is transformed into a nightmare: the sea again invades the sleeper's room, the white horses reach him. Full of anguish and anxiety he turns towards the wall, and riding on the waves, obscuring the moon as it goes down on the horizon, there appears the gigantic, swollen glove like a sail blown by a storm. Strange sea creatures rise from the water and gesticulate hostilely at the sleeper who seeks to profane their beloved glove. But then the sea nightmare fades away and the sleeper sees the glove, which has returned to normal, lying on a table in an elegant shop. Behind the table a row of rigid and gigantic gloves, hanging from a rail, forms a sort of barrier and guard of honour. But now a monstrous bird passes through the barrier, seizes the glove in its beak, and flies out of the window. The sleeper jumps out of bed and dashes after it, but the bird is already far away. In the last etching we see the epilogue of the story. The sleeper has wakened, the glove still lies on the little table near the bed, and a smiling cupid approaches as if to say that it was all nothing but a nasty dream.

## THE PAINTING

Like all painters gifted with profound and clairvoyant minds, Klinger has sought in his painting to express with the utmost clarity, solidity and perfection precisely those visions, sentiments and thoughts that disturbed him. Consequently he has never come under the influence of the French impressionists. On the other hand, he has drawn useful lessons from Pompeian painting and from the works of our fifteenth-century painters. He has always sought spirituality and completeness in drawing, and solidity of form. He has painted in oil and tempera, tried many methods and over a long period he has studied the complicated problem of colours and that of paints.

One of Klinger's major works is the *Crucifixion*. In this painting he has sought to exploit a certain bizarre and metaphysical appearance that actors assume upon the stage, especially in old melodramas, in which there are moments when all is arranged symmetrically, when one sees the principal characters in the middle of the stage and at the sides the chorus and secondary characters.

The whole picture is *theatrical,* but not in the way usually connected with this word. In fact, while in some artists the theatricality of the work is an element that creeps in without the intervention of the artist's will, and diminishes the aesthetic and spiritual value of the work, in this painting by Klinger the theatrical aspect is *desired* and *conscious* since only the metaphysical side has been used, and, as I mentioned, this element, rather than diminishing the spiritual power of the work, augments it.

Behind the figures in the painting one sees, as if on a stage back-drop, a panorama of the houses and towers of Jerusalem. The characters are all arranged on practically the same plane, above a sort of terrace that resembles the lower slope of a mountain, covered in flagstones and destined to be a place of execution.

The three crucified men are nailed to low crosses, with their feet almost touching the ground. Christ, who is seen in profile, does not seem to be a dying man, but rather one who lives and suffers, a symbol of the extraordinary man and of his destiny. In front of Christ is a group among which is the sorrowing Magdalene, and standing apart from the group, his mother, severe, spectral and statuelike. On the left are spectators who have the strange appearance of fairground wrestlers, or of extras in a melodrama. A group of rabbis and Jewish scribes completes the composition.

The *Crucifixion* was exhibited in Paris, and, in spite of its high spiritual and painterly value, it passed unnoticed, as was only to be expected in that city. On its return to Germany, the canvas was acquired by the Hanover Museum where it can be seen now. The circle of attention and interest became wider and wider, and today it is considered to be one of the masterpieces of modern German art.

Another profound work by Klinger is entitled *The Walk*. In front of a long, low wall constructed of tiles are a few men who are walking in the sun, and their shadows are thrown in profile on to the earth and rise on the wall. The horizon is empty. That wall seems to mark the end of the world, it seems that behind it there must be the void. The sense of boredom and of infinite dismay, the question posed by the line of the horizon infuses the whole painting: the figures, the earth, the shadows and the light.

The works in which Klinger goes somewhat astray are the large compositions concerned with social philosophical thought, like the *Christ on Olympus* and the frescoes in the University of Leipzig representing the heroic period of Greek history, with a naked Homer singing his poems to the Greeks. He goes astray in his treatment of the postures of the figures, in the sumptuousness of the overloaded composition, and falls into a hazy labyrinth that was not what he felt most intimately and profoundly. But in the Leipzig frescoes, as compensation for these mistakes, there is a marvellous coastal landscape of islands and gulfs that expresses the Mediterranean spirit I mentioned before.

SCULPTURE

Klinger's sculpture is absolutely classical. In many polychrome statues, like the marvellous *Cassandra*, for example, he attempted to find again the feeling of the *statue as jewel* as it must have been in Greece's golden age. One thinks for instance of the ivory Jove, and the diamond-eyed Pallas. With great skill he avoided the banality of sculpture into which nearly all those who practise this art fall irredeemably. Even with marble he always sought to fix the human figure in its spectral and eternal appearance, and to encourage out of it an apparition that was not destined to the fleeting moment, but belonged to the past and the future, an apparition that had already existed and was yet to exist.

But at times Klinger descends to 'forced' effects, as in the monument to Beethoven, in which in order to give a feeling of inaccessible height, he has sculpted an exhausted eagle grappling wearily with its claws at the rocks on the base below the composer's seated figure. This work is at the same level as his mural paintings and the *Christ on Olympus*.

CONCLUSION

Max Klinger was born on 18 February 1857 in Leipzig. He died last year on 4 July at Jena. He fell gravely ill in November 1919, and the newspapers mistakenly published notice of his death, which was later denied.

He was a painter, sculptor, engraver, philosopher, writer, musician and poet. He left a book of thoughts on drawing and painting. He wrote numerous articles and studies on ancient and modern art.

Even today, in spite of his fame, he can be considered misunderstood. In Italy the ingenuous crudely confuse him with Franz Stuck and with all that is generally labelled disparagingly as 'German art'. In northern countries he is more respected, if not completely understood. In France no one talks of him, even though he had exhibited more than once at the Salon and collections of his etchings are to be found in the libraries of Paris.

Apart from this, one can hardly expect the mass of French critics and writers to appreciate the work of Klinger, when one of the most clear-sighted French minds, Jules Laforgue, who, when acting as reader to the Empress Augusta, had occasion to become acquainted personally with Klinger, and whose attention was drawn by the artist himself to his works, speaks of them with an exasperating lightness and dismisses them in a few lines. The same writer cannot find words sufficient to praise the studies by Pissarro and Berthe Morisot.

I quote as an example a few excerpts from letters written from Berlin to his friend M. Ephrussis. 'Have I told you about an artist here, Max Klinger, who possesses a sort of genius for the bizarre? He has sent a canvas entitled *Cerné* to the Salon de Paris which I myself have not seen, but from the descriptions I have heard of it, it must be amazing. He is afraid it will be refused, and is sending four etchings and two other paintings. Take note of them – you will be amazed. They are painfully executed and very laboured but so controlled, so profound. Anyway, if you see —— he will tell you about him, and you will witness how he waxes lyrical.'

A few days later he wrote to the same friend: 'I've seen a catalogue of the Salon, have a vague suspicion that Max Klinger's canvas has been rejected. What have you to say about his etchings at least? The ideas are curious, though painful, over-prepared and grainy, lacking in bravura.'

The last three words should be noted. They are proof of a man unsure of his own opinions. The judgment of the Salon jury was enough to make him doubt and to withdraw the slight interest and esteem he had felt for Klinger.

Klinger was the modern artist par excellence. Modern not in the sense that is currently given to this word, but in the sense of a man of awareness who feels the heritage of centuries and centuries of art and thought, who sees clearly into the past, into the present, and into himself.

Referring again to the words of Leopardi at the beginning of this study one could say that the moment has arrived for a definitive evaluation of Klinger.

Published in *Il Convegno,* Milan, May 1921

# Arnold Böcklin

There are men whose greatness is inevitably associated with certain misunderstandings that arise during or after the evolution of their work. These misunderstandings are created by false interpretations of their art by imprudent or unintelligent admirers. The commonplaces born of such misunderstandings, the tone of the praise paid to the above-mentioned men, and especially the category of men who pay such praise, leads to these men acquiring a reputation for exceptional intelligence, and a good nose for talent. Those affected by such compromising praise are regarded with diffidence and kept at a certain distance. The shrewd avoid speaking of them because of a sort of prudence, or rather through the etiquette of a cunning clique.

In literature the case of Ibsen is typical. He was entirely traduced by the Ibsenites, and was misinterpreted even by Nietzsche. Nietzsche himself, in turn, was traduced and declared undesirable by many people. In music the classic case is that of Richard Wagner, and in painting, that of Arnold Böcklin.

Ibsen's case, which contains several analogies with that of Böcklin, has been clarified in a masterly way by Otto Weininger, the most profound psychologist I know, in the first pages of his book 'Concerning Supreme Things'. Limited space prevents me quoting from this beautiful piece of writing by the Austrian thinker, but I refer the reader to it because it clarifies Böcklin's position better than I can.

The most obvious side of Böcklin's work, which has misled many into considering him a romantic, has filled a whole legion of individuals with enthusiasm, and among them women are by no means a minority. This legion with its writings, conferences and conversations etc., compromised the work of the great painter, compromised it as far as more intelligent people were concerned. I must add that by intelligent I do not mean intelligent in its absolute sense, since an absolutely intelligent man has the courage to ignore the opinions of others and to see true value beneath the crust of compromise, as Otto Weininger did in the case of Ibsen and as I do today in the case of Arnold Böcklin. In France aversion for Böcklin's work reaches a peak. Gourmont, the prototype of the cunning characters I mentioned previously, and the only leper in Europe, was, apart from this, semi-intelligent. In his *Epilogues*, speaking of Böcklin, he used precisely these words: 'Böcklin seems to me to be one of those powerful imitators encountered in the history of art of all ages.' Here the true Frenchman reveals himself: in a 'more-or-less' founded on the scepticism of impotence, he disposes of the matter. But Gourmont fails to mention who it was that Böcklin imitated. I am not a hater of the French, who have always treated me well, but nevertheless I think I am justified in revealing their deficiencies and weaknesses, all the more because in recent years they have led astray many of our countrymen whom we would prefer to see travelling a major and more Italian road.

In the first issue of *Rete Mediterranea* Ardengo Soffici labelled the painter of Basle 'a failed master', together with Puvis de Chavannes and De Karolis. A friend of mine, a painter of exceptional talent and a man of intelligence, told me recently that he found excessive Wagnerism in Böcklin.

These are gross misunderstandings. It is wrong to consider him a failed master since he possessed a formidable skill, which was born slowly and evolved as a result of his profound study of nature and of the painting of the past, a study carried out with method and philosophical patience, with love and with the clearsightedness of a poet. Unlike the painting of all the moderns which is based on the immediate, neglecting method and technique, the work of Böcklin is based on prolonged elaboration. A few of the portraits in the Basle museum are sufficient proof of his force and intelligence; solid and clear and executed with a technique that follows the precepts of the great masters, they have the power of some of Dürer's and Holbein's works.

The accusation of Wagnerism is patently unjustified. Böcklin's spirit was at the antipodes of Wagner's. In Wagner everything is indefinite, everything rumbles and is confused, and the power of cosmic evocation is born of a sort of indefinite and inaffirmable incantation; whereas in Böcklin's work the metaphysical power is always released by the exactness and clarity of a definite apparition. He never painted a mist, and never drew an undecided outline: in this lies his classicism and his greatness. He was aware of the weak side of Wagner's work, of its anti-profound and anti-human elements, of its aestheticism and evasiveness, in short of its D'Annunzian side. Proof of this awareness is an episode in his life when he was in Munich and met Wagner, who requested him to design the scenery and costumes for his operas. Böcklin refused categorically, saying that he neither understood nor felt the plastic side of Wagnerian creation.

Arnold Böcklin was classical in the purest sense of the word. In every one of his works one can feel the vision that repeatedly presents itself to the spirit, carried in the claws of a dove, as Nietzsche said: the revelation of that inexplicable something that fills the creative artist with divine joy, perhaps the deepest and purest joy granted to us mortals.

In Böcklin there is always little composition and very little embellishment, no more than is absolutely necessary to consolidate the preliminary vision during its ultimate elaboration. The use of some embellishments is in fact indispensable, and is apparent not only in painters, but in all poets in general. The more classical an artist is, the less evidence there is in his work of compositional effort. In ages of artistic decadence composition forms the principal part. One can, for curiosity's sake, compare a fresco by Paulo Uccello with a composition by Annibale Carracci. In a work by Uccello every figure is in the position allotted to it by an inevitable law and the spiritual power of the whole would be disturbed, indeed diminished, and perhaps absolutely destroyed, if even one figure or object were to be moved a single centimetre. In the case of Carracci, on the other hand, bodies and figures can be moved without diminishing the value of the composition. Characteristic of modern painting, decadent among the decadents, is the effect of chance combination that constitutes the main part of every conclusion. I know of avant-garde painters capable of changing three or four times on the same canvas not only the positions and movements of one or more figures, but even the very subject of the painting.

This does not happen in Böcklin's case.

Every one of his works gives that sense of surprise and unease that one feels when finding oneself confronted with an unknown person, but one whom one seems to have seen before, without being able to remember the time or the place, or when one enters a strange city for the first time, and finds a square, a street, a house in which one seems to have been already. These are strange and inexplicable phenomena which made Heraclitus meditate under the portico of the temple of Diana in ancient Ephesus, and perhaps in those moments his figure assumed the sorrowing solemnity of Ulysses as represented by Böcklin on the edge of the sea, upright above the black reefs of the island of Calypso.

One of the paintings that gives this sense of surprise is that entitled *Centaur at the Blacksmith's*. The inspiration for this work must have come to him in a flash, and its strangeness is rendered even more potent by the classical solemnity of the composition. The figures of the peasants who have come with their children to look at the centaur have the composed spectrality of some figures painted by Giotto or Uccello. The centaur's body is treated with impressive reality. This perfect being, with his hoof laid on the block to point out the necessary repair to the blacksmith, is anything but a 'monster', indeed, he awakens feelings of sympathy. He is friendly, like the Hermes Dionysophoros of Praxiteles; and he is *good*, too, but not in the pious sense of the word.

The sky is marvellously profound, and makes one think of the skies painted by certain old masters, for example the sky of the *St Sebastian* by Antonello da Messina. Details like the drawings and instructions scratched on the walls of the smithy, the white houses of the hamlet profiled in the distance, the square of firmament framed by the window that can be glimpsed through the open door, add to the metaphysical intensity of the work.

With his profound soul and acute intelligence, Böcklin knew how to make use of the teachings of the old masters. Perhaps more skilfully than any other painter, he interpreted the great lessons of the primitive and classic painters of Italy, the Low Countries and Germany.

The French accuse him of being insufficiently painterly. This is a superficial way of judging him, and derives from the fact that Böcklin, a man of profound imagination and restless spirit, having always disdained the facile subjects of the current naturalism and of petty realism, came to be considered, by those who did not understand the power of his imagination, as a literary painter. Since for ages past literary painters have been held in poor esteem as mediocre workmen by our Latin brothers, who judge without examining the works closely, not even the material of its construction, and who follow only the impression made upon them by the subject matter, they concluded without further reflection that Böcklin was a bad painter. But I would like to see a painting by Böcklin hung in a museum, next to an old master, and along with these a work by one of those painters of whom they admiringly declare *'c'est un peintre!'* Then one would see which of the two paintings stood up to antiquity better.

Böcklin, as I said before, had made a deep study of the old masters. When he left the academy in Düsseldorf to which he had been sent by his father to learn the rudiments of painting, he set out with a friend to wander from country to country. When they reached Paris the painter who impressed him most was Nicolas Poussin. He copied his works lovingly and went in search of those wonderful landscapes, *die wunderschönen Landschaften,* as he himself was wont to call them. A few years later he found those landscapes in Italy where he came to conquer and to die. From the old masters he learnt solidity and cleanliness of technique and also that feeling of vibration and the internal life of pictorial materials that renders a painting strange and beautiful, and holds the beholder for a long time. All his paintings are classically drawn, the heads, hands and feet of the figures are of small dimensions, unlike the work of those pedestrian minds which are always strongly inclined to enlarge these parts of the body. Examples of this are Michetti's great heads, and the Tuscan painter Fattori's mania, when correcting his pupils' work, for lengthening hands and feet beyond proportion. As for technique, Böcklin used a very fine and close veil of paint over solid impastos; the use of this veil has completely disappeared nowadays.

He studied those old masters from whom he could learn most. Thus the Venetian, Spanish and Flemish schools derived from Rubens seem to have been of little interest to him. These schools generally enrapture superficial and spiritually poor painters. On the other hand, he learnt a great deal from the Tuscan primitives and the great sixteenth century masters, as well as from some of the powerful German painters like Dürer and Holbein. With rare intelligence he knew how to draw the maximum effect out of certain subject matter, and out of certain aspects of wall-painting. His *Self-portrait,* with Death behind him playing the violin, is taken from the portrait of Sir Brian Tuke by Holbein, in the Alte Pinakothek in Munich.

*The Play of the Waves,* the largest canvas painted by Böcklin, recalls some of the fragments of Pompeian painting, and is full of the same feeling of dryness and flatness as the *Aldobrandine Wedding,* which was also admired and copied by Poussin. He knew too, how to use to advantage the tragic aspect of statues, those of the classical Greek era as well as those of Hellenic Greece and of Rome. In his *Prometheus* he interpreted marvellously the appearance of a gigantic divinity come down to inhabit the earth, the idea for which was perhaps initiated by seeing Poussin's *Sicilian Landscape,* now in the museum of St Petersburg, in which, in the distance, beyond a valley inhabited by nymphs, and on the peak of a high rock, is the gigantic back of Polyphemus who is playing the pipe.

He knew how to create his own world of lyricism, combining the appearance of the Italian landscape with architectural elements.

Few have really understood the profundity of his work. Like all exceptional spirits he is destined, with the passing of time, to be continually compromised by misunderstandings.

I was still a child when I saw a reproduction of his work for the first time. I retained an impression of it that I have never forgotten and even today, with all the experience I have acquired, even though I have forgotten several of the painters I admired in years past, every time I see a painting by Böcklin I feel again that strange joy, that happy excitement, that encourage me to do better. I feel that sense of happiness and faith that only great painting gives me.

It is probable that after all the idiocies that have suffocated us, after all the hatred for all that belongs to the imagination and to spiritual power, after the triumph of the filthy apples and the crooked dishes, it is probable that the great painter of Basle will be regarded with more attention and with cleaner eyes.

Not for nothing are these three words from Ovid's prophecy carved over the tomb where he rests in Italy: *Non Omnis Moriar.*

Published in *Il Convegno* (Milan), May 1920

## The Return to the Craft

*Savoir pour pouvoir*
GUSTAVE COURBET

By now it is quite apparent: the painters who have been agitating for half a century, who have been racking their brains to invent schools and systems, who have sweated with the continual effort of seeming original, of presenting their personalities, now hide like rabbits behind the banner of multifarious fancy-work, and press ahead the latest defence of their ignorance and impotence: the pretence of spirituality. (This is an uncontrollable phenomenon, but only for the majority, including the writers on art; a few intelligent men, whom you and I know, are capable of understanding of what this spirituality consists and of esteeming it for what it is worth.) These painters, then, are returning prudently, with outstretched hands like men walking in the dark, towards an art less obstructed by fancy-work, towards clearer and more concrete forms, and towards surfaces that can testify without too many equivocations, just what one knows and what one can do. In my opinion this is a good sign. Such a turn of events was inevitable.

It is curious to note how this return came about. It was effectuated with prudence, or to be plain, with fear. It seems that the painters feared that in going back, they would stumble and fall into the same snares and traps that they themselves had laid during the previous advance. Such fear is justified by the fact that they are unarmed, vulnerable and weak. While returning it is necessary, too, that they grasp hold of a few of those same fancy tricks: that they make use of the shields they used during the advance. And so the great problem that terrifies them most in this return is that of the human figure.

Man who with his canons rises again like a spectre in front of man.

The neglect of anthropomorphic representation, and the deformation of it, encouraged entire legions of painters to turn out stupid and facile reproductions.

With its return the problem of animal-man looms larger and more terrible than ever, since, this time, the right weapons to confront it are lacking, or rather they are in existence, but they are blunt, and many have forgotten how to use them.

These painters can no longer hide behind the excuse of primitive artifice.

The case of the penitent painter of today is tragic, but amidst such puerile confusion there is also a comic side to it that encourages an ironic smile from beneath the observer's moustache.

Some of the penitents limit themselves to the still-life, which, as everyone knows, was a great refuge and an immense outlet for all those who participated in the revolutionary era. One need only think of the thousands of still-lifes painted by all Cézanne's little followers, the apple with the knife and the crooked dish on the table with its false perspective, then onwards, following this so-called progress towards the cubist still-life: the famous trick of the guitar and the skeletal violin without bridge or strings, and the no less famous trick of the thick black number reproduced with a stencil, and then the bottles and the playing-cards (the less complicated ones), the piece of newspaper glued on to the canvas, the imitations of wood and marble. (When this imitation proved too difficult, or time was pressing and a painting had to be sold to raise the monthly wage, instead of working with the brush like every good painter with some self-respect, they glued on to the canvas a piece of the printed imitations used by decorators.) And so now a section of the painters turn again to the still-life, seeking, of course, to be *honest* this time and to represent the objects with clearer forms. Others, the daring and the bold, even tackle the human figure. But now, dear me, things cease to go smoothly, the snags come to light; there are holes and rocks in the road, and footsteps begin to stray. They need the support of walls and lampposts, and the trees in the avenues, otherwise disaster befalls and they crash to the ground with all four paws in the air like inexpert skaters. They feel like arthritics, or like a violinist who attempts a tempestuous sonata after leaving the instrument in its little coffin for centuries of silence. And yet a beginning must be made! And so, little by little, they tentatively take up primitivism again. They paint heads, hands, feet and torsos which, although they do not belong to cubism, futurism, secessionism, or fauvism, nevertheless, they stiffen into deficiencies and mistakes which are prudishly veiled with stylistic contortions.

By now the phenomenon is as apparent in France as in Italy. I do not know as yet what is happening in Germany, but from the few German reviews I have seen, including *Jugend,* it would seem that our former enemies still live in the *Status quo ante bellum*. I would wager, however, that within six months the transformation that has already taken place in the Entente countries is also apparent in that of the divine Wolfgang.

In France, then, in the country which up to now has laid down the law in matters of art, in France the geniuses whose praise Apollinaire sang in his lyrical book on cubism, in France these much-lauded geniuses are busy drawing careful drafts of the human figure. To think, that what these painters are doing now was being done a few years ago by others whom they then considered absolute imbeciles! I quote as an example an acquaintance of mine in Paris, a painter called Zack, a Polish Jew transplanted with all his household goods on to the left bank of the Seine. This Zack painted pictures similar to those we today see produced by the little hands of the cubists and the penitent avant-garde. Strictly between ourselves, as a painter this Mr Zack was not worth a worm-eaten walnut. This was also the opinion of my good friend Apollinaire, who used to clutch his chest in mirth when the Polish painter's name was mentioned. He would have been dumbfounded if someone had predicted that in 1919 his favourite painters would be producing work of a quality approximately identical to that of the derided Pole. But what can one do? The history of art has its paradoxical turns just like the history of a race. There is no need to be discouraged, however, for time, the best judge of all, will put things in their rightful places.

To return to the craft! This will not be easy and will demand time and toil. The schools and the masters are deficient, or rather they are vilified by the colouristic riot that has invaded Europe in this half-century. The academies exist, full of methods and systems, but, alas, what results they produce! What on earth would the weakest student of 1600 say if he could see a masterpiece by a *professore* of an Italian academy, or by a *cher maître* of the Ecole des Beaux-Arts of Paris? Let us take as an example, the Academy of Munich, which is perhaps the best organized of all and offers its students the most elaborate means of learning the complicated and difficult arts of drawing and painting. A student is admitted after a practical test which consists of making a charcoal copy of a head or nude of small dimensions, the copy being direct from nature.

If this is well received the student is admitted to one or other of the professors' classes and immediately begins to copy live models in colour. The majority of students who begin the extraordinarily complicated science of painting in such a way are completely unprepared: they do not know how to draw.

And yet the art of drawing is considered to necessitate lengthy and wearisome preparation. The student should begin by copying figures reproduced in prints, paying particular attention to the details of the human body – the hands, feet, eyes, nose, ears – and from this he progresses gradually to making copies of sculpture, first of busts and then of entire statues, first the draped ones and then the nudes. Such a preparation takes not less than four or five years, and *then* he can tackle the direct copy from nature.

And so it happens that these raw painters, finding themselves in the academies with palette in hand in front of a live model, being ignorant, through lack of practice, of the science of drawing, modelling and chiaroscuro, are inevitably attracted by the superficial lure of colour, and in this they are encouraged by their teachers, who for the most part are secessionists. The official academies are controlled by secessionists, that is, by that idiotic band of daubers who reduce the severe magic and the complicated art of painting to a sort of decorative trick, to an ornament of ephemeral aestheticism, the value of which could be compared with that of a piece of Art Nouveau furniture, with cushions and carpets decorated in accord with the facile refinements of Russian popular art, the elegance of which does not go beyond the taste of the boudoirs of international society.

In Munich such teachers include Angelo Jank, Leo Putz Samberger, Otto Wirsching, etc., in Paris, Henri Martin, Lucien Simon, Besnard, Laprade, etc., and in Italy we have our dear Sartorios, Tito and Co. This is the point we have reached. This is the state of confusion, ignorance and overwhelming stupidity in the midst of which the very few painters whose brains are clear and whose eyes are clean are preparing to return to pictorial science following the principles and teachings of our old masters. Their first lesson was drawing; drawing, the divine art, the foundation of every plastic construction, skeleton of every good work, eternal law that every artifice must follow. Drawing, ignored, neglected and deformed by all modern painters ( I say all, including the decorators of parliamentary halls and the various professors of the realm), drawing, I say, will return not as a *fashion* as those who talk of artistic events are accustomed to say, but as an inevitable necessity, as a condition *sine qua non* of good creation. '*Un tableau bien dessiné est toujours assez bien peint*', said Jean Dominique Ingres, and I think he knew more about it than all the modern painters. Just as in elections voters are exhorted to go to the polls, we, who were the first to set a good example in painting, summon those painters who have been or can be redeemed to *go to the statues*. Yes, to the statues to learn the nobility and the religion of drawing, to the statues to dehumanize you a little, you who in spite of all your puerile devilries were still *too human*. If you lack the time and the means to go and copy in the sculpture museums, if the academies have not yet adopted the system of shutting the future painter up for at least five years in a room in which there is nothing but marble and plaster statues, if the dawn of laws and canons has not yet arisen, have patience; and meanwhile, so as not to lose time, buy a plaster copy – though it need not be a reproduction of an antique masterpiece. Buy your plaster copy, and then in the silence of your room copy it ten, twenty, a hundred times. Copy it until you manage to produce a satisfying work, to draw a hand or a foot in such a way that if they were to come alive miraculously, the bones, muscles, nerves and tendons would all be correct.

To return to the craft, our painters must be extremely diligent in the perfection of their means: canvas, colours, brushes, oils and varnishes must be of the highest quality. Colours, unfortunately, are of very poor quality nowadays because the roguery and immorality of the manufacturers and the modern painters' mania for speed have encouraged the distribution of very poor products, since no painter was likely to protest. It would be a good thing if painters again took up the habit of making their own canvas and colours. Rather more patience and effort is necessary: but, when the painter has understood once and for all that the execution of a painting is not a thing to be carried out in the shortest possible time, a thing merely to be exhibited or sold to a dealer; when he has understood that the same painting should be worked on for months, even years, until it is completely smooth and polished; and until the painter's conscience is completely clear; when he has understood this he will not find it difficult to sacrifice a few hours a day to the preparation of his own canvases and colours. He will do it with care and with love, it will cost him less, and will provide him with safer and more consistent colours.

When this transformation comes about, the finest painters, who will be considered the *masters,* will be able to exert control and act as judges and inspectors for the minor painters. It would be wise to adopt the discipline current in the era of the great Flemish painters who, united in societies, used to elect a president who had the power to inflict punishments, to impose fines and even to expel from the society a painter who was guilty of negligence or who had used inferior materials.

When Ingres painted, he had within reach one hundred paintbrushes of the finest quality, perfectly washed and dried and ready for use the moment the artist needed them. Today our avant-garde boasts of using a couple of rough decorator's brushes, clogged with dried paint, hard and never washed. It has often been repeated that in Italy futurism, although it did not produce complete artists or definitive works, and although it furnished excessive encouragement for the ignorant and the impotent, nevertheless served to rid Italian art of the academic spirit, of a considerable amount of old and rotten things, and of the maniacal cult of the museums, etc.

When I heard such chit-chat I think of what was said about the war, that the war *was necessary,* that in spite of all the risks Italy could not have avoided entering the war, etc., but what if the war had not in fact been necessary? To go back to futurism: in my opinion futurism was as necessary to Italy as the war. It came, like the war, because it was ordained by destiny, but we could perfectly well have done without it. Humanity needed anything but war. And art needed anything but futurism! Apart from anything else, futurism got rid of nothing and liberated no one. The painters liberated by futurism are like the men liberated by the war: *they do not exist.*

The people who had silly ideas about art before futurism still have them, and as for those very rare intelligent beings who live in this peninsula, I believe they have learnt little from futurism, and the small amount of good they have done and are doing, they would have done just the same without the futurist interlude. Spiritually, futurism was of no use at all to Italian painting. Results in Italy therefore were quite the opposite to those in France, where cubism, and before this, the work of a few individuals like Cézanne and Gauguin – painters really possessed by the demon of art – definitely enriched painting by opening up new metaphysical possibilities.

Futurism, on the other hand, is a sort of confused D'Annunzianism and contains the same deficiencies and falsities as his work: lack of profundity, no sense of humanity, absence of construction, hermaphroditism of feeling, homosexual plasticity, false historical interpretation and false lyricism.

As far as material and craft are concerned, futurism dealt the final blow to Italian painting. Even before the advent of futurism it was navigating murky waters, but the futurist revels made the bucket overflow.

Now night falls on everything. We have reached the second half of the parabola. Hysteria and roguery are condemned. I think that by now we are all satiated with roguery, whether it be political, literary, or painterly. With the sunset of hysteria more than one painter will return to the craft, and those who have already done so can work with freer hands, and their work will be more adequately recognized and recompensed.

As for me, I am calm, and I decorate myself with three words that I wish to be the seal of all my work: *Pictor classicus sum*.

Published in *Valori Plastici* (Rome), 1920

## Seventeenth-century Mania

For those of us who are accustomed to live on deep emotions, on ideas and thoughts, always seeking the clearest and purest aspects of the surprise-packed forest of painting, the swarm of Italians who insist on praising and promoting the seventeenth century, the least Italian of all periods of painting and the beginning of the decadence around us, cannot but arouse our pity and our legitimate protests.

Luxury magazines dedicate their glossy pages to the study and reproduction of seventeenth-century paintings, and those who sing their praise under the banner of the potent word 'Tradition' draw the attention of a swarm of young painters to the hazy century of bitumen and cracks.

Now we who, setting modesty aside, have some idea of what constitutes the Italian pictorial tradition, want above all to study this phenomenon psychologically and to see what are the elements of instinct, education, interest, comprehension, insensibility, obtuseness, deficiency, cunning, etc., that caused the birth in our country of this complicated pro-seventeenth-century movement.

Most people see in it motives of self-interest: the desire to increase the value of certain paintings, little known or forgotten painters who are put in the limelight for speculative reasons, obscure pacts between critics and antique dealers or collectors. But in my opinion there are other, perhaps more important motives. To begin with, for many writers lacking in imagination and spirit, and therefore incapable of treating painting from the critical and philosophical side, the seventeenth century offers excellent outlets for the churning out of vast quantities of articles, studies, monographs, etc. It should not be forgotten that at the present moment the magnificent abundance of reviews and paying newspapers makes this as remunerative an activity as it has ever been.

One should also note that the seventeenth century is easily understood, more easily accessible than those that preceded it, and closer to the intelligence, taste, sensibility and artistic education of the majority of our contemporaries. In fact, what does one see in the antique shops? Seventeenth century, be it authentic or fake, and the same in private collections. The restorers' studios regurgitate seventeenth-century canvases. It suffices for a speculator or a maniac to acquire a figure thrown into violent chiaroscuro, with a white-flecked shirt and deep shadows, to think he has laid hands on an authentic Caravaggio. And all this is explained by the fact that it is easier to imitate a Caravaggio than a Botticelli or a Piero della Francesca, and this explains in turn the vast number of Caravaggesque figures and Ruoppolesque apples and cabbages that one sees around.

The habit of painting on canvas that spread in the seventeenth century permits all the counterfeiting of today, and added to this is the fact that the materials produced by Italian and foreign factories are more suitable to the imitation of a seventeenth-century painting than of a fourteenth-century one, especially since the latter consisted of tempera mixed with oil or resin, but never of pure oil paint, and today painters do not even know what tempera is. In the seventeenth century the use of oil paint spread, the painting against which Michelangelo, who was present at its birth, so rightly railed, calling it *arte di femminucce*, 'street-walkers' art'. These paints, too, are more suitable for the imitation of seventeenth-century than of fifteenth-century paintings, if only because of the inevitable cracking they produce.

The seventeenth century was the prelude to today's decadence of painting. In it are already solidly rooted the vices and defects which are widespread in contemporary art, and which instead of rendering it a source of enjoyment, surprise, joy and spiritual uplift, make it dull, muddy, lugubrious and immensely boring.

In the seventeenth century we see the birth, and robust growth, with all the stupidity of a bard-killer boy Hercules, of that banal and weak bourgeois feeling that still survives, both here and abroad.

In the seventeenth century we see every principle of revelation and discovery extinguished, together with every element of lively curiosity for the world around, to be replaced by a sort of cowardice both in technical research and spiritual content. The painter ceased to *seek*, he lost the instinct of the traveller and explorer. The inheritance of the past masters, of his fathers, grandfathers and great-grandfathers, had indeed given him a certain technical facility, but this inheritance, amassed with such toil by his forebears, was stupidly defiled and frittered away in chiaroscuro and tricks of violent contrast. The problem of composition, in its spiritual sense, no longer tormented him. He looked around with sleepy eyes, became easily satisfied, began to fear complications, and sought to portray things *as he saw them,* to use an expression frequently used by the worshippers of realism.

Thus was born Realism, the deplorable consequences of which are apparent today in our country to those who have clean eyes and a clear mind.

In the seventeenth century the human figure lost all power of expression, every element of spectrality, all spiritual value, and became a *still-life*. It is curious to note the affinity in painting of this century between animate and inanimate objects, between a head, for example, and an apple or cabbage. There are people little accustomed to the world of the spirit who find facile and instinctive enjoyment in the contemplation of such works and of such logic; indeed, in France, realist painting is always destined to achieve the greatest success. But what amazes, or rather revolts us, is that certain people try, in one way or another, to identify in the seventeenth century the foundations of the Italian artistic tradition. They do not state or write this clearly, but if one reads between the lines it becomes obvious.

And now I ask of this select legion of critics, of failed writers, aesthetes and gallery inspectors who seek to promote the seventeenth century, have they ever thought of the possible existence of an *Italian spirit* determined by inevitable reasons of geographic configuration, of climate and history, of the physical and metaphysical appearance of our peninsula? And if they admit to having thought of the existence of such a spirit, even if in an obscure and confused way, have they ever wondered what would be the most faithful representation of it translated into the plastic arts, and particularly into painting? I know an Italian spirit that is the spirit of the traveller and the discoverer of new worlds, I know an Italian spirit that is sad, even in its joy, and more profound in its joy than in its sadness, I know a classical Italian nature which is languid and adventurous, and in which I find elements of every country of the world: from the clear, immobile beauty of ancient Greece to the demons of Africa and of the North. I find this spirit, with all the inevitable complications and deformations and additions born of painting (the most magical art), in the work of a Fra Angelico, of a Carpaccio, of a Signorelli, of a Botticelli, of a Piero della Francesca; but I do not find even a shadow of it in any painting of the seventeenth century.

Caravaggio is the painter most frequently and gladly cited by the seventeenth century fanatics, who seek to find in his painting a justification for the exaggerated panegyric they offer to his greater or lesser contemporaries. It does not seem to me that he merits such praise.

In Italian seventeenth-century painting we cannot even boast of a Poussin or a Claude Lorrain, who, even though they lack the solid clarity of a Fra Angelico or a Botticelli, nevertheless arouse our admiration and sympathy for their great breadth of poetry, for the idyllic and heroic sense, that is always infused into their canvases, and which they learnt from Italian landscapes and buildings. There were seventeenth-century Italian painters who followed this example, the most interesting of whom in my opinion is Francesco Grimaldi, dubbed Bolognese; but they were only imitators.

If an Italian spirit exists in painting, I can see it only in the fifteenth century. In this century the toil and labour of the medieval ages, the midnight dreams and magnificent nightmares of Masaccio and Uccello were resolved in the immobile clarity and adamantine transparency of a happy and tranquil art that nevertheless contained an element of unease, like a ship that reaches the calm port of a sunny land after battling through dark seas and contrary winds.

The fifteenth century offers this, the most beautiful painting in the history of art, an art that is clear and solid, in which figures and objects appear as if washed and purified, resplendent with internal light. Phenomena of metaphysical beauty that contains something springlike and yet autumnal at the same time. Works of this century offer themselves to us with the sonorous clarity of palaces, of stones and Roman walks washed by a nocturnal storm, or against the purity of an October afternoon sky.

This magnificent feeling was still apparent in the youthful work of Raphael (*The Wedding of the Virgin*), and then the selfsame painter of Urbino degenerated gradually in the last years of his life, the prelude to the darkness of the sixteenth century.

Published in '*Valori Plastici*' (Rome), No. 3, 1921

# Statues, Furniture and Generals

*'The world is full of daemons.*
HERACLITUS OF EPHESUS

When walking through a museum of antique sculpture and coming across a deserted room we often receive the impression that the statues take on a new appearance. A statue on the façade of a palace, or in a temple, as opposed to a garden or a public place, reveals different metaphysical characteristics; on top of a palace against the southern sky it acquires a Homeric quality, a sort of severe and distant joy, mingled with melancholy. In public places its appearance comes as a surprise, especially if its pedestal is low, for then it seems to merge into the swirling of the crowd and of everyday town life.

In a museum a statue looks different, and then it is its phantomatic appearance that strikes us, an appearance like that of people suddenly noticed in a room we had at first thought to be empty.

The lines of the walls, floor and ceiling separate the statue from the exterior world: it is no longer a figure destined to mingle with nature, or with the beauty of a landscape or to complete the aesthetic harmony of an architectural construction. It appears in its most solitary aspect and becomes a ghost that appears before us and surprises us.

And yet a statue is not destined always to stand in a place enclosed by well-defined lines. In ancient times statues were to be seen everywhere: in and outside palaces and temples, in gardens and towns, in harbours and the courtyards of houses.

We have long been accustomed to seeing statues in museums, and the appearances of statues standing in the above-mentioned places has long been known and often exploited by poets as well as painters. To discover newer and more mysterious aspects we must have access to new combinations. For example: a statue in a room, whether it be alone or in the company of living people, could give us a new emotion if it were made in such a way that its feet rested on the floor and not on a base. The same impression could be produced by a statue sitting in a *real* armchair or leaning against a *real* window.

The furniture to which we have been accustomed since our childhood awakens in us feelings with which many of us are familiar. And yet as far as I know furniture is not credited with the power of being able to awaken ideas of any particular strangeness within us. For some time I have known from experience that this is often possible.

The reader may have noticed the singular appearance of beds, mirror-fronted wardrobes, armchairs, divans, and tables when one comes across them unexpectedly in a street in the midst of unaccustomed surroundings, as happens when people are moving house, or in areas where dealers show their merchandise on the pavement. The pieces of furniture then appear in a new light; they are reclothed in a strange solitude, a great intimacy grows between them, and one could say that a strange happiness hovers in the narrow space they occupy on the pavement in the midst of the fevered life of the town and the hasty comings and going of men. An immense and strange happiness is radiated by this blessed and mysterious little island against which the thundering waves of the raging sea crash in vain. One can imagine that if a passer-by somewhere down there in the crowd in the town, where people mill in ever greater numbers and the roar of man's activity and obsessive work is even more intense, if such a passer-by were suddenly to be seized by an indescribable terror and panic, like Orestes pursued by the Furies, or a deposed tyrant fleeing from the unleashed anger of his rebelling people, and were to seek refuge in the little island formed by the furniture displayed on the pavement and let himself sink into an armchair in their midst, then he would suddenly find himself sheltered from all the persecutions of gods and men, and could contemplate the thundering of the clouds or the wrath of an unleashed mob, as a Sunday stroller in the zoo contemplates the cruel tiger gnawing angrily and in vain at the bars of his cage.

Furniture, removed from the atmosphere of our rooms and shown outside, awakens in us an emotion that also reveals a new aspect of the street in which it stands.

The effect of furniture placed in deserted countryside, in the midst of infinite Nature, is also very profound: like an armchair, a divan and chairs grouped together on a Greek plain, or on the traditionless prairies of distant America.

And by contrast the countryside surrounding the furniture reveals to us an aspect of itself that we did not know.

Furniture abandoned in the midst of great Nature: this is innocence, tenderness, and sweetness in the midst of blind and destructive forces, children and pure virgins in a circus full of famished lions; protected by their innocence they are there, distant and solitary. And in the same way we see great armchairs and large divans on the shore of the roaring sea, or at the bottom of valleys surrounded by high mountains.

But these are only a few of the impressions and emotions that such things can impart. There are others even more solitary and mysterious. The furniture in the street is, as I said, the temple into which Orestes flings himself. On the threshold of these temples the Furies come impotent to a halt, and in the boredom of the wait they finally fall asleep and snore.

For some time now I have been obsessed by the appearance of such furniture left standing outside houses, and in some of my recent paintings I have tried to express the emotion I feel.

I find a reflection of all these emotions in this strange image expressed by the poet Jean Cocteau: 'In this landscape we saw two screens and a chair. It was the opposite of a ruin. Fragments of a palace of the future.'

The funerals of senior officers, generals, field-marshals, etc., have always made a very strange impression on me . . . Above all at the moment when the body of the dead man is still in the house, whilst below, in the street, the cortège is being formed amidst the manœuvres of a military or marine detachment; the arrival of the civil servants and dignitaries, the movement of the crowd, etc., all this has always made a very deep and mysterious impression upon me. I imagine that the burial of a king, or a prince, or a pope would have the same effect on me.

I think the origin of this must reside in the fact that all these characters are basically phantoms. This phantomlike nature appears even more when they mingle with the life of the crowd, for they seem to belong to another element, and to find themselves there due only to a strange combination of enigmatic circumstances. And so, when we are present at their funerals what strikes us above all is the idea of the *death of a phantom*. We think: a phantom is dead, and men – who did not know him – come to honour and mourn him!

And yet painting concerns us as much for its material and craft[1] side as for its enigmatic and disturbing aspects.

The one side enriches the other and makes painting worthy of existence. Painting demonstrates not only the enigmatic and the disturbing, but also the lyrical and consoling, and it is good that it should be so, otherwise we would be forced to leave our studios and dedicate ourselves to pure meditation, as did Socrates Deliomachos on the memorable night that preceded the battle.

[Written in French]

## Epode

Return, O my first happiness!
Joy inhabits the strange cities,
A new magic has descended to earth
City of undreamed dreams,
Constructed by daemons with such patience,
Faithful to you will I sing!
One day I too will be a man of stone,
Bridegroom, widower on an Etruscan tomb . . .
That day, maternal goddess, hold me tight
In your great embrace, of stone.

Ferrara 1917

## Zeuxis the Explorer

To Mario Broglio

Once the openings in the idiotic stockade that enclosed the various bleating or bellowing groups had been broken through, the new Zeuxises departed alone in search of curiosity, and like moles they found nooks for themselves all over the crust of the globe.

153

[1] I say this for the benefit of all those who think of us painters, poets, and philosophers as alchemists and cabalists continually plunged in reveries of mumbo-jumbo.

'The world is full of daemons,' said Heraclitus of Ephesus, walking in the shadow of the porticoes at the mystery-fraught noonday hour, whilst in the dry embrace of the Asiatic gulf, the salt water simmered under the south-west wind.

*The daemon in everything must be discovered.*

The ancient Cretans stamped an enormous eye in the midst of the emaciated profiles that ran round their vases, domestic utensils and the walls of their houses.

And the foetus of a man, of a fish, of a chicken, of a snake, in the earliest stage, is all eye.

*The daemon in everything must be discovered.*

I already thought in this way in Paris in the last years before the explosion of the conflict.

Around me the international set of 'Modern' painters were struggling stupidly amid exploited formulas and sterile systems.

I alone, in my squalid studio in the Rue Campagne-Première, had begun to perceive the first ghosts of an art that was more complete, more profound and more complicated, and, to pronounce the word at the risk of throwing a French critic into a fit of liver-gripe: *more metaphysical*.

New lands appeared on the horizon.

The great glove of painted zinc, with its terrible gilded nails, swinging on the workshop door in the sad breeze of an urban afternoon, pointed with its index finger at the stones of the pavement, indicating to me the hermetic signs of a new melancholy.

The *papier mâché* skull in the middle of the hairdresser's window, carved in the strident heroism of shadowy prehistory, seared into my heart and my brain like a reoccurring song.

The daemons of the city opened the street before me.

When I entered the house again more harbinger ghosts came to meet me.

On the ceiling I noticed new signs of the zodiac, when I stared at the desperate flight that ended in death at the back of the room in the rectangle of the window open on to the mystery of the street.

The door half-closed to the night of the ante-chamber had the sepulchral solemnity of the stone moved from the empty tomb of the risen man.

And the new paintings arose in annunciation.

Like autumn fruits we are ripe for new metaphysics.

Powerful gusts come from beyond the troubled seas.

Our summons reaches the densely-populated cities of the far-off continents.

We must not grow complacent in the happiness of our new creations.

We are explorers ready for new departures.

Under the corrugated roofs resounding with metallic blows the quadrants are touched at the sign of casting-off time.

In the walled-up boxes the bells vibrate.

It is time. . . .

All aboard, gentlemen, *please*!

Rome, April 1918; published in Valori Plastici (Rome), 15 November 1918

# Alberto Savinio

## Anadyomenon: Principles in the Evaluation of Contemporary Art

We live in a phantasmic world with which we are gradually becoming familiar.

I shall now dispense with this use of the plural: there were, are and always will be very few of us who feel the completeness of life.

Let us not limit ourselves to the repercussions of Nature's effects which act on the diminished receptive senses of such and such a man. We attempt to encounter the generous embrace of Nature in her fullness and to know the reasons that govern everything by penetrating everything.

At this point I should return to my opening sentence and above all to the word *phantasmic* in order to avoid suspicion or those misunderstandings which cause truth to be shattered as it collides with the brick wall of obtuseness.

The intellectual deficiency of my contemporaries becomes daily more apparent to me – the darkness in which they heedlessly grope, and the error into which they often plunge.

Over the world there hangs a low and heavy sky; there hangs over the world a low sky that precludes the starry verticals and makes beings doubt, even fall into forgetfulness.

The darkness, rather than lightening, is made much denser by this new smoke: in it there contend the falsities, the mistaken interpretations, the total miscarriage of justice, and especially the secularism in which we live, the usurped liberty to spread rumours and expectorate judgments; the stupid amnesty conceded to thoughtlessness, the free will reigning beast-like in the world of Art and of the spirit.

Every connection between *phantasmic* – as I mean it – and any unnatural aberration is to be excluded.

Besides, what is the unnatural?

(Let us extinguish the artificial lights beneath the saving circle of the lampshade and open the shutters to the moon.)

*Phantasmic* meaning *incipient phenomenon of representation*; genesis of every aspect. And, in the case of man: the initial state of the moment of discovery, when man found himself in the presence of a reality hitherto unknown to him.

The world is still – like Venus – *anadyomenon*: beyond some sea that brought him forth, amid mysterious travail, there rises a new god.

Every mind – in good spiritual, or, one could say, cosmic, order – is never separated from the equally cosmic motivation of continual change. And for this reason the sense of the phantasmic will never be dulled, like the spirit that touches the borders of an unexplored region.

In this breast there converge the extremes of the systems that lead man to every exterior richness, and once the new aspect has been grasped, they grind it down and nourish themselves on it, and eventually resolve it in the precise sweetness of the assimilated element.

Such is the genesis of art in its exact truth.

Once this unique thread has been established, the neutral zones that commonly separate the real from the unreal, fact from supposition and the physical from the metaphysical, are filled in.

Let us pause to consider the adjective 'metaphysical' in as far as it concerns art, and in this case, painting.

This word, already used in philosophical language to signify a balance more substantially physical than otherwise and then taken up by theologians, finds free spiritual existence for the first time in the work of Nietzsche.

With the acquisition of this new and vast meaning in a vaster reality, it no longer suggests the hypothetical after-natural. It signifies everything that continues the existence of reality, beyond the crudely apparent aspects of reality itself.

All disquiet inevitably prepares the way for a calm in which the very element that provoked this uneasiness spreads and extends in all its truth: this is the natural process that leads from barbarism to classicism.

This premise sums up the psychology of an artistic period, from its beginning to its conclusion.

After pictorial art had become uniform in a regularity without contrasts, after it had condensed from that state of calm into an inactive coagulation, it gradually began to lose all its power of spiritual consolation, and every element of sustaining vitality was little by little extinguished. Through lack of internal nourishment the external form became sterile.

Like vegetation lacking water, pictorial art came to be reduced to this extreme, to a scabby superficiality, an inelastic exterior which, because it was dry, fell to pieces.

There remained that heap of bones called academicism; there remained those scattered bones which the arrogant society of brush-wielding imbeciles avidly shared out among themselves, and dragged along with them, and sucked and scratched, and which they still continue to gnaw, conjuring up the horror of those bureaucratic panoramas that constitute official art, here as everywhere else.

But meanwhile, new forms were being extracted from the real meaning of art, and Cézanne was undertaking new lines that arose from the true aspect of that truth. He achieved this by means of the lively adoption of classical rudiments, whilst twisting them in the grip of an enlivening irony. And apart from this he managed to examine the atmosphere plastically, and to condense this almost into the solidity of form. His art can be defined as dissection of natural appearances, reproduced pictorially with the mechanism of a technique that I would qualify as *primitive anatomy*.

After Cézanne, painting expanded and broke through its barriers, but not in just one stream that led it immediately to complete fulfilment; indeed, it was divided into many individual investigations. But this does not demonstrate, and this point is of the utmost importance, that the phenomenon of inquietude had not yet appeared.

And it is this inquietude that finally makes us stop and turn our eyes to different proofs: manifestations of the certainty of a new birth.

If is this anxiety that forms a prelude to a strangeness that will come to pass in the world. Let us pause: Saturn mutilated Uranus in his sleep, and from his spilt blood there germinated a new fecundity, fructifying in nymphs on the Earth and the appearance of Venus on the sea.

Indeed, there was a rebirth, in the total fever of its delivery.

But on close examination of the period (now that distance permits it) one must conclude that unease and great restlessness, the continual drive to investigate, to break and to search, are like a barbarism that could only have motivation in a subsequent fulfilment, and that this could only happen when it was superseded by something superior to it: its spiritual reason.

Whereas the impressionists devoted themselves above all to atmospheric representation, and moulded light, and abolished deceptive contours, completing the picture by means of interpenetration of atmospheric and solid substances, and let themselves be led by an increasingly animal, sensual delight in the seduction of light and colour – whilst others, with equally unilateral limitations, submitted themselves to the geometric examination of form, and decomposed it, penetrating its innermost parts, a true reason for art was reborn, an opening appeared in the midst of all the fragments, aiming to surpass formalism and draw to itself, from among existing elements, the correct form with which to cover itself.

The various contortions, multiple fragmentations, and infinite deformations that occurred during this period of genesis show how hasty and barbarous was the development of this germ of the new spirituality.

We can see this great anguish impressed on all the painting that presents itself in its painful monstrosity. It reveals to us its supremely taciturn and dark character, in the midst of which we perceive the tremor of a living nucleus still confined and constricted in bitter disorder.

We could also establish the barbarism of those painters anthropologically, for even though they are European men they are primitive; their inspiration is drawn from true and physiognomically exact barbarism, from being nourished on the Negro, the primitive, the archaic, until the breath of the spiritual alighted on them and became a prime necessity, carrying them beyond formalism. When this had happened the same spiritual breath reduced the form to its own demands, and, exposed to such superior and liberated demands, form condensed little by little to achieve the precise limits of necessary representation. Form became mellower, broke its corners, stretched out in its true contours – to contain the spiritual necessity that had created it, elaborated it, softened it, and placed it in its total fullness.

Here we arrive at metaphysical art.

This general survey of pictorial evolution, from Cézanne to today is based, of course, on precise historical references. It seems to me to be superfluous to list the stages in this development and the men who represented them. All that matters to me is to establish them historically, psychologically and philosophically.

All this period of preparation leading towards a new pictorial art can be attributed mainly to the French. Not that corresponding examples cannot be found elsewhere than in Paris, but they were limited to sporadic events, isolated attempts, and individual cases, whereas in Paris these researches came together in such contingent efforts that, united, they all proceeded in the same way. The French are by character particularly suited to being initiators, since, so to speak, *they have their hands free of any spiritual preoccupation*. I do not deny their priority in the formal transformation of recent painting, but since every such transformation springs of necessity from a spiritual movement, I will later on demonstrate that this particular aspect germinated outside France.

By virtue of the very fact that, for the French, the spirit does not impede the free management of form, French art never transcends the limits of the naturalistic.

If one analyses the whole of French painting (and the same can be said of poetry and literature) one will see that it always remains irredeemably naturalistic.

Naturalism in art corresponds to positivism in philosophy.

Now, without embarking on an extended discussion of philosophy, one can nevertheless establish that positivism, in the totality of philosophy, represents a deficient form. Psychologically, positivism is motivated by the impossibility of rising to the vastness of the volume of philosophy, and as far as France is concerned it is curious to observe that, basically, the only philosophy that is purely and naturally positivist is the French one.

France affirmed positivism. Analysing the course of philosophy throughout the ages in a psychological way, it will be realized that my assertion is anything but rash.

The cases of positivism to be found in Greek philosophy (mostly before Socrates) contain this curious phenomenon: the Greek positivist became so through an act that could be called an act of rebellion. Far from being unaware of the vastness of philosophy, he perceived it to such a degree that he came to hate and repudiate it, to withdraw to the intelligible zone of positivism. Phenomenon of weakness, or of fear.

And in this one can recognize the effort such men made to restrict themselves to such narrow limits, for their positivism is as fierce as a sort of vendetta.

Not so the French positivist. If one considers Montaigne, Descartes, Comte – they are natural positivists in whom there is no trace of regret for anything recognized and voluntarily abandoned.

And Pascal?

The case of Pascal is much less complex than one may think. Not even Pascal was a spiritualist. Pascal presents us with the phenomenon of reversed positivism: he is a positivist who throws himself into the mystical. Now, the mystical is not the spiritual, and just as positivism is deficient in terms of philosophical totality, so is mysticism.

The most important part of philosophy – need one say it? – is certainly not positivism. And so why, in art, should naturalism prevail over the spiritual form?

Spiritualist philosophy, after its great flowering in Greece, emigrated to the west and flourished there. It did not reach France, but spread widely in Germany where it achieved its extreme form in Nietzsche's formula of the *metaphysical*.

It would be interesting to establish the 'political' reasons that even now prevent France from attaining spirituality, though it is true that natural reasons are even stronger.

Political reasons because in modern times spirituality finds true expression in Germany, and is also cultivated on Italian soil.

Oh, what a blow to their nationalism my French friends receive from the bugbear of *metaphysical art*!

'Why in art, should naturalism prevail over the spiritual form?'

Let us pause to consider this *spiritual form*.

Just as I qualified positivism as *a deficient form* in the totality of philosophy, so there exists a form that is exclusively spiritual, that is to say *abstract*.

And yet I declare, once and for all, that I cannot accept a spirituality that refers directly to material things, and establishes an indivisible unity with them.

I would like to insist on this point to dispel the frequent misunderstandings that have gradually gathered round the work of Carrà and of De Chirico, that these are representations of the abstract. This is as absurd as an attempt to establish the existence of the abstract, and is a misunderstanding as crude as the mentalities that conceived it.

Once the final moments of the past period of painting have been established, at the time of its collapse into fossilized academicism, the name of Cézanne appears at the beginning of the period of renewal. This may be true chronologically, but not psychologically.

The work of Cézanne is irretrievably chained to a certain compromise that renders it transitory. Cézanne was never able to free himself entirely from the vestiges of decadence, and so return to a pure state, which would have given his work a precise historical value.

The unique aspect of Cézanne's work is his ability to penetrate the bodily structure of volume. This penetration confers on the objects represented the full and fleshy appearance that makes his painting so pleasing and so sonorous.

Cézanne was obsessed by a tormenting desire to establish a balance between the weight of solids and of the atmosphere. And it was this that led him astray.

For these reasons I cannot consider Cézanne to be the initiator of the rebirth of painting.

His art serves what one could call a diplomatic purpose, more than anything else: it provides a link between the last vestiges of classicism – dried up in the academies – and the origins of a new art tending towards a new classicism. What was needed was a courageous plunge into the most primitive origins, into the most genuine barbarism possible, and it was Gauguin who took this plunge.

This painter was a pupil of Cézanne's, and had not really set about deliberately returning to the primitive. This happened through a blind instinct and was not confirmed by his conscience. In fact, he returned to formal crudeness only as a reaction to what could be called 'the graciousness of classicism', demonstrating in so doing that he was unaware that primitivism does not go beyond classicism, indeed that the element of graciousness that he condemned in Raphael, for example, was only the natural and therefore superior conclusion of a line descending from primitivism which Raphael himself had left behind.

Nevertheless, Gauguin's achievement remains a fact, even if it was unconscious: he succeeded in indicating the origins of a new art, truer than that achieved by the impressionists, or by the abstract decompositions of the cubists, etc., reduced and limited forms, bereft of progressive relationships, and transitory, as history shows.

Man's natural progress is also symptomatic in Gauguin: he withdrew first to Brittany, that is, to the primitive region that was geographically closest to hand, and then, dissatisfied with that, he left for Tahiti to immerse himself in a more radical primitivism.

Having established the origins of the new art in primitivism, we can follow its evolution through the work of the fauves, most particularly in that of Matisse, and then of Derain, touching first on the work of Rousseau. Then finally we will see it widening out into a new classicism, which appears for the first time in the paintings of Giorgio de Chirico and of Carlo Carrà.

This evolution, considered in its progressive stages, seems to be complicated by all the various elements that belong specifically and inevitably to it. That monstrous suffering, and that anguished sadness, mentioned before are the most obvious symptoms of that very fatality in which one can detect a necessity that is clearly anthropological. The characteristics noted with regard to the last pictorial period emphasize the physiognomic difference between the barbarian and the civilized man, and similar characteristics are verified in all previous artistic periods. To offer but one parallel: in the history of Greek statuary one can establish with chronological exactness the progress of the gradual dissolving of the element of sadness, so darkly affirmed throughout the entire archaic period (the closed phase), until one arrives step by step at a levelling-out of that sadness; from the *xoanon,* monoform and hermetic, to the first freeing of a limb from the body, to progressive movement, and, where expression is concerned, to the first statue that *smiles,* precluding classicism – and which attains the fulfilment of its organic and spiritual impulse.

Since France is precluded from spirituality it was obvious that as soon as she had reached the stage in her development of touching the edge of spiritual fulfilment, painting in France should come to a halt. And, in fact, painting did pass into other hands.

When considering the work of the painters who led the progressive stages of the last period of painting, it becomes apparent that each of them remained rigidly restricted to the limitations of his respective stage; individual action, therefore, is limited.

It remains to consider this evolution as far as it concerns two Italian painters who passed all these stages to arrive beyond them, to achieve pictorial spirituality.

In the work of Carrà we find summarized the entire development of painting from Gauguin onwards. He does not stop at one particular stage of formal development, but attacks all of them, progressively, in order to go beyond them, to acquire experience through them, to assimilate them and to achieve the quality that constituted the definitive form he was seeking and which he finally made his own.

The genesis of De Chirico's art is not dissimilar. This painter, who lived for the most part outside the major artistic circles, did not have occasion to be swept away to the same extent by the mechanisms of formal evolution.

One could say that, right from the beginning, he was concerned with spiritual affirmation. Nevertheless, since I was present during his time in Paris, I can state that he too, at this time, felt obliged to work through the course of the formal transformation of painting for his own benefit, and through all this to return again to a spiritual aim, which he was then able to affirm with complete organic plasticity.

The unique element in the art of this painter is: representational completeness of spiritual necessity within its plastic limitations; expressive potential of the spectrality of appearances; irony.

The *representational completeness* of spiritual necessity, within its plastic limitations, is on the whole, the definition of the definitive form which art achieved in the course of its classical period.

I wish to explain the character of *spectrality* in order to avoid any suspicion of witchcraft. Spectrality is the true, spiritual and substantial essence of every appearance. To reproduce this essence in its complete genuineness is the highest aim of art.

Here the painter achieves the representation of an appearance in its original apparition, that is, cleansed of all impositions of heterogeneous elements.

A common cause of the destruction of spectrality is banality, that is, the disappearance through forgetfulness, or through paralysis of the discerning faculties, of the complete truth of an appearance; the obscuring of precise vision.

Appearances – all of them – are also forgotten or neglected values which the artist uncovers little by little. In other words, he reveals them.

*Irony*

Heraclitus says that Nature loves to conceal herself.

This fragment can be interpreted in a wide variety of ways:

That Nature loves to hide from herself – through a phenomenon of self-directed modesty, motivated by a constricted ethical scale. Then, that this modesty is born of Nature's relationship with man. Here I will pause and reveal the chief factor that generates irony.

Basically, it is nothing but the effect of nudity – and consequently of morality.

In painting irony occupies a most important position, once the mind of the artist achieves the maximum degree of clarity. Then he perceives exactly the original precision of Nature. This precision is reflected in man, and is destined, through him, to be externalized in subsequent representation, producing a very subtle but elementary and human reaction, which, I repeat, can be called modesty. This is what induces the artist, in spite of himself to deform in some way as he reproduces them the terribly clear appearances he perceives.

Here I have unfolded the origins of metaphysical painting and touched fleetingly on its fundamental qualities.

Milan, May 1919; published in Valori Plastici (Rome), Nos. IV–V, 1919

## Preludes

*Head-antechamber of a minister*

Through my head there passes a charming coming and going of Pretty things. Joyful round-about: my ideas come at the gallop, caracoling, steeplechasing. . . .

For this reason I do not have time to become too familiar with them or to weary of them. Fresh when they arrive, they are still rippling with freshness when they leave me. I am left panting, trembling, unassuaged, like the lover touched by sublime love, like Tristan! . . . I conserve the emotion they impart in all its purity. They leave me with all the nostalgia of ardent and fleeting friendship.

> 'Farewell my mouse
> you're leaving for the Mississippi.
> Farewell my mouse
> dear mouse!'

> (Doctor Doyen! Make all haste to give an emergency injection of oxygen to the skeleton of Victor Hugo, for he's about to have an attack of locomotor ataxia.)

– How can one flute in your jargon,
anthropomorphic mousie? . . .
The voice of half-death is sweet
Far from the spirit of the grapefruit
too easy to gather.

        the coconut
          or the apricot.
A strange gourd serves me as nourishment,
a sort of cashew – a thousand infinite tastes,
soft flesh, –
my teeth without decay
run over it . . .
then sink into it until oblivion . . .
Horror! – hide under the waterproof
the plant they call: '. . . .!'
    Futile star that grows
    in the wooden chests.

I cast my truths in your teeth!
    You, sir, with the rigid morals,
    turn your frigid gaze
    towards the strange vegetation . . .
        – raise an oration
          to my heart's flowering,
          cities, aediles . . . –

underwater plant,
coral-red flower . . .
its roots are in the aorta
I steep it in my bile
so thick and black-sensitive coal-tar.
        Now I rise to the altar
        adorned with *Kepta* pearls.

Pity! Pity!
My entrails crave an augurer . . .
Oh, the deep entrails
of passion!
let us slide . . .

      – Silence!
      for Soffici is meditating
      in front of the brazier . . . tally ho!

          (the cries of a deer-hunt in the night)

                    – Silence!
                    his soul is dedicated
                    to mournful pleasure . . . tally ho! . .
Oh, look at that Afrikhan! . . .
– I grasp his hand, like this:
                    I shake the hand
                    of my friend,
                    sweet Afrikhan
                    may you be blessed.
The man with the ferruginous morals
turns on me his wrinkled eye
                    his antarctic stare.
Touch my lungs with your austral hands
                    – a diplomatic friendship –
I will present you with my equatorial *victory*
I will nominate you superintendent of my estates!
I give my quid of tobacco to the urchin, to you,
                    Sir,
a great fluorine-filled balloon
surrounded with multiflowered ribbons
there you will read your future,
the success of your affairs,
and whether Madame will deceive you.


                    Farewell, it will be so!
The man free from lies has had his day,
witness the hopeless return of a mad round of visits.
                    What do you want, anyway?
                    Oh, the eiderdown is stifling me! . . .
Return, o voyage!
Orage!
Rivage!
Virage!
Mirage!


(The hour in which I await you has arrived, noble Orient, Phoenician prince; you, demon lover, you who know how to caress the beautiful forty-year old ladies with the magical exhalations of your jaw swollen with gingivitis, as they sleep under the canopies envied by the undersigned, ascetic through greater effort – noblesse oblige! – Orient, the time has come! Come, Orient, genius of the tiny blond pyramids! Come, Orient, charitable satan of the Zampironi!)

164

Sir, I shall sleep now
I have confessed my faults . . .
I leave for a journey without luggage.
Be so kind as to bolt the door.
One day I shall see you, but I know not where.
The donkey sleeps in the stable
My port's lighthouse is extinguished.
Respect me, for I am worthy of respect
like a pope on his death bed.

Published in French in *Les Soirées de Paris* (Paris), May 1914

## Drama of Noonday Town

*'Por la gracia de los fantasmas.'*

*It is midday. Three-quarters of the stage is occupied by an immense slab of excessively white and polished marble, veined in places with thin lines of darker colour, carmine or opal. Further back, a group of tin soldiers. Piles of polychrome boxes. Iron palm trees. A variety of vegetation: medlar trees, pineapple plants, coconut trees. The sky is heraldic green, traversed by white storks describing long spirals.*

*A man enters, wearing a minister's frock coat. In place of his missing head he wears a little flag implanted in a steel antenna. He has three rigid legs, unarticulated and inflexible like the legs of a photographer's tripod. He skates on metal rollers that squeak horribly.*

*On arriving at the centre of the marble plaque he unbuttons his frock coat, and his waistcoat and then a third layer of clothing that, when opened, reveals two wings of living flesh and all the anatomical details of his thorax with its play of organs.*

*The man rummages in his lungs and extracts from them an enormous heart, as red as a black-pudding swollen with blood.*

MAN (*Sings*)

I have a very limpid heart, friends
a mind like chrysoprase
strange channels of waves
I can sing the songs of the city
the terrible dream
watched over: by the traffic lights
and the asinine guard.
　　I saw the statues of the politicians die
their heads bent over and they uttered
their last song, then,
their flanks broken, they fell
like Ariadne abandoned . . .

*The man dressed in a minister's frock coat produces a hammer from his pocket. With an*
*atrocious noise he nails his bleeding heart to the middle of the marble plaque.*
*Then he goes away, gliding on the skates that produce a terrible squeak.)*

       — The house! the house! friends;
       who amongst us will ever know how to untie
       the enigmatic knot of stone?
       I saw a bald woman
       like an enamelled lizard
       climbing up the column
       of Emanuele Filiberto in pure Turin;
       I stabbed the Prince in his jacket
       there flowed out garnet blood
       of dried-up bronze . . .
       The pigeons sung, like
       Ariadne sorrowing . . .
         — The sun, friends, black, and the long shadows
       run dramas over the city.
       I saw the beautiful, tragic, terrible houses;
       Defeated, exhausted, bereft of love
       and of hatred, stripped of all nostalgia,
       tranquil, both violence
       and passion overcome, lying
       at peace, calm
       like Ariadne sleeping . . .

WOMAN

*(Rushes on to the stage: she cries out to the character who has just left)*

Sir! Sir! I have just seen an enormous zinc fish in the square outside the station;
he had come out of an ice cream shop and was running off on all fours . . .

*(She stays nailed to the spot, immobile, like a turkey.)*

JOURNAL OF EVERYDAY VOYAGES

Yesterday was the night of St John. Outside, a tenement building. On the third
floor there is light in three windows. Beyond the window panes can be seen the
butcher, his wife, her lover and an old man who was dancing like the dead.
    No one.
    The American women above my head . . . For three long minutes could be heard
the rhythmic noise of several people dancing *without music*.
    Oh! the insupportable malediction of bourgeois life! . . .

               VII GIORGIO MORANDI *Still-life* 1918

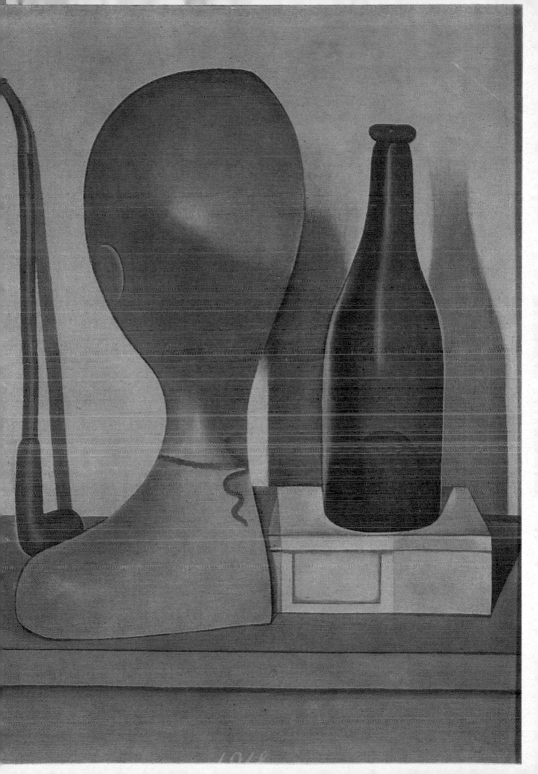

Statue. Castle of red putty.
Pascal, the needle moved on that quadrant;
*ten minutes to midday!*

## DIALOGUE BETWEEN ITALIAN SOLDIERS

A: Io ti dico sinceramente, Pasqualino che non ne posso più!
B: T'han fatto sergente perche hai messo la firma.

## MONOLOGUE

But I am not alone. I am walking . .
the track is double.
Destiny!
can you give me back Guillaume the Parisian? . . .
I would like to have him here with me and say to him 'look!
I am thirsty with unknown delights . . .
    he who passes does not know . . .
    but you, since you wear a cockade . . . '
(and afterwards thinks: I who made you a knight; I rested my sword on your shoulder.
You, there on your knees, submissive to the educating steel, murmured with juicy
lips: 'You, my prophet! you my suzerain!')

*The author himself crosses the stage. He has just climbed out of his hammock; he lives in lodgings
in the house numbered 43, rue de Chaillot. He enters. In the kitchen the sterilized water he will
use for his daily douche sings gently on the gas ring.*

## THE AUTHOR

– I saw M. Chevillard in a dream.
He said to me: your ballets will not be
staged. He was shaking his head, M. Chevillard . . .
Ah, Miss Florence Cook, why did
you drive such misery
into my skull?

*The woman has flights of fancy: she goes out to attend to her intimate toilet. The author slips
craftily behind a low door. He is going to digest his clyster.*

*The tin soldiers present arms; blood runs down the flash of their bayonets. The storks take
flight again in spirals in the green sky. A chorus of viole d'amore passes like a draught. Nature
whimpers as if seized by colic. Gustavo says: 'One o'clock!'*

Published in French in *La Voce* (Florence), 31 March 1916

## Topping Out

Today I feel the need to criticize bitterly the faulty architecture of my body. My head is heavy. I find it strangely humiliating to feel myself the victim of such structural academicism. Besides all my other battles I also have to combat this primordial lack of proportion. . . . And I feel utterly unsuited for such athletics.

In this mountebank city I will wear a flesh-coloured jersey. I want to arouse diluvian storms of applause. I am a terrible violator: the incalculable weight at the top of my leg – One metre and sixty-nine centimetres.

I too am destined for the variegated tragedy of the acrobats. For me, too, the crowd sits mute and in its midst totemism creates havoc.

And I remember you – Egypt – most perfect representer of men.

Like the idols of the Nile, I see all around me, but all around, men with beastly faces, whimpering animals, dressed in black, terribly tragic. Who knows what tragedy? They certainly are not acquainted with the tragedy I know, and yet I am as gay as the public fountains on holidays. . . .

Indeed, what power the Egyptians had in capturing the current image of man; and they esteemed only the full black profile. They found the means to print man and his face, like a trademark, everywhere.

And they rebuked physiognomy. And they revealed the *type* like the veins in the skeleton of a leaf; and they did not fall into the muddy fullness of entirety.

The elementary law of gravity acts powerfully on my shoulders, pressing me gently and inexorably into the horizontal of sleep.

The propeller that becomes insane with speed spins in front of my forehead, nothing bites and nothing remains, just as in the empty void of the elements.

And little by little I resign myself to my seven days of passion, separated by an entire lifetime. . . .

In my pocket I find no keys. I cannot open the door of any house that I can call *mine,* or enter *my rooms,* or arrive at the heart of my isolation, an isolation built of plaster and stone.

At the moment I haunt the great toll-house gates – black hands rigid on telegraph poles show me the road – in the scholastic solemnity of the halls of the Post Office, in the town hall, the police station, the registry office.

And so now I have returned to the age of the pharaohs. I feel I am the chief heir of a long dynasty, since others have scattered so much sand obscuring the geometric foundations like those of cities buried by earthquakes.

After the epoch of the assassins comes the time of the constructors, who traditionally possess the poetry of the profession of aerial balance.

Scaffolding, then, skeletons, towering anatomies. And at last the roof is thrown across. The time for the topping-out celebration has come. Wine flows freely.

On the highest beams – lightning conductors gathering joyfulness – we will hoist the flags amid the branches.

Ferrara 22 May 1917; published in Antologia della Diana, Naples 1918

# The Dramatic in Painting

A spirit of genius that has not yet reached complete maturity is a spirit that composes rather than one which creates.

In modern painting:

Representation of the dramatic is the supreme preoccupation of the best of the modern painters. According to the degree of their talent or of their clearsightedness, they have set themselves the task of incorporating into their work, by means of line and colour, the innumerable dramas that mature and explode in our modern life.

The cubists are still wavering between two divergent paths: the dramatic appearance of things and objects, and a residual feeling, however admirably they have attempted to purge themselves of it, for the scruples of refined aesthetic sensibility.

The Italian futurists limit themselves to the purity of dramatic appearance.

For evidence of the most advanced stage, we must look to the painter Giorgio de Chirico, who has penetrated the *mystery* of the dramatic today. His canvases do not reproduce the mute visibility of the object chosen for the dramatic elements of its appearance, of its shape, of its nature, of its material, of its utility. He succeeds in going *beyond* the object itself. He strips off the coverings from the metaphysical anatomy of drama.

He is the modern painter; but, more precisely, he is the modern sorcerer.

Before the dawn of this golden age, authentic elements of spectral drama can be traced in the work of some of the painters of past eras. Among these the most significant are Dürer, Holbein and Rembrandt.

Rembrandt conjured up the dramatic aspect of spectrality, even though he relied on realism, in his *Anatomy Lesson of Dr Tulp*. An early example of this imaginative, though naturally grotesque, feeling is offered by the *Rape of Ganymede*; and this was to achieve its full flowering in the work of Böcklin.

I would point out that in Rembrandt's painting there is a most obvious principle of creation, indeed of *revelation,* even though this is sustained by literary, historical and biblical mysticism, as in the *Sacrifice of Isaac* and the *Pilgrims of Emmaus*. These very same paintings owe so much to the feeling in them which is very closely linked with such a perfect understanding of Judaism — of that arid feeling for the burnt bush — that I suspect the painter of *Semitic* atavism.

This sentiment is so natural to him that it is manifest even in canvases with no biblical pretext to justify the presence of such feeling – as in his *Landscape with Ruins*. I would be most surprised if anyone were to try to convince me that the painter of Leyden was a native of the Low Countries . . . I would maintain against everything that Rembrandt was no more Dutch than was Spinoza. Both of them belong to that race of tardy examples of ancestral patriarchalism which roams the world. The Zionists who dream of the restoration of Israel should be grateful to these two, for they have done more to spread knowledge of the history of Israel than any effete historian like the hopelessly Gallic Renan.

What a pleasure it is to remove the veil from certain little truths on which writers and critics have never dared to rest their little fingers. They have incessantly praised the ingenious play of light in the work of Rembrandt and the skill of his chiaroscuro, but they have never been able to seek out this painter's real qualities.

The painting of the Latin Renaissance is of very little interest to us.

One must be wary of the primitives. Researchers into art, and people with a good nose for smelling out such things, claim to be able to find exceptional qualities in the works of the primitives.

In my opinion, the primitives were simply artists who experienced great difficulty in painting. Since they lacked mastery they became *stylists* . . . of necessity! Their works possess no greater *occult qualities* than the shameless daubs of their tardy descendants over the English Channel – the chinoiseries of Rossetti, and Burne-Jones, and all the Pre-Raphaelite gang.

### ORIGINALITY

The audacity of the artists who have drawn the attention of the world to themselves in these recent years, this audacity is a childish game compared to the discovery of *a truth*.

In my opinion, all the so-called modern artists whose work I have seen are nothing but the constructors, and at times the inventors, of certain new mechanics. But deep down, I doubt whether this is a virtue, a quality. The very fact of *invention* demonstrates the inanity of their work. It is no exaggeration to say that they are concerned exclusively with *style*.

Basically, all the transformations in art that led to 'cubism', and to the various forms of 'Modern Art' in general, were minimal. And besides, the transformation was only partial.

Because of my convictions, I defend 'cubism', and hence all 'Modern Art', for a purely material and so to speak diplomatic reason.

In short, 'Modern Art' will have served no purpose except that of sweeping out of artistic affairs a certain suffocating bourgeois attitude which had settled heavily over them. Cubism will at least have sent to the devil once and for all an opinion that was formerly dominant: that art is the search for, and the representation of, the beautiful. This, at least, has widened the scope of art. It has raised new possibilities. And even if they had succeeded only in revealing to a certain group of men the beastliness in which they were immersed and of which they were proud, even this would have been an important achievement.

But alas! alas! not even this has revealed a new art, not even in the smallest degree. We Italians have a song:

> *You can change the leader of the band*
> *but the music stays the same.*

An artistic transformation can only be achieved through a preliminary transformation of men's mentality and of their intellectual education.

Art is not a side-issue. It is a form of materialization of the soul, of the temperament, of the feelings of a man who is an artist. Causes: soul, temperament, feelings. Result: art. Now, a *result* cannot be changed unless the *causes* that produce it are changed first.

As far as I know, the mentality of a cubist is not substantially different from that of a painter fifty years ago. Indeed, I would go so far as to say that they are exactly alike. If by chance there are differences at times, the will of the cubist is in no way responsible. . .

Modern artists have in no way achieved a transformation of art. Their 'renewal' only consists of a simple variation of sensory taste.

This 'renewal' is a pitiful thing. We still have a maimed art, the creation of maimed spirits.

For the modern artist, like the majority of the artists of the past, has not realised that our intuition of the external world is not only *sensory*, but above all *intellectual*, or, to express this in more objective terms, *cerebral*.

In artistic matters originality has no real value.

Nearly all these modern artists whose audacious works have astounded the world are *feeble minds*.

No great prophetic insight is necessary to foresee that their works will very soon be lost in oblivion, and that they themselves will disappear like flies in autumn.

The only thing these audacious artists have achieved is that the influence of their works has liberated the world from *traditional aestheticism*. This is an excellent achievement, and for this reason these *good liberators* are worthy of our highest esteem.

The question of *originality* can only appertain to the external and superficial aspect of a work of art: the least noble part.

The desire to appear original at all costs is a social ambition, too weak and too grossly human to be taken seriously. Besides, if a work of art is to be presented to the public in an *original* form, according to the current interpretation of the word, it must renounce all substantial truth. Here, too (and above all in the great artistic centres like Paris), the rarefied tastes of a whole tribe of dilettantes and pretentious bourgeois come into play. These are the misdeeds of liberalism. The disorder inflicted on society by the eruption of the Third Estate has assigned to art the duty of titillating the public. For some years now in Paris there has been a great misunderstanding where 'Modern Art' is concerned: those who practise it firmly believe that they constitute an intellectual élite, creating a sort of kingdom inaccessible to the populace and to common men. Their conviction found confirmation in the hostility that the non-modern artists (commonly called *pompiers* or hacks), and all their cortège of admirers, manifested towards the new arrivals. In fact, however, this entire modern aesthetic movement contains the germs of the most crass vulgarity, and the influence of the female sex (the great propagator of popular taste) is naturally well to the fore.

This rash of originality has brought about the hatching and multiplication to infinity of a bizarre, though banal, type of man, of which numerous examples throng every era of decadence. This is the artist type – the martyr – poor, degenerate, almost always ill, alcoholic, armoured in ignorance, incapable of anything, destitute of all talent, who grotesquely recites the role of the renewer, of the misunderstood genius, calculating on the absence of scruples that characterizes contemporary society. These sad individuals dragged along in the vortex of general irresponsibility, always living together in a sort of artistic ghetto, have the task of untiringly furnishing a pastiche of art for the insatiable bourgeoisie, who cannot admit to lunching on the same food two days running.

Originality in art represents business acumen; this is pure feminism. One becomes original to please the ladies. It is a sort of gallantry.

In the sixteenth century, Palestrina, the musical genius of the era, restricted himself within severe forms of his art, whilst his contemporaries, the madrigalists, far surpassed him according to the then-current canons of originality and modernity.

An *artist-creator* would not even know how to be original in the sense of playing to the gallery; he has far more important things to do, and therefore *no time to lose.*

What one must seek in a work of art is the *degree of intelligence.* Not an extravagantly original appearance which, in order to escape from the monotony of tradition, takes easy ways out, of a sort that have always led to decadence as in seventeenth-century poetry, with Marini in Italy and Góngora in Spain.

*Original* form, apparently strange, peculiar unto itself, rebelling against previously known forms, is only authentic when it is necessary in terms of the singular psychological state of the creative man who through such expression finds himself in an intellective state that is peculiar to himself. This is the state of *genius.* But then the forms of expression are usually assigned to a position of secondary importance, and the *trivial* form, however low and vulgar, is by no means excluded. This is why Dante wrote verses 'in the vulgar tongue' that are far from being illustrious, and for the same reason in music Palestrina, Bach, Mozart and Beethoven were far from being original artists in the sense of creators of new forms, or stylists. They were reformers who used all the means available to *construct* their works. And for this very same reason the appearance of Böcklin's works is so very far from original that in France, above all, his reputation is that of a *pompier.*

A work of art must not make concessions to the motivations of artistic tendencies or to aesthetics, or science, to manners, or to taste, elegance or *chic.* . . If one makes a close examination of the majority of well-known works of art, one will have no difficulty in realizing that they exist only by virtue of this feigned necessity. In hardly any of them is to be found true *tragic multiplicity.* Can it all be dilettantism? . . .

I acknowledge true value in a work of art only when it is *intelligent.* And there is a case for setting up codes and dogmas for works and for the men who create them. Universalism is not for us. The *good* and the *bad* must be named. Art as abstraction does not exist. It is a general idea and therefore a circular one. If its two extremes meet it is because they have no existence *in accordance with fatality.* . . . Let us oppose Pythagoras' theory: the circle, far from representing *everything,* represents *nothing,* the *void.*

Published in *Valori Plastici* (Florence), 15 November 1918

# Surrealism and the Metaphysical

**Patrick Waldberg**

The metaphysical school, in the strict sense of the term, was born in 1917, in Ferrara, when Giorgio de Chirico met Carlo Carrà, and came to an end in 1920, when they parted company. In fact, however, the unexpected, enigmatic quality of this form of art, its essential unnaturalness, were already clearly evident in De Chirico's works of 1910, such as *The Enigma of the Oracle* and *The Enigma of Autumn*. Apollinaire, struck by De Chirico's work in the 1914 Salon des Indépendants, quoted Ardengo Soffici: 'The painting of De Chirico is certainly not painting in today's sense of the term. It might be defined as "dream writing". Juxtaposing almost infinite recessions of arcades and façades, of long straight lines, of immanent masses of simple colour, he expresses those sensations of vastness, solitude, immobility, ecstasy, which our visual memory sometimes conjures up in our souls when we are falling asleep.'

Never had art been in such a state of upheaval as in the years of De Chirico's first stay in Paris, 1911–15. Fauves, futurists, cubists, orphicists, suprematists, vorticists and all the others were competing for the perilous joy of carrying to its ultimate conclusion the certitude of being right. In this orgy of experimentation a few masterpieces stand out among a host of those sad canvases that seem destined to hang in the corridors of great museums.

From today's standpoint, the work of De Chirico stands out triumphantly amid all this monotony. An anecdote may help to illustrate its extraordinary power. For many years I have been a frequent guest in the house of Vicomtesse de N., in Paris, who has a magnificent collection of paintings of all periods. One room in particular, a little dining-room, contains a number of works ranging from Watteau to Moreau by way of Magnasco, Géricault, Delacroix, Bonington and many others: one of them is a copy by Degas of Bellini's *Souls in Purgatory*. In the midst of these historic works of art, there stands out, by virtue of its unusual format as well as the hallucinatory aggressiveness of its colour and its subject matter, the tall, narrow canvas by De Chirico entitled *The Philosopher's Outing* [83]. A hundred times I have paused in this room, among all these marvels; but in the end I am always drawn to the De Chirico, which holds me fascinated. At these moments it is as if the conversation around me were receding into the distance, while the other paintings fade into a haze – with the exception of the Degas-Bellini, which, although derived from an entirely different inspiration, possesses the same silent, crepuscular power.

What is it that gives this work its hypnotic force? At first sight there is nothing in particular to be seen. A plaster bust of Jupiter and two artichokes rest on an inclined plane which forms the upper surface of a right-angled parallelepiped which might be a building stone or a mysterious piece of luggage. This base is placed obliquely, so that one can see part of one of its sides, on which are cast the shadows of geometrical forms, together with a curved dotted line. In the background, far away, is a dismal sky in which rises a tall factory chimney. On the right, in perspective, the wall of a palazzo recedes into the night. The light of a setting sun enters from the right, and the bust and the artichokes cast violent shadows; the livid light endows them with a spectral atmosphere, as if they were on the point of vanishing into the shadows from which some mysterious enchantment has brought them forth. The whole is bathed in what Soffici defines as 'immanent masses of simple colour': in this case pallid green, a green which cannot be identified with any that is known in Nature. It might be described as 'lunar', if the moon had not now lost all its mystery; it would perhaps best be described as extra-terrestrial. A subtle stratum of colour; a drawing with a clear cut, almost schematic line; a uniform tonality; a layout in which the solidity of the objects represented is virtually negated by the abnormal angle of the surface on which they rest, although they logically ought to slide off: all these elements account for something of the nature of the fascination which this work holds. Three elements converge and combine to disorientate the mind, achieving a spiritual intensity which is effective in proportion to the simplicity of the means that are used to give it external expression. The ancient world (Jupiter) and the modern world (the chimney) coexist in a moment of highly-charged emotion which the painter has fixed for all eternity. Furthermore, the juxtaposition of the plaster bust, that antiquated academic prop, with two artichokes, banal articles of everyday consumption, forces us to look at each object as if we had never seen it before, and endows them with an 'apparitional' power which tears them away from their humdrum destiny.

Finally, the profoundly static nature of the composition, contradicted by the violent slant given to the plane surface, seems to me to express, without too much emphasis, a dialectic of tranquillity and dizzy panic, of time and its passing.

If I have dwelt at some length on this *Philosopher's Outing,* this is not only because I know this picture better than any other, but also because it seems to me to contain, in essence, all that was to constitute the compelling message of metaphysical art. It contains that quality which lies 'Beyond Painting', and which Max Ernst later took as the basis of his own personal world: that ambivalence between stability and collapse, between closeness and remoteness, which was the great merit of the posters created by the Cassandre studio between 1925 and 1939. It is not by chance, furthermore, that the name of Cassandre comes to mind more readily than that of any poet; Giorgio de Chirico has always seemed to me, at least as far as his metaphysical painting is concerned, a great designer of posters for a world of the imagination.

It was through the painting of Giorgio de Chirico that the term 'metaphysical art' came into use. For Carrà, Morandi, Sironi and the rest 'metaphysical art' was a relatively short episode, and their reputation was made through their later work. Carrà, who had been one of the first futurists, was the only one to match De Chirico for a brief period on his own ground. In the last analysis, however, it was in Paris that, in three different periods, the metaphysical legend grew up; and its centre and inspiration was De Chirico alone.

First period: Apollinaire discovers De Chirico. De Chirico exhibited at the Salon d'Automne in 1912 and 1913, then at the Salon des Indépendants in 1913 and 1914, the principal works exhibited were: *The Enigma of the Oracle*, *The Red Tower*, *Melancholy of Departure*, *The Enigma of the Hour*, *The Nostalgia of the Infinite*, *Joy and Enigma of a Strange Hour*. The poetic dignity of the titles exactly matches the strange beauty of the paintings, charged with a 'solitary and profound lyricism' (in the words of De Chirico himself).

It was certainly not their *manner* that attracted attention, in those years of artistic revolution. De Chirico's technique is archaic, i.e. 'academic', and takes no account of the problems that concerned the abstract handlers of space. For him what counts is the content, the power of the image, the ability to carry the spirit beyond the every-day world towards the shores of the land of Hypnos. Apollinaire, always an intent observer of new departures, immediately recognized Giorgio de Chirico as a brother-poet. His support of De Chirico strongly influenced the members of that youthful élite whom he had captured with his irresistible charm. In *Les Soirées de Paris* (15 November 1913 to 15 March 1914), in *L'Intransigent* (28 February to 3 March 1914), in the *Journal de Paris* (23 June, 14 July, 23 July, 1 August 1914), Apollinaire, with the authority of a prophet, raised De Chirico to his just place among the most important artists of the age.

Meanwhile, De Chirico went to all the poet's 'Saturdays' in the Boulevard Saint-Germain, where he met Picasso, Marie Laurencin, Brancusi, Derain, Max Jacob and many other avant-garde artists and writers. There is no doubt that this group, few in numbers but extremely influential, acted as a springboard to launch the reputation of De Chirico and to spread the metaphysical idea.

On the walls of Apollinaire's house hang two works by De Chirico; one is the famous and disturbing premonitory portrait in which Apollinaire is shown in profile, with a target on his temple marking the exact spot where, two years later, he was to be struck by the bullet which eventually killed him. It was more or less at this time, I believe, that Jean Paulhan followed Giuseppe Ungharetti as De Chirico's co-tenant of the studio in the rue Campagne-Première, and acquired two works that he kept all his life. For a painter to be bought by such an influential figure was better than to be bought by a museum. De Chirico was thus very much appreciated by the real leaders of intellectual life in Paris.

The second period of expansion of the metaphysical idea came in about 1921, with the appearance of those who were soon afterwards to become the surrealists. André Breton and Paul Eluard, stimulated by Apollinaire's example, were fascinated by De Chirico's painting, which represented, better than any other, what they looked for in art.

Later, in *Genèse et perspectives artistiques du surréalisme,* Breton summarized what metaphysical art had meant to him and his friends: 'The evolution of De Chirico, in the four [sic] years in which inspiration favoured him as it did at no other time, is no less impetuous, no less fated, no less dramatic, than that of the equally brief life's work of Rimbaud. This art of establishing places that are *eternal*, which become spectral (phantasms, horoscopes) where the object exists only by virtue of its symbolic and enigmatic value (the period of arcades and towers), endows the human figure with a structure which excludes all individual character, reducing it to a framework and a mask (the manikin period). Then this same framework dissolves: the living being disappears and is merely suggested by inanimate objects which have to do with his function (as a king, a general, a sailor, etc.). Finally these objects themselves are linked in compositions with measuring instruments, and have no apparent connection with human life except through the symbolic presence of an easily preserved article of food, the dry biscuit; the great cycle of De Chirico's work is completed by the period of the *Metaphysical Interiors*.'

As is well known, when De Chirico came to Paris again in 1925–26 he fell out with the surrealists; and they always bitterly attacked the work he did after 1917. For his part, De Chirico rejected the poetic and Freudian interpretations that the surrealists placed upon his metaphysical painting. Whatever the rights and wrongs of the dispute, it remains true that it was through surrealism that metaphysical art became widely known. There has been no major surrealist exhibition since the 1920s in which De Chirico does not appear as the principal precursor. Four great pioneers of surrealism owe to De Chirico the discovery of a new dream world: Max Ernst, Yves Tanguy, René Magritte and Salvador Dalí.

About 1920, Ernst found some reproductions of metaphysical drawings and paintings in an issue of *Valori Plastici*. The impact was immediately apparent in his work. The prints of the *Fiat Modes* series, with their eyeless manikins, the great compositions of 1921–23, including *Revolution at Night* and *Oedipus Rex,* and the extraordinary montage painting *Two Children are Menaced by a Nightingale* of 1924, carry the unmistakable signs of metaphysical influence. The same spirit is present in the 'collage novels', *La Femme 100 Têtes* (1929), *Rêve d'une petite fille qui voulait entrer au Carmel* (1930), and *Une Semaine de bonté* (1934). Reminiscences of De Chirico reappear in Ernst's work at various later periods, as in 1942–43 with *Painting for Youth* and *Day and Night,* and also in 1948 with a return to the use of manikins: *The Feast of the Gods* and *The Chemical Wedding.* De Chirico's example was a major and lasting inspiration for Ernst.

One day in 1926, Yves Tanguy was riding in a Paris bus which passed the Galerie Paul Guillaume, then showing a De Chirico retrospective. He spotted the four canvases in the gallery window, leaped off the moving bus, and spent the rest of the day in contemplation. In his own later work he was never to forget the suggestive power of cast shadows, or the *angst* conjured up by infinite perspective recessions, or the use of crepuscular, melancholy colour, bathing a timeless setting.

At the same period, in the mid-1920s, René Magritte was in a state of uncertainty and indecision, dissatisfied with his own work in which cubism and futurism came together in a way which failed to carry conviction. One day his friend the poet Marcel Lecomte brought him a reproduction of De Chirico's painting *The Song of*

*Love*. He was moved to tears. From then on, all Magritte's work is a continuation of De Chirico's. 'This', wrote Magritte, 'is a new vision, in which the spectator recovers his own isolation and listens to the silence of the world.' He is of course speaking for De Chirico as much as for himself. He was the only painter of the mid-twentieth century who might have laid claim to the title 'metaphysical' – if the metaphysical school had survived, if it had not been repudiated by its own founder.

In the work of Salvador Dalí the influence of De Chirico is evident between the years 1929 and 1938: walls and arches in perspective, outsize shadows, much of the metaphysical repertoire is re-used in a systematic process of denaturalization. The same can be said of the first period of Victor Brauner, up to about 1933. And, finally, in Paul Delvaux the influence of De Chirico and that of Magritte coincide in a mannerism which recalls that of the post-Renaissance Italian painters.

Thus, notwithstanding all the conflicts and the exchanges of denunciations and venomous insinuations, there undeniably exists between metaphysical painting and surrealism a blood tie, transcending individuality, which links them for ever on the loftiest plane of the spirit, that of poetry.

The third period of metaphysical influence was that in which Jean Cocteau admitted De Chirico to his gallery of personal myths alongside Picasso and Stravinsky. In 1928 Cocteau published a little book, illustrated by De Chirico, entitled *Le Mystère laïc*, in which he extolled the 'Master of the Enigmas'. 'It is not a matter of looking without understanding and enjoying without reason, through a mere decorative attraction. It is a matter of paying a high price, and of comprehending through a special sense: the sense of the marvellous.' Cocteau added no new ideas to those of Breton, who had already spoken of the 'inner model' and 'the marvellous at any price'. However, he did do something to shelter De Chirico from the torrent of abuse which the surrealists were heaping on him. Cocteau came on the scene a little late, as he realized himself; but he did have a considerable reputation, and he was very much admired in quite a few circles to which the painter's earlier admirers had no access: lovers of the theatre and the ballet, night-people in general, professional socialites and the world of fashion. He was sensitive enough to feel just how much theatrical quality (in the fullest sense of the word) there was in this painting which is a stage peopled by materialized phantoms, lost desires, latent obsessions, places beyond time, in which present, past and future merge. 'Death is the only representation which moves freely in all directions on De Chirico's chessboard.'

Is it certain that the strictly metaphysical work of De Chirico came to an end in 1917, as the surrealists claimed? I do not think so. It is true that he yielded to the temptation of a painting style inspired by classical tradition, but there are many moments in which the myth-creating, angst-ridden inspiration of his early work reappears. Even some late works – *Horses on the Seashore, The Return of the Prodigal, The Archaeologists, The Gladiators,* as well as the bathing-machine compositions and those showing pieces of furniture in a valley, remain charged with a subtle mystery. It remains that this more recent output did not, for his contemporaries, exert the same hypnotic fascination as the *Enigmas*, the *Nostalgias* and the *Melancholies* which made his reputation.

The true influence of metaphysical art is a psychic one; the lesson that can be learned from it is not pictorial but poetic. Its obvious imitators, like Pierre Roy, weakened rather than reinforced the lesson. 'Art', wrote De Chirico, 'is the fatal snare which catches in flight, like mysterious butterflies, those moments of strangeness which elude the innocence or the absent-mindedness of common men.' In the confusion which reigns today as to the destiny of the arts, there still exist a few artists, generally solitary ones, who have accepted this view. And it is thanks to them that the great surge of energy which possessed De Chirico and the other metaphysicals, in the years between 1910 and 1920, continues on its course through the starry night.

# Magic Realism and the Metaphysical

## Ewald Rathke

The First World War marked a decisive break in the development of German painting. Afterwards, while the older expressionists turned to a deeper involvement in the world of Nature, the younger generation involved itself with the social, intellectual and political conditions of contemporary life. The Dada idea reached Cologne, Berlin and Hanover from Zurich and Paris, and produced a violent and passionate movement of social criticism and polemic. Dada dealt with everyday life, went straight to the realities of the social situation, and adopted expressive forms, including collage and photomontage, which were entirely new to German art. Dada in Zurich had shown itself to be receptive to all the artistic tendencies of the day, and its Zurich exhibitions contained works by the futurists Marinetti and Prampolini, and by De Chirico; the influence of futurism was felt in Germany both before and after the First World War.

Soon after 1918 a new kind of realism, more direct than that of German Dada, began to make itself evident in the work of the younger generation of artists, who had made a clean break with the Brücke and Blaue Reiter traditions. The art historian Franz Roh found a name for this new tendency as early as 1925; 'magic realism'. He also pointed out its affinity with Italian metaphysical painting.

The thematic range of 'magic realism' is wide, embracing the allegory and symbolism of Max Beckmann, the caustic energy of Otto Dix, the magical awareness of concrete reality in Anton Raederscheidt, and the almost naïve world of Georg Schrimpf. What they all have in common is the endeavour to transform the pictorial representation of reality in such a way as to make visible the concealed reality that lies beyond. Themes and subjects were drawn from reality, but they were assembled in such a way as to endow the representation with a general, exemplary significance. Universal significance now no longer sprang from a process of generalization and abstraction, as it had done in pre-war expressionism, but from the very reverse: a careful and precise representation of the specific. The common factor was not the subject matter but the expressive function with which it is endowed.

Two main tendencies may be distinguished within magic realism: those who sought essentially dramatic effects, and those whose interpretations of reality was poetic or lyrical. The principal figures on the 'dramatic' side of the fence were Max Beckmann, Otto Dix and George Grosz, besides Karl Günther, Rudolf Schlichter, Karl Hubbuch and several others. The 'poetic' magic realists included Heinrich Davringhausen, Herbert Böttcher, Karl Grossberg, Alexander Kanoldt, Carlo Mense, Franz Radziwill, Anton Raederscheidt, Georg Scholz and Georg Schrimpf.

Obviously Dix, Grosz and Beckmann have had the most lasting success (although the recent growth of interest in the Germany of the 1920s is bound to lead to the rescue of some of the other names from their oblivion). It was these three that brought the human figure firmly back into its central role in painting.

Max Beckmann said in the 1920s that the artist's place was in the midst of a great city, where he could become aware of the headlong rush of events in which the bestiality of human passions manifests itself. Beckmann, Grosz and Dix concentrated on the shadowy, dark side of life, situations of human crisis, emblems of transience and poverty, hardship and torment. Acute and vigorous though the treatment of these themes may have been, this painting remained primarily social criticism or propaganda for reform. The artists were cast in the role of recorders, fixing on the sensitive point amid the torrent of reality. This did not free their pictures from the appeal to human feeling; but it was left to the individual spectator to draw the moral. George Grosz, in a whole series of picture books, revealed 'The New Face of the Governing Class'; but his *Ecce Homo* is fact, not sermon.


The key to the work of Max Beckmann lies in his monumental *The Night*, of 1918–19, on which he had started work during the war. Its content is hard to describe; it is essentially an allegory of man's inhumanity to man. Its magic lies in the symbolic overtones of all the individual elements of reality within it. The cramped attic room in which the scene is set symbolizes the prison in which man is confined, the prison of the human condition. All the objects – the candle which has fallen over and still burns, the gramophone on the floor, the torn clothes – are symbols, as are the human figures themselves and their gestures. The cramped representation of space is symbolic in itself. In the middle of the picture there is an empty space. The figures are forced outwards against the walls that hold them like an iron clamp. Despite the clear directionality of the arms and legs, there is no depth in the painting; the rigidity of the lines themselves is a symbol of bondage. It is a picture full of activity which conveys no sense of an event; it conveys only the rigidity of death. The colour is far from realistic. It is used partly to add compositional accents, partly to convey drabness, deadness and immobility. The effect rests largely on a combination of individual elements which are drawn from reality but can never be found in reality in just this arrangement.

There is no chance of proving a direct link between Beckmann and Italian metaphysical art; but there is a spiritual affinity. This lies in the reality of the details and the combination of these details to form an entirely new and artificial whole which carries conviction precisely because it looks as if it might be real. This also applies to the spatial conception, which involves, in Beckmann as in De Chirico, either unnatural breadth or unnatural compression. The forms, too, have the same sharp edges and smooth curves as they have in De Chirico; the choice of viewpoint, obliquely upwards or downwards, and the use of colour, are also common factors. The affinity lies above all in the creation of new experimental possibilities. The tensions and dislocations imposed on the normal experience of reality evoke in the spectator a new inner tension, a new intensity of feeling, which brings the metaphysical within reach.

Beckmann's almost entirely unpeopled townscapes are really still-lifes, in which the interstices are full of the tensions set up by the objects: houses, bridges, towers and trees. There are practically no figures; but one senses that these are cities marked by the hand of man, cities which set their mark on man in return. These relationships lead the spectator to the hidden quality which lies behind the external form; they make the life behind the façades real.

All this presents analogies with De Chirico, as does the use of distorted perspective; both painters, working independently, filled their paintings with the same sense of the reality of the dream.

Beckmann's portraits, too, are infused with an aura of magic. He does not characterize his figures as actors on the stage of life; nor does he cast light on the depths of their psyche. In his portraits they appear inhibited, intensely composed, and remote as if a barrier stood between them and the spectator. On one hand they are alien, impossible fully to comprehend; on the other they are generalized types whose being holds within itself basic potentialities of human life. Beckmann's own relationship to reality was distanced in the same way. He observed it with extraordinary acuity, as his drawings show, but without passion, as is clear from his paintings. He concentrated on the decisive element; his painting reveals the world through a choice of aspects which always point in the direction of penetrating the apparent aspect in order to make possible a magical awareness. Significantly, Beckmann habitually chose to observe reality in the circumstances in which it stood at one remove from itself: in the masquerades of Carnival, or in the circus or the music-hall, with the studied artifice of its gestures and poses.

Otto Dix, who started his career with an intensified impressionist technique influenced by Van Gogh, began even before the war to turn to a totally different, smooth old-masterly, technique, using glazes, which was inspired by the Quattrocento painters. During the war the influence of cubism and futurism became apparent, although this was much more a matter of form than of spirit.

The subject matter of Dix's art is aggressive. His uncompromising treatment of controversial themes must have shocked many people (as in *War Cripples playing Cards*, 1920; *The Salon*, 1921; *Remembrance of the Halls of Mirrors in Brussels*, 1920; *Butcher's Shop*, 1920). Dix concentrates on everyday life in all its banality; however, his concern is not with the banality itself but with what lies beyond. Dix takes the commonplaces that everybody repeats without really being conscious of them, and takes them seriously: the ugliness of whores, the brutality of a butcher, the repulsiveness of the war cripples' wounds. He also takes seriously the primitive emotions that exist within this banal everyday world: the brutish faces, the spontaneous gestures, the grubby rooms, the garish clothes.

But can there be anything 'magical' in such a world? Can anything emerge from it but a set of clichés? Dix endows each of his subjects – and he studied them with great subtlety in numerous drawings – with a generalized significance. They stand in each case for a whole category; in this way Dix removes his subject matter from its banal context. His constant theme is human potential and its limitations. Each of his figures reflects a fate which is imposed on him from outside, a fate which he cannot evade. Dix works with the utmost realism, thus firmly establishing the statement 'That is so'. He confronts the spectator with stimuli which do not differ in character from those which affect him in the real world.

Of course there is more to his painting than this. Like Beckmann and like De Chirico, he distorts perspective, leaving the line of floor and ceiling unspecified, and endowing his objects and figures, whatever their purely anecdotal relationship, with the isolation and formal tension of items in a still-life. His compositions are based on the accumulation of points of emphasis, rather than on overall principles; often they seem arbitrary, almost like snapshots, but the metallic hardness of the forms, the smoothness of the surfaces, produce a sculptural quality of permanence which is one of the essential constituents of magic realism in Germany.

Dix's evolution as an artist culminated in the monumental triptych *Big City* of 1927–8. This mighty work is a summation of Dix's thematic concerns: man as a victim of man, and man as a victim of fate. The realism of the individual forms is combined with a weirdly unreal use of colour; the result is at once visually credible and intensely visionary and dreamlike. This is the combination of factors through which Dix attains a magical quality.

Almost inevitably, this period in Dix's career came to an end about 1930. His pictorial world in the 1920s, and the profound insights that it contains, had been the products of a certain political, historical and economic context. German society in 1930, which was, among other things, much more static and rigid, did not provide the essential stimulus. Dix turned to a lyrical preoccupation with Nature, retaining the old-masterly technique but abandoning the search for a 'magical reality' behind appearances.

Of all the magic realist painters, George Grosz was the most directly political. He represents a fractured world in uncompromisingly polemical terms; sarcasm and irony play a central part in his drawings, often to the extent of caricature. Grosz was first and foremost a draughtsman, with an economical and wickedly incisive line.

Grosz, like Dix, had stood in pre-war days somewhere between expressionism and impressionism. The war had a decisive affect on his development. Temperamentally well suited to directness and forcefulness of expression, he played an important part in the Berlin Dada movement. Around 1920 he was painting pictures like the untitled townscape now in Chicago [216], in which the affinity with metaphysical painting is evident. De Chirico and Carrà are the sources of the conceptions of space in these works, of their sharp and intense treatment of form, and above all of their attainment of an alienation effect through the juxtaposition of dummy figures and industrial settings. The absence of human content is the same, as are the eerie silence and the dead, dumb architecture.

For Grosz this was only a first step. Like Dix and Beckmann, he soon turned his attention to the depiction of human figures. He both characterized and caricatured

178 Giorgio Morandi, photographed by the sculptor Messina

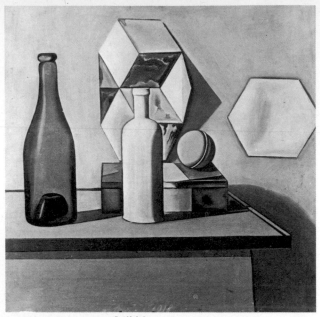

179 GIORGIO MORANDI *Still-life* 1918

180 GIORGIO MORANDI *Cactus* 1917

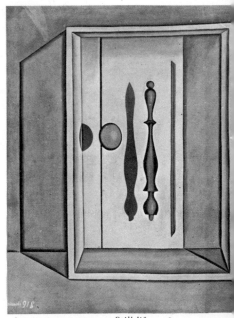

181 GIORGIO MORANDI *Still-life* 1918

182 GIORGIO MORANDI *Self-portrait* 1919

*Morandi*

183 GIORGIO MORANDI *Still-life* 19?

184 Arrangement of objects in Morandi's studio, photographed by L. Lionni

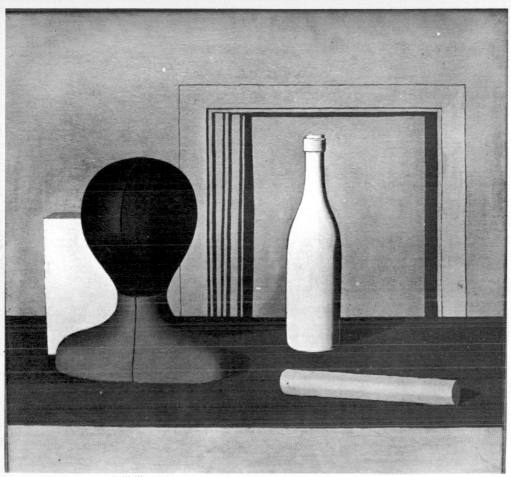

185 GIORGIO MORANDI *Still-life* 1918

186 Arrangement of objects in Morandi's studio, photographed by L. Lionni

187 GIORGIO MORANDI *Still-life* 1918

188 GIORGIO MORANDI *Still-life* 1919

189 GIORGIO MORANDI *Still-life* 1919

190 GIORGIO MORANDI *Still-life* 1919

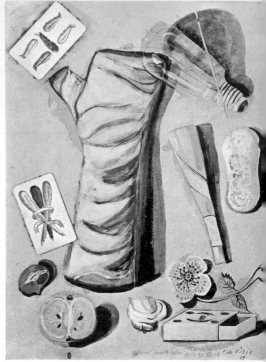

191 FILIPPO DE PISIS *The Mad Poet* 1919

192 FILIPPO DE PISIS *Hysterical Still-life* 1919

193 Raffaele Carrieri and Filippo de Pisis

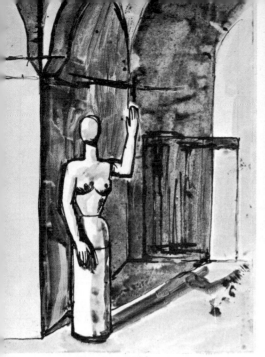

MARIO SIRONI *Metaphysical Idol* 1918

195 MARIO SIRONI *Metaphysical Idol* 1916

96 Alberto Savinio

197 ALBERTO SAVINIO *Alphabetical Morning* 1929

198 ALBERTO SAVINIO *Untitled* 1928

199 ALBERTO SAVINIO *The Death of Pompey* 1929

200 ALBERTO SAVINIO *Prometheus* 1929

201 Alberto Savinio with Bontempelli and Cardare. 1922

202 ALBERTO SAVINIO *The Battling Angels* 1939

203 FELICE CASORATI *Female Nude* 1926

204 RENÉ MAGRITTE *The Migratory Angel* 1926

205 RENÉ MAGRITTE *The Great News* 1926

206 RENÉ MAGRITTE
*The Difficult Crossing* 1926

207 MAX ERNST *Two Children Menaced by a Nightingale* 1924

208 MAX ERNST *The Elephant Celebes* 1921

209 YVES TANGUY *Mummy, Daddy's Hurt* 1926

210 YVES TANGUY *Promontory Palace* 1939

11 SALVADOR DALÍ *Nostalgic Echo* 1935

212 SALVADOR DALÍ *The Dismal Sport* 1929

13 MAX BECKMANN *Night* 1918/19

214 MAX BECKMANN *Pierrette and Clown* 1925

215 MAX BECKMANN
*Spring Landscape* 1924

216 GEORGE GROSZ *Untitled*
1920

217 GEORGE GROSZ
*Sportsman* 1922

218 OTTO DIX *Sailor on Shore
Leave from the 'Hamburg'* 1921

219 OTTO DIX *Worker* 1921

220 OTTO DIX *Metropolis* 1927

221 GEORG SCHRIMPF *Girl on Balcony* 1927

222 OTTO DIX *Salon* 1922

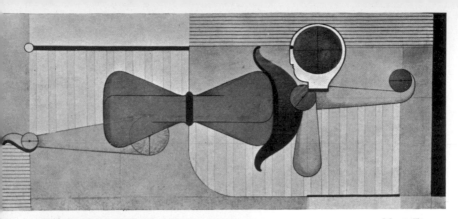

223 OSKAR SCHLEMMER *Mystic Figure* 1923

224 OSKAR SCHLEMMER *Nude* 1925

225 OSKAR SCHLEMMER *Five Men in a Room* 1928

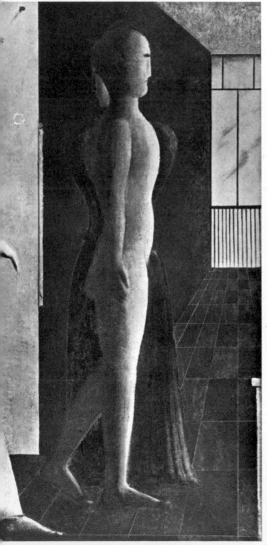

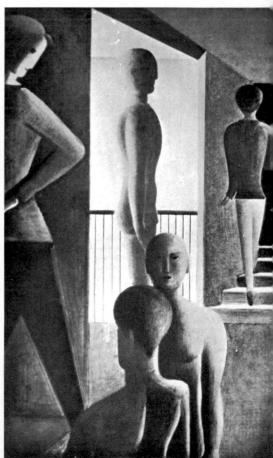

human types. The stimulus of cubism was present in his work. But one element remained that sprang from metaphysical art: the achievement of thematic tension through the juxtaposition of elements which do not belong together in the real world. From metaphysical painting, too, he had learned the essential lesson of the value of a forceful line in driving home a point. On the whole, however, he remained within the bounds of reality; he violated the existing taboos which governed the choice of themes in art, but he did not overstep the mark nearly as far as Otto Dix had done.

German magic realism in the work of these three artists is characterized by its discursive and narrative content, and particularly by its emphasis on drama: in the work of Beckmann and Grosz the drama takes the form of action, while Dix sets out to stress the dramatic, crisis-ridden quality of the human condition as a whole. A number of the artists shared both the ideas and the techniques of these three; they include Kurt Günther, Karl Hubbuch and Rudolf Schlichter, all predominantly draughtsmen, whose incisive and economical style stood in more direct and intellectually less demanding relationship to external reality than did those of Dix, Grosz and Beckmann. Günther, Hubbuch and Schlichter were consequently rather more popular in the 1920s than the others, and seem a lot less interesting now.

The other major group of magic realist painters consists of those artists whose approach to reality was rather 'poetic' than dramatic. The senior member of the group was Alexander Kanoldt, a founder member of the Künstlervereinigung in Munich in 1909, and the earliest opponent within the association, of the abstractionist ideas of Kandinsky. Kanoldt's artistic ideals were objectivity, impersonality and truth to reality. His models were the Italian Quattrocento painters, and Ingres; and his work itself carries reminiscences of the *naïf* painters.

Georg Schrimpf [222] was a genuine *naïf* who started out as a Sunday painter; his aim was to create an impression of absolute stillness, a total absence of dynamics. The 'Munich group', Kanoldt, Schrimpf and their friend Carlo Mense, were united in their admiration for the Douanier Rousseau and in their emphasis on atmosphere, their endeavour to capture the feeling emanating from objects and from the landscape. Magic realism in their hands turned not only in the direction of poetry but in that of sentiment. All three shared with Heinrich Davringhausen, a painter who made a speciality of strict linear constructions in exaggerated perspective, one dominant quality: that of airlessness. Their objects are treated as if totally independent of atmosphere and light.

There were a number of like-minded painters in North Germany as well. Franz Radziwill had been decisively influenced by the German romantics he had seen in the Gemäldegalerie in Dresden: his way of painting is derived largely from Caspar David Friedrich. Nature is weird and menacing. Sombre skies loom over landscapes in which spectral events take place; his shimmering colour has a dreamlike quality. Karl Grossberg, on the other hand, gave his paintings an ironic twist. Representational exactitude is carried to the point of deliberately emphasizing the trivial and irrelevant.

A more important figure altogether was the Cologne painter Anton Raederscheidt. He took up a central idea of metaphysical painting: that of unlikely juxtapositions of objects. He did not invent such entirely unexpected combinations as did the Italians; but there is in his paintings always a tension between figure and setting which gives the impression of bringing to light some hidden essence. The paintings are airless, like those of the Munich group; but this airlessness is used to underline the tensions between objects rather than to emphasize their individuality. Raederscheidt goes less into detail; he emphasizes the overall form.

Whereas surrealism, in France, was a coherent and indeed organized movement, magic realism was the product of the shared preoccupation of a number of separate and individual artistic personalities; it follows that the term is relevant to the work of some artists who were never included in the group as originally defined. The greatest of these was without a doubt Oskar Schlemmer [223–5]. His early work recalls the late Cézanne, with its firm shapes and emphasis on the plane. During and after the First World War, he narrowed his scope to the exploration of the relationship between the human figure and the surrounding space. His figures are compact and firmly delimited; his space seems infinite; and the strong contrast powerfully recalls De Chirico and Carrà, both of whose work Schlemmer knew well, as his writings show. He set out to grasp, in clearly defined forms, the unconscious part of the human experience of reality. Schlemmer was another artist who concerned himself more with mood than with events, more with feeling than with narration. The colour scale of his painting ranges from brilliant variety to tonal variations on a single colour. This last feature is a link with cubism; but it is done for entirely different reasons. The limitation of the colour intensifies the emphasis on plastic qualities, and clarifies the relationships between the individual elements of the picture.

The wide stylistic differences between the individual artists whose work belongs to magic realism are partly accounted for by the isolation in which they all worked. In the 1920s there was no artistic metropolis in Germany, and they had no theorist to act as their spokesman. They had, for once in the history of modern art, no programme. And even today the German art of the period has not received any general recognition. It is only in the last few years that two of these artists, George Grosz and Max Beckmann, have aroused attention in the United States.

The organic evolution of the group was cut short by the coming of the Nazis in 1933. Both those artists who went into exile and those who stayed behind were forced into positions of even greater isolation; while the Third Reich's preoccupation with 'popular' realism had the effect of diverting the magic realist tradition in the direction of mere platitude. This turn of events has since had the effect, in Germany itself, of causing people to underrate the art of the 1920s, which differed from Third Reich realism in content but often not in style. It is now time to take a new view, free from political considerations, which will assess the achievements of magic realism at their true worth.

# Chronological Table

**1881**  Carlo Carrà born in Quargnento (Alessandria), 11 February.

**1888**  Giorgio de Chirico born of Italian parents in Volo (Greece), 10 July.

**1890**  Giorgio Morandi born in Bologna, 20 July.

**1891**  Andrea de Chirico (Alberto Savinio) born in Athens, 25 August.

**1905**  On the father's death the De Chirico family moved to Munich. Carrà was in Milan, working as a decorator, after trips to Paris and London in 1899 and 1900. Morandi was employed in his father's office in Bologna.

**1909**  His studies at the Brera Academy over, Carrà became friends with Boccioni, Bonzagni, Romani and Russolo, and experimented briefly with Pointillism. De Chirico came to Italy and lived in Milan, Turin and Florence, living monastically and painting under the influence of Böcklin and Klinger. Morandi saw Cézanne's work for the first time, reproduced in Vittorio Pica's book on impressionism; he also read articles by Soffici in *Voce*.

**1910**  On 11 February the Futurist Manifesto, signed by Balla, Boccioni, Carrà, Russolo and Severini, was issued. De Chirico moved to Paris: he painted the first *Places d'Italie*. Savinio, still in Paris, continued his musical activities. Morandi saw 37 Renoir works at the 9th Biennale in Venice; he also went to Florence to study the works of Giotto, Masaccio and Paolo Uccello.

**1914**  The futurist movement was at its height; by arrangement with the Florentine group of *Voce* a new review was begun under the direction of Papini and Soffici, who at once made contact with the French cubists, enlisting the cooperation of Apollinaire, Braque, Picasso. Carrà's futurist crisis began: this was the year of his collages. At the futurist evening at the Teatro del Corso in Bologna on 20 January, he met Morandi for the first time; Morandi, though he kept aloof, was nevertheless interested in the futurist movement. In Paris, De Chirico devoted himself to paintings in which disparate objects were united in a magical association related to dream and memory. Apollinaire published Savinio's 'Chants de la mi-mort' in the May issue of the review *Les Soirées de Paris*.

**1915**    War broke out and De Chirico and Savinio returned to Italy to enter the army.

**1916**    Carrà published his 'Discourse on Giotto' and 'Paolo Uccello, Constructor' in *Voce*; it was the time of his 'anti-graceful' (*antigrazioso*) painting, in which a new rhythmic balance between movement and stasis, a geometrical structure, and an aura of magic, already presaged the painting of the following years. He painted *Composition TA* and *Il Gentiluomo Ubriaco* (*The Drunken Gentleman*). De Chirico, in the army in Ferrara, painted *The Disquieting Muses, Metaphysical Interior* and many other works. Savinio, also in Ferrara, published the literary work 'Hermaphrodito' in *Voce*. Morandi, in Bologna, painted some still-lifes which showed a decisive divergence from his earlier cubist principles. Arp, Tzara and others founded the Dada movement in Zurich.

**1917**    Carrà, also serving in Ferrara, met De Chirico, Savinio, De Pisis, Govoni and Ravegnani; new opportunities for discussion arose. At the military hospital in Villa Seminario, Carrà and De Chirico painted together. There they also met the young Bolognese writer Guiseppe Raimondi. Meanwhile, Bino Binassi's little review, *La Brigata,* to which Carrà and Savinio, as well as other ex-futurists, contributed, was being published in Bologna. In December Carrà had a large one-man show in Milan (Galleria Chini), where he also showed, under the umbrella of futurist painting, several metaphysical works painted in Ferrara.

**1918**    The review *La Raccolta,* for which Raimondi, Cardarelli, Bachelli, Carrà and Ungaretti wrote, was being published in Bologna. Morandi encountered De Chirico's and Carrà's metaphysical painting in reproductions shown him by Raimondi; he himself was inclined towards a form of metaphysical painting closer to Carrà's than De Chirico's. In July Carrà and De Chirico had an exhibition in Rome, at the Galleria dell'Epoca. The first issue of the new art periodical *Valori Plastici,* edited by Mario Broglio, was issued on 15 November. Various critics and Italian and foreign artists were contributors; among the principal ones were De Chirico, Savinio, Tavolato and Soffici.

    Morandi painted the first metaphysical still-lifes, four canvases showing a manikin's head. In Paris Ozenfant and Jeanneret (alias Le Corbusier) founded the purist movement.

**1919**    De Chirico painted *The Pumpkins,* in which he revealed a new interest in reality in an almost neoclassical sense: it was the first example of the third phase of his painting, in which classicism and romanticism merged in a curious combination of contradictory elements. Savinio published *Hermaphrodito* in book form. De Pisis published *Pittura moderna,* in which he enthusiastically hailed the paintings of De Chirico and Carrà; he also published *Prose,* on the subject of Boine, and painted a *Still-life* in the Ferrarese metaphysical style. Bontempelli, a friend of Carrà's since the early days of futurism, published two books of verse, *Il Purosangue* and *L'Ubriaco,* which signalled the transition from futurist poetry to a poetry incorporating magical and grotesque elements. He also wrote some of his *Viaggi e Scoperte,* which were to be published in 1920 and 1921. Gropius founded the Bauhaus at Weimar. Carrà published *Pittura metafisica.* Morandi, in Rome, became acquainted with De Chirico.

1920     This was a year of crises for Carrà and Morandi: the former did not show any paintings, although he painted many, in a simplified style which the critics were to call his purist phase; the second abandoned the metaphysical approach and resumed his study of Cézanne, 28 of whose works he had seen at the Venice Biennale. De Pisis left Ferrara for Rome. Ozenfant and Jeanneret published *L'Esprit Nouveau.*

1921     The principles set forth in *Valori Plastici* were acted upon, though not unanimously. In the beginning of April the exhibition promised by the periodical took place in Berlin, with the metaphysical works of De Chirico, Carrà, Morandi, Arturo Martini, Melli, Edita Zur Mühlen and Zadkine. The show introduced the new Italian painting to German artists and art students and had important repercussions. After Berlin the show went to Hanover and Hamburg. *Valori Plastici* ceased publication. Carrà's new painting style was launched; he had taken up naturalism: the critics were to call it 'magic realism' or 'archaic' or 'mythical realism'. Bontempelli wrote *La Scacchiera davanti allo specchio,* which was to be published in 1922: it was a kind of literary answer to Ferrarese metaphysical painting.

1922     De Chirico, in Rome, painted self-portraits and compositions with clear classical references, the first *Ville romane,* and *Return of the Prodigal,* which was metaphysical in style. De Pisis praised the painting. Carrà became the art critic for the new Milanese daily *L'Ambrosiano.* Carrà, De Chirico, Martini and Morandi contributed to the Florentine spring exhibition. Max Ernst moved to Paris.

1924     De Chirico was in his 'classical romantic' period. Carrà painted landscapes in Valsesia and continued to ponder the work of Cézanne and that of Giotto, about whom he wrote a long monograph issued by the publishers of *Valori Plastici.* Second exhibition in Germany of works of the *Valori Plastici* school: increased interest in the German art world. De Pisis painted *Still-life with Eyes,* in a half-metaphysical, half-surrealist manner. Mondadori reissued Bontempelli's metaphysical fable *Eva ultima,* written in 1922. De Chirico went to Paris, where he met, not always amicably, the surrealists and their leader Breton. The first Surrealist Manifesto was issued, and the review *La Révolution surréaliste,* to which even De Chirico contributed, was launched.

**1925** Wilhelm Worringer published, in *Wissen und Leben,* an article on Carrà's painting *The Pine Tree by the Sea.* Franz Roh published his *Nach-Expressionismus, Magischer Realismus,* in which he concentrated on Carrà's and De Chirico's painting. 'New Realism' exhibition held in Mannheim, and the first surrealist exhibition in Paris. De Pisis moved to Paris.

**1926** De Chirico, still in Paris, formed an alliance with the art dealer Léonce Rosenberg: he painted works of both surrealist and magical or metaphysical character. Savinio, who had some time ago begun to paint, had a show at Bernheim's Paris gallery. Carrà painted his first canvases of Venice, of seascapes and landscapes. The Milan exhibition of '20th Century Italians' included works by Carrà and Morandi.

**1928** Carrà's first one-man show at the 16th Venice Biennale; Morandi showed etchings. De Chirico painted his *Archaeologists, Warriors, Amazons, Gladiators* and *Furniture in a Valley.* Jean Cocteau dedicated his *Mystère laïc* to them. De Pisis too was living in Paris, and in his works there was still an echo of Ferrarese metaphysics.

# Bibliography

\*\*\*. 'Carrà'. *La Sera* (Milan 10 February 1918).

APOLLONIO, U. 'La pittura metafisica di De Chirico'. *Popolo di Trieste* (3 January 1940).

——. 'Le grandi mostre retrospettive: Pittura metafisica'. *Ulisse* (Rome July 1948).

——. *Pittura metafisica*. Venice 1950.

ARCANGELI, F. 'Sulla pittura metafisica'. *Vernice* (Trieste April–May 1948).

——. 'Carlo Carrà'. *La rassegna d'Italia* (Milan 1948).

——. *Giorgio Morandi*. Milan 1965.

BALLO, G. *L'opera grafica di Carrà*. Milan 1967.

BARDI, P. M. *Carrà e Soffici*. Milan 1930.

BELLONCI, G. 'La mostra di Carrà e De Chirico'. *Tempo* (Rome 2 July 1918).

BONTEMPELLI, MASSIMO. *L'avventura novecentista*. Florence 1938.

BRANDI, C. 'De Chirico metafisico al Milione'. *Le Arti* (Rome December 1939–January 1940).

BRANZI, S. 'La pittura metafisica'. *Camere* (Catania July 1948).

BRIZIO, A. M. *Ottocento e Novecento*. Turin 1939.

BRUGHETTI, R. *Pintura italiana del siglo XX*. Buenos Aires 1967.

CAFFÉ, R. *Giorgio de Chirico le voyant*. Brussels 1946.

CALZINI, R. 'Ventennio 1914–1934'. *Domus* (Milan 1934).

CARRÀ, CARLO. *Pittura Metafisica*. Florence 1919.

——. *La mia vita*. Rome 1943.

CARRÀ, M. *Tutta l'opera pittorica di Carrà*. Milan 1967/68.

CARRIERI, R. *Giorgio de Chirico*. Milan 1942.

——. *Pittura e scultura italiana d'avanguardia*. Milan 1950.

CASTELFRANCO, G. 'Giorgio de Chirico'. *Der Cicerone* (Berlin May 1924).

——. *La pittura moderna*. Florence 1934.

——, and M. Valsecchi. *Pittura e scultura italiana dal 1910 al 1930*. Rome 1956.

CATALANO, S. *Carrà*. Milan 1945.

COCTEAU, JEAN. *Le mystère laïc*. Paris 1928.

COSTANTINI, V. *Pittura italiana contemporanea*. Milan 1934.

——. 'La peinture italienne après le Futurisme' in *Histoire de l'art contemporain*, R. Huyghe, Paris 1935.

COURTHION, P. 'Le rêve: De Chirico', in *Panorama de la peinture française*, Paris 1927.

DE CHIRICO, GIORGIO. *Hebdomeros*. Paris 1929.

DELL'ACQUA, G. A. 'Peinture Metaphysique', *Cahiers d'art* 1 (Paris 1950).

DE PISIS, FILIPPO. 'C. Carrà, G. de Chirico'. *Gazzetta Ferrarese* (Ferrara 12 February 1918).

——. *Pittura moderna*. Ferrara 1919.

DEUBLER, T. 'Neueste Kunst in Italien'. *Der Cicerone* (Leipzig May 1920).

EINSTEIN, C. *Die Kunst des 20. Jahrhunderts*. Berlin 1931.

FALDI, I. *Il primo De Chirico*. Venice 1949.

FANCIULLI, G. 'La mostra di Carrà'. *La Perseveranza* (Milan 10 January 1918).

FANTUZZI, G. *Carrà*. Milan 1964.

FAR, I. *Giorgio de Chirico*. Rome 1953.

FRANCHI, RAFFAELLO. *La pittura italiana dall' 800 al 900*. Palermo 1929.

GEORGE, W. *La peinture italienne et le destin d'un art*. Paris 1935.

GUZZI, V. *Pittura italiana contemporanea*. Milan 1931.

HAMANN, R. *Geschichte der Kunst*. Berlin 1933.

HAUTECOEUR, L. *Réflections sur la peinture d'aujourd'hui*. Paris 1929.

HEILMEYER, H. 'Die moderne Italienische Malerei'. *Deutsche Kunst und Dekoration* (Leipzig 1920).

HILDEBRANDT, H. *Die Kunst des 19. und 20. Jahrhunderts*. Potsdam 1924.

KOVARNA, F. *Soukasné Malirstvi*. Prague 1932.

LANCELLOTTI, A. *L'arte italiana contemporanea*. Rome 1928.

LO DUCA, G. *Dipinti di Giorgio de Chirico*. Milan 1936.

LONGHI, R. *Carlo Carrà*. Milan 1937.

MARCHIORI, G. 'Cocteau e De Chirico'. *Emporium* (Bergamo March 1946).

MASCIOTTA, M. 'La pittura metafisica'. *Letteratura* (Florence 1941).

MEIER-GRAEFE, JULIUS. *Entwicklungsgeschichte der modernen Kunst*. Berlin 1927.

MORISE, M. 'A propos de l'exposition Chirico'. *La Révolution Surréaliste* (Paris 15 July 1925).

NEBBIA, U. *La pittura italiana del Novecento*. Turin 1939.

N.F. 'L'exposition de Chirico-Carrà'. *Art Vivant* (Paris 15 March 1926).

OPPO, C. E. 'La mostra d'arte indipendente'. *L'idea nazionale* (Rome 25 May 1918).

ORS, E. D'. 'De Chirico y la inteligencia sarcástica'. *La Gaceta Literaria* (Madrid 1 April 1930).

PACCHIONI, G. *Carlo Carrà*. Milan 1945.

PAPINI, G. 'Carlo Carrà'. *La Vraie Italie* (Florence April 1919).

PICA, A. *Giorgio de Chirico*. Milan 1944.

PIOVENE, G. *La raccolta Feroldi*. Milan 1942.

RAGGHIANTI, C. L. 'Giorgio de Chirico'. *Critica d'arte* (Florence October 1935).

———. 'Carlo Carrà'. *Critica d'arte* (Florence 1936).

RAIMONDI, Giuseppe. *Carlo Carrà*. Bologna 1916.

———. 'Carlo Carrà'. *La Ronda* (Rome January 1920).

READ, H. *A Concise History of Modern Painting*. London 1959.

RIBEMONT-DESSAIGNES, G. 'Giorgio de Chirico'. *Documents* (1930).

ROH, F. *Nach-Expressionismus, Magischer Realismus*. Leipzig 1925.

ROM, L. *Der unbestechliche Minos*. Hamburg 1925.

———. *Neue Kunst in Italien*. Hamburg 1925.

SARFATTI, M. *Storia della pittura moderna*. Rome 1930.

SAVINIO, ALBERTO. *Anadioménon, Principes d'évolution de l'art contemporain*. Rome 1923.

SCHEIWILLER, G. *Art italien moderne*. Paris 1930.

SHELDON, C. *A World History of Art*. New York 1937.

ŠIBLIK, J. *Carlo Carrà*. Prague 1968.

SOBY, J. THRALL. *Giorgio de Chirico*. New York 1966.

———, and A. H. Barr. *Twentieth-Century Italian Art*. New York 1949.

SOFFICI, A. 'Pittura metafisica'. *Rete mediterranea* (Florence 1920).

———. *Carlo Carrà*. Milan 1928.

SOMARE, E. 'Carlo Carrà'. *Il Primato* (Milan February–March 1920).

TERNOVETZ, B. *Giorgio de Chirico*. Milan 1928.

TORRIANO, P. *Carrà*. Milan 1942.

VALSECCHI, M. *Maestri moderni*. Milan 1957.

———. *La pittura metafisica*. Milan 1958.

———. *Carrà*. Milan 1962.

VENTURI, L. *Pittori moderni*. Florence 1946.

———. *Pittura contemporanea*. Milan 1947.

VITALI, L. 'Variazioni metafisiche di Carrà'. *Le Tre Arti* (Milan 1945).

———. *Morandi*. Milan 1964.

———. *L'opera grafica di G. Morandi*. Turin 1964.

VITRAC, R. *G. de Chirico*. Paris 1927.

WALDEN, H. *Einblick in die Kunst*. Berlin 1924.

WORRINGER, W. 'Carlo Carrà's Pinie am Meer'. *Wissen und Leben* (Zurich 10 November 1925).

ZERVOS, C. *Histoire de l'art contemporain*. Paris 1938.

———. in *Cahiers d'art* 1 (Paris 1950).

# List of Illustrations

33  *The Man with a Glass*, 1920.

34  *The Engineer's Mistress*, 1921.

35  *Study for 'The Engineer's Mistress'*, 1921.

36  *St Anne's Mill*, 1921. Oil on canvas, 91 × 80. E. Gabbrielli Scalini, Varese.

37  *The Pine Tree by the Sea*, 1921. Oil on canvas, 68 × 52·5. A. Casella, Rome.

38  Carlo Carrà at work at Belgirate, Lago Maggiore, summer 1922.

39  *The House of Love*, 1922. Oil on canvas, 90 × 70. Emilio Jesi, Milan.

GIORGIO DE CHIRICO

40  Giorgio de Chirico, photographed by Man Ray.

41  Signora Gemma de Chirico with her sons Giorgio and Andrea (Alberto Savinio).

42  Arnold Böcklin. *Triton and Mermaids*. Etching.

43  De Chirico. *The Dying Centaur*, 1909. Private collection, Milan.

44  *Seascape with Mermaid*, 1909.

45  *The Convent on the Mountain*, 1909. Private collection, Milan.

46  Arnold Böcklin. *Odysseus and Calypso*, 1881–3. Kunstmuseum, Basle.

47  De Chirico. *The Enigma of the Oracle*, 1910. Approx. 35·5 × 46. Private collection, Italy.

48  Group of *Garibaldini* with Giorgio de Chirico and Alberto Savinio as children.

49  *Melancholy of a Beautiful Afternoon*, 1913. 89 × 106. Benedict Goldschmidt, Brussels.

50  *Portrait of Andrea de Chirico (Alberto Savinio)*, 1910.

51  *The Tower*, 1911–12. 155 × 45. Bernard Poissonier, Paris.

52  *Self-portrait (What shall I love if not the Enigma?)*, 1911. 72 × 55. Mrs Stanley Resor, Greenwich, Conn.

53  *Nude (Study)*, 1911–12. 71 × 55. The Pierre Matisse Gallery, New York, N.Y.

54  *Meditation of an Early Morning*, 1912. 52 × 71. R. Jucker, Milan.

55  *The Great Tower*, 1913. 117·5 × 50. Bernard Poissonier, Paris.

56  *The Enigma of the Hour*, 1912. 55 × 71. Gianni Mattioli, Milan; formerly Feroldi collection.

57  *Drawing*, 1913.

58  *The Delights of the Poet*, 1913. 69 × 86. The Museum of Modern Art, New York.

59  *Melancholy*, 1912(?). 79 × 63·5. Peter Watson, London.

60  *The Song of Love*, 1913. 73 × 60. Nelson A. Rockefeller, New York, N.Y.

61  *The Square*, 1913. 57 × 48. Bernard Poissonier, Paris.

62  *The Uncertainty of the Poet*, 1913. 105 × 94. Sir Roland Penrose, London.

63  *Self-portrait*, 1913. 81 × 55. Richard S. Zeisler, New York.

64  *The Pink Tower*, 1913. 75 × 100. Peggy Guggenheim, Venice.

65  *The Chimney*, 1913. Private collection, Paris.

66  *The Silent Statue*, 1913. 101 × 124. Jean Paulhan, Paris.

67  *Nostalgia of the Infinite*, 1913/14. 135 × 65. The Museum of Modern Art, New York, N.Y.

68  *The Dream Transformed*, 1913. 63·5 × 157·7. The City Art Museum, St Louis, Mo.

69  *The Weariness of the Infinite*, 1913(?). 44 × 112. Mrs John Stephan, New York, N.Y.

70  *The Anxious Journey*, 1913. 75 × 106. The Museum of Modern Art, New York, N.Y.

71  *Ariadne's Afternoon*, 1913. Yvon Delbos, Paris.

72  *Ariadne*, 1913. 135 × 180. Jean Paulhan, Paris.

73  *The Joys and Enigmas of a Strange Hour*, 1913. 84 × 129·5. Wright S. Ludington, Santa Barbara, Calif.

74 *The Poet's Recompense,* 1913. 134 × 179. The Philadelphia Museum of Art.

75 *Ariadne, c.* 1913. Plaster, 17 × 56·5. Jeanneret, Geneva.

76 *I will be there . . . The Glass Dog,* 1914 68·5 × 57. Mr and Mrs Bernard Reis, New York, N.Y.

77 *Gare Montparnasse (The Melancholy of Departure),* 1914. 140 × 183. Private collection, New Canaan, Conn.

78 *The Child's Brain,* 1914. 81 × 65. Formerly André Breton, Paris.

79 André Breton. *The Reawakening of the Child's Brain,* 1950. Retouched reproduction of De Chirico's *The Child's Brain,* published in the *Almanach Surréaliste du Demi-Siècle,* Paris 1950.

80 De Chirico. *Memory of Italy, c.* 1914. Oil on canvas, 91 × 64. Herbert Rothschild, Kitchawan, N.Y.

81 *Portrait of Guillaume Apollinaire,* 1914. 89 × 69. Mme Guillaume Apollinaire, Paris.

82 *The Dream of the Poet,* 1914. Peggy Guggenheim, Venice.

83 *The Philosopher's Outing,* 1914. 135 × 65. Vicomte Charles de Noailles, Paris.

84 *The Endless Journey,* 1914. 88 × 39. Mrs Marcel Duchamp, New York, N.Y.

85 *The Evil Genius of a King,* 1914–15. 61 × 50. The Museum of Modern Art, New York, N.Y.

86 *The Sailors' Barracks,* 1914. 81 × 65. The Norton Gallery of Art, West Palm Beach, Fla.

87 *The Great Tower,* 1914. 33 × 33. Gianni Mattioli, Milan.

88 *The General's Illness,* 1914–15. 50 × 44. The Wadsworth Atheneum, Hartford, Conn.

89 *The Enigma of Fatality,* 1914. 138 × 94. Bernard Poissonier, Paris.

90 *The Enigma of a Day,* 1914. 185 × 141. Private collection, New Canaan, Conn.

91 *Mystery and Melancholy of a Street,* 1914. 87 × 71. Stanley R. Resor, New Canaan, Conn.

92 *The Scholar's Serenity,* 1914. 132 × 73 overall. Gordon Onslow-Ford, Mill Valley, Calif.

93 *The Poet's Departure,* 1914. 86 × 41. Mrs L. M. Maitland, Brentwood, Calif.

94 *The Day of the Fête,* 1914. 81 × 65. The Carstairs Gallery, New York, N.Y.

95 *A Span of Black Barbed Wire.* Mme Eyre, Paris.

96 *The Destiny of a Poet,* 1914. 88 × 32·5. Pierre Matisse, New York, N.Y.

97 *Still-life: Turin, Spring,* 1914. 123 × 100. Vicomte Charles de Noailles, Paris.

98 *The Philosopher's Conquest,* 1914. 126 × 100. The Art Institute of Chicago.

99 *Melancholy of Turin,* 1915. Private collection, Milan.

100 *The Poet's Torment,* 1914. 53 × 41. Mrs Yves Tanguy, Woodbury, Conn.

101 *The Anguish of Departure,* 1914. 85 × 70. The Albright Art Gallery, Buffalo, N.Y.

102 *The Fatal Light,* 1915. 55 × 38. Peggy Guggenheim, Venice.

103 *The Philosopher and the Poet,* 1915(?). Pencil.

104 *The Philosopher and the Poet,* 1915(?). 73 × 52. Conte Don Alfonso Orombelli, Milan.

105 *The Soothsayer,* 1915. 88·5 × 69·5. Private collection, New Canaan, Conn.

106 *The Double Dream of Spring,* 1915. 56 × 53. Private collection, New Canaan, Conn.

107 *A Girl's Pastimes,* 1915. 38·5 × 45. Private collection, USA.

108 *The Duet,* 1915. 79 × 58. Private collection, New Canaan, Conn.

109 *The Astronomer (The Anxiety of Life),* 1915. 41 × 31. Mr and Mrs Burton F. Cumming, Westport, Conn.

110 *The Sage's Prophecy,* 1915. 46 × 38. Mr and Mrs Burton F. Cumming, Westport, Conn.

111 *The Inconsistency of the Thinker,* 1915. 46 × 38. The San Francisco Museum of Art.

112 *The Prince's Toys*, 1914–15. 55 × 26. Mrs Pierre Matisse, New York, N.Y.

113 *Metaphysical Interior with Small Factory*, 1916. 46 × 36. Private collection, Milan.

114 *The Two Sisters*, 1915. 66 × 43. Sir Roland Penrose, London.

115 *The Joy of Return*, 1915. 85 × 68·5. Mrs L. M. Maitland, Brentwood, Calif.

116 *The Purity of a Dream*, 1915. 65 × 50. Bernard Poissonier, Paris.

117 *Two Masks*, 1916(?). Oil on canvas, 56 × 47. Emilio Jesi, Milan.

118 *Hector and Andromache*, 1916(?). Private collection, Germany.

119 *Metaphysical Interior* 1, 1916. 31 × 25. Sir Roland Penrose, London.

120 *The Melancholy of Departure*, 1916. 53 × 36. Sir Roland Penrose, London.

121 *Metaphysical City*, 1916(?). 64 × 50. Private collection, Milan.

122 *Grief*, 1916. 46 × 34. Munson-Williams-Proctor Institute, Utica, N.Y.

123 *War*, 1916. 34 × 27. Gordon Onslow-Ford, Mill Valley, Calif.

124 *The Language of a Child*, 1916(?). 41 × 28. Pierre Matisse, New York, N.Y.

125 *The Engineer's Homesickness*, 1916. 32 × 24. Mrs Stanley Resor, Greenwich, Conn.

126 *Metaphysical Still-life*, 1916. Private collection, Paris(?).

127 *Evangelical Still-life*, 1918. 80 × 71. Sidney Janis, New York, N.Y.

128 *Politics*, 1916. 33 × 26. Gordon Onslow-Ford, Mill Valley, Calif.

129 *Metaphysical Interior with Large Factory*, 1916. 96 × 73·5. Private collection, Milan.

130 *Death of a Spirit*, 1916. 37 × 33. E. L. T. Mesens, London.

131 *The Faithful Servant*, 1916. 38 × 35. Private collection, New Canaan, Conn.

132 *The Temperate Afternoon*, 1916. 64 × 59. Peggy Guggenheim, Venice.

133 *Greetings from a Distant Friend*, 1916. Eric Estorick, London.

134 *The Sage's Revolt*, 1916. 59 × 59. Sidney Janis, New York, N.Y.

135 *Metaphysical Interior*, 1917. 43 × 30·5. Sidney Janis, New York, N.Y.

136 *Metaphysical Interior*, 1917. 42 × 30. Sidney Janis, New York, N.Y.

137 *Great Metaphysical Interior*, 1917. 94 × 68. Private collection, New Canaan, Conn.

138 *The Disquieting Muses*, 1917. Oil on canvas, 97 × 66. Fondazione Gianni Mattioli, Milan. (At later periods De Chirico made almost identical replicas of this and very many of the works of the metaphysical period. See Nos 139–40.)

139 *The Disquieting Muses*, 1924. Oil on canvas. Mrs Jonathan Tichenor, New York.

140 *The Disquieting Muses*, 1947(?). Oil on canvas. A. Deana, Venice.

141 *A Scholar's Toys*, 1917. 89·5 × 51. The Pierre Matisse Gallery, New York, N.Y.

142 *The Great Metaphysician*, 1917. 105 × 70. Philip L. Goodwin, New York, N.Y.

143 *Metaphysical Interior with Biscuit and Cigarette Holder*, 1917. 55 × 35. Private collection, Milan.

144 *Evangelical Still-life*, 1917. 90 × 60. Private collection, Milan.

145 *Metaphysical Interior*, c. 1917. Sir Roland Penrose, London.

146 *Troubadour*, 1917. 88 × 52. Private collection, Milan.

147 *Hector and Andromache*, 1917. 90 × 60. Gianni Mattioli, Milan; formerly Feroldi collection.

148 *Metaphysical Interior with Waterfall*, 1918. 62 × 46. Private collection, Milan.

149 *Hector and Andromache*, 1918(?). 99·5 × 70. Mr and Mrs Jean de Menil, Houston, Texas.

150 *Hermetic Melancholy*, 1919. Previously Mario Girardon, Rome. (Destroyed by fire in America.)

151 *Still-life with Salami*, 1919. 30 × 40. Giulio Laudisa, Rome.

152 *The Sacred Fish,* 1919. 75 × 62. The Museum of Modern Art, New York.

153 *Lucretia,* 1921.

154 *The Return of the Prodigal Son,* 1922. Tempera. 88·5 × 60. Private collection, Milan.

155 *Hector and Andromache,* 1924. 99 × 73. R. Toninelli, Milan.

156 *Memories of the Iliad,* 1924.

157 *The Poet and his Muse, c.* 1925(?). 89·5 × 72. The Philadelphia Museum of Art.

158 *The Contemplation of the Infinite,* 1925. Private collection, Paris.

159 *The Great Metaphysician, c.* 1925(?). 113 × 81. Formerly Adriano Pallini, Milan.

160 *Day and Night,* 1925. Della.

161 *Seated Manikin,* 1926. Tega, Milan.

162 *The Archaeologists,* 1926. 72 × 96. Private collection, Milan.

163 *Interior in a Valley,* 1927. Léonce Rosenberg, Paris.

164 *The Gentleman in City Clothes,* undated. Tosi, Milan.

165 *Lion and Gladiators,* 1927. Léonce Rosenberg, Paris.

166 *Furniture in the Valley, c.* 1927. 96 × 130. Giovanni Silva, Modena.

167 *Furniture in the Valley,* 1927. 96 × 130. Formerly Pallini, Milan.

168 *Victory,* 1928. 242 × 162. Cardazzo.

169 *Warriors Resting,* 1929. Léonce Rosenberg, Paris.

170 *The Construction of Trophies,* 1928. 74 × 91. Private collection, Milan.

171 *Warriors,* 1928. Léonce Rosenberg, Paris.

172 *Horse and Gladiators,* 1930. Petit Palais, Paris.

173 *The Boat,* undated. Pecci Blunt, Marlia.

174 *Gladiators,* 1931. Formerly Ery Aeschlimann, Milan.

175 *The Mysterious Swimmer,* undated.

176 *The Dioscuri,* 1934.

177 Giorgio de Chirico.

GIORGIO MORANDI

178 Giorgio Morandi, photographed by the sculptor Messina.

179 *Still-life,* 1918. 52 × 47. Formerly A. Orombelli, Milan.

180 *Cactus,* 1917. 32·5 × 44. Gianni Mattioli, Milan.

181 *Still-life,* 1918. 66 × 80. R. Jucker, Milan.

182 *Self-portrait,* 1919. (Untraced.)

183 *Still-life,* 1918. 54 × 47. R. Jucker, Milan.

184 Arrangement of objects in Morandi's studio, photographed by L. Lionni.

185 *Still-life,* 1918. 71·5 × 68. E. Jesi, Milan.

186 Arrangement of objects in Morandi's studio, photographed by L. Lionni.

187 *Still-life,* 1918. 51 × 71. State Hermitage Museum, Leningrad.

188 *Still-life,* 1919. 60 × 59·5. E. Jesi, Milan.

189 *Still-life,* 1919. 55 × 52. R. Longhi, Florence.

190 *Still-life,* 1919. 47 × 56. E. Jesi, Milan.

FILIPPO DE PISIS

191 *The Mad Poet,* 1919. 23 × 31. Levi, Turin.

192 *Hysterical Still-life,* 1919. 32 × 44. Private collection, Milan.

193 Raffaele Carrieri and Filippo de Pisis.

MARIO SIRONI

194 *Metaphysical Idol,* 1918. 20 × 14·5. Private collection, Milan.

195 *Metaphysical Idol,* 1916. Ink, 21·5 × 15. Private collection, Milan.

ALBERTO SAVINIO

196 Alberto Savinio.

197 *Alphabetical Morning,* 1929. 73 × 60. Private collection, Milan.

198 *Untitled,* 1928. 35 × 45. Private collection, Milan.

199 *The Death of Pompey,* 1929. 80 × 65. Private collection, Milan.

200 *Prometheus,* 1929. 79·5 × 65. Tega, Milan.

201 Alberto Savinio with Bontempelli and Cardarelli, 1922.
202 *The Battling Angels*, 1939. 100 × 80. Tega, Milan.

FELICE CASORATI
203 *Female Nude*, 1921. P. Rossini, Turin.

PAINTERS OUTSIDE ITALY
204 René Magritte. *The Migratory Angel*, 1926. 64 × 149. William N. Copley, New York, N.Y.
205 René Magritte. *The Great News*, 1926. 62 × 80. Gustave Nellens, Paris.
206 René Magritte. *The Difficult Crossing*, 1926. 81 × 65. G. Niels, Brussels.
207 Max Ernst. *Two Children Menaced by a Nightingale*, 1924. 46 × 33. Museum of Modern Art, New York, N.Y.
208 Max Ernst. *The Elephant Celebes*, 1921. Sir Roland Penrose, London.
209 Yves Tanguy. *Mummy, Daddy's Hurt*, 1926. 72 × 93. Museum of Modern Art, New York, N.Y.
210 Yves Tanguy. *Promontory Palace*, 1939. 58·5 × 71·5. The Peggy Guggenheim Foundation, Venice.
211 Salvador Dalí. *Nostalgic Echo*, 1935. 95 × 95. L. M. Maitland, Brentwood, Calif.

212 Salvador Dalí. *The Dismal Sport*, 1929. 30·8 × 44·8. Claude Hersaint, Paris.
213 Max Beckmann. *Night*, 1918/19. Günter Franke, Munich.
214 Max Beckmann. *Pierrette and Clown*, 1925. 160 × 100. Kunsthalle, Mannheim.
215 Max Beckmann. *Spring Landscape*, 1924. 95·5 × 55·5. Lilly V. Schnitzler.
216 George Grosz. *Untitled*, 1920. 81 × 61. Richard Feigen Gallery, Chicago, Ill.
217 George Grosz. *Sportsman*, 1922. Watercolour. Unknown collection.
218 Otto Dix. *Sailor on Shore Leave from the 'Hamburg'*, 1921. 59 × 84. Unknown collection.
219 Otto Dix. *Worker*, 1921. 57·5 × 78·5. Unknown collection.
220 Otto Dix. *Metropolis*, right panel of triptych, 1927. Private collection.
221 George Schrimpf. *Girl on Balcony*, 1927.
222 Otto Dix. *Salon*, 1922. 120·5 × 86.
223 Oskar Schlemmer. *Mystic Figure*, 1923. 80 × 170.
224 Oskar Schlemmer. *Nude*, 1925. 128 × 64·2. Dr Richard Merz, Stuttgart.
225 Oskar Schlemmer. *Five Men in a Room*, 1928. 150 × 90.

*Italic figures are illustration numbers.*